Intentional and
Targeted Teaching

ASCD MEMBER BOOK

Many ASCD members received this book as a
member benefit upon its initial release.

Learn more at: **www.ascd.org/memberbooks**

Intentional and Targeted Teaching

A Framework for Teacher Growth and Leadership

Douglas **FISHER** | Nancy **FREY** | Stefani Arzonetti **HITE**

 | Alexandria, VA USA

1703 N. Beauregard St. • Alexandria, VA 22311-1714 USA
Phone: 800-933-2723 or 703-578-9600 • Fax: 703-575-5400
Website: www.ascd.org • E-mail: member@ascd.org
Author guidelines: www.ascd.org/write

Deborah S. Delisle, *Executive Director;* Robert D. Clouse, *Managing Director, Digital Content & Publications;* Stefani Roth, *Publisher;* Genny Ostertag, *Director, Content Acquisitions;* Julie Houtz, *Director, Book Editing & Production;* Katie Martin, *Editor;* Donald Ely, *Senior Graphic Designer;* Mike Kalyan, *Manager, Production Services;* Cynthia Stock, *Typesetter;* Kyle Steichen, *Senior Production Specialist*

All web links in this book are correct as of the publication date below but may have become inactive or otherwise modified since that time. If you notice a deactivated or changed link, please e-mail books@ascd.org with the words "Link Update" in the subject line. In your message, please specify the web link, the book title, and the page number on which the link appears.

PAPERBACK ISBN: 978-1-4166-2111-9   ASCD product #116008
PDF E-BOOK ISBN: 978-1-4166-2113-3; see Books in Print for other formats.
Quantity discounts: 10–49, 10%; 50+, 15%; 1,000+, special discounts (e-mail programteam@ascd.org or call 800-933-2723, ext. 5773, or 703-575-5773). For desk copies, go to www.ascd.org/deskcopy.

ASCD Member Book No. FY16-7 (May 2016, P). ASCD Member Books mail to Premium (P), Select (S), and Institutional Plus (I+) members on this schedule: Jan, PSI+; Feb, P; Apr, PSI+; May, P; Jul, PSI+; Aug, P; Sep, PSI+; Nov, PSI+; Dec, P. For current details on membership, see www.ascd.org/membership.

Library of Congress Cataloging-in-Publication Data

Names: Fisher, Douglas, 1965-, author. | Frey, Nancy, 1959- author. | Hite, Stefani Arzonetti, author.
Title: Intentional and targeted teaching : a framework for teacher growth and leadership / Douglas Fisher, Nancy Frey, Stefani Arzonetti Hite.
Description: Alexandria, VA : ASCD, 2016. | Includes bibliographical references and index.
Identifiers: LCCN 2015049292 (print) | LCCN 2016010993 (ebook) | ISBN 9781416621119 (pbk.) | ISBN 9781416621133 (ebook) | ISBN 9781416621133 (PDF)
Subjects: LCSH: Effective teaching. | Classroom environment. | Educational leadership.
Classification: LCC LB1025.3 .F575 2016 (print) | LCC LB1025.3 (ebook) | DDC 371.102--dc23
LC record available at http://lccn.loc.gov/2015049292

25 24 23 22 21 20 19 18 17 16   1 2 3 4 5 6 7 8 9 10 11 12

Intentional and Targeted Teaching

A Framework for Teacher Growth and Leadership

Introduction: Becoming a FIT Teacher 1

1. Planning with Purpose 15

2. Cultivating a Learning Climate 45

3. Instructing with Intention 81

4. Assessing with a System 115

5. Impacting Student Learning 142

Conclusion: Taking Up the Challenge 165

Acknowledgments 166

Appendix: The FIT Teaching Growth and Leadership Tool 167

References 181

Index 185

About the Authors 190

Introduction
Becoming a FIT Teacher

Recently we hosted a guest speaker for an evening gathering at a local hotel. It was a great event, with stimulating conversations about teaching and learning and hors d'oeuvres for the 160 or so people who attended. The speaker had used Nancy's computer and cables to share his stories, and one of the participants helped pack up at the end of the evening so that we could thank our guest. When we got to the car, Nancy realized that she did not have the connector that allows her computer to communicate with the projector. We went back inside the hotel to retrieve it.

When we entered the room, we saw the catering manager, the banquet manager, and a person wearing a chef's hat standing at the food table. One was literally counting tomatoes that had been left on a tray, while another counted fruit sticks. They stopped when they saw us, but Nancy had to ask what they were doing.

The banquet manager responded first, saying, "We always do a postmortem after an event like yours. We have different things we look for so that we can make changes for future events. I'm looking at the places trash was left and the number of remaining utensils. See right here, there's a pile of trash. That tells me that we need to put some sort of receptacle there, because that's where people are going to put their trash. We didn't make it obvious enough where they could dispose of things."

The catering manager added, "We're also counting leftover food. We look for trends and then make decisions about how much of what to offer groups. Your group didn't eat much of the desserts, but they demolished the hummus

1

and finger sandwiches. There are more than 20 tomatoes left. We used them for decoration, but obviously there were too many, and we don't need to waste money on extra tomatoes in the future."

The person in the chef's hat chimed in, "It's all part of our self-evaluation process. We learn from every group we host, and we make it better for the next time. If people leave hungry, they tell other people, who then don't want to have their events here. When our boss comes around, he wants to see a clean environment, so this little pile of trash is a problem, and we can address it the next time we set up the room this way. And see the utensils? There aren't any forks left, so some people probably had to use a spoon instead. That's a problem. The silverware plan wasn't matched very well to the type of food served. We will definitely fix that for next time."

We looked at one another, silently making the same connections. Although not having a fork for one's hors d'oeuvres isn't too big a problem in the larger scheme of things, not reaching students is. Not getting them to grasp algebra is. Not engaging them in the subject matter you love is. Not preparing them to be critical thinkers and strong citizens is. You get the point.

The three people in this hotel spent time collecting and analyzing data because they wanted to improve the experience their guests had. The same should be true for teachers, coaches, and administrators. We certainly care as much about our students' learning as the catering manager, the banquet manager, and the chef care about the food they serve and the environment they create. But do we routinely invest in the same kind of analysis of our practices, situations, and outcomes? Are these based in the same kind of collaborative and dialogic problem solving? The hotel team's process wasn't about filling out forms; it was about communicating with one another to reach solutions. But, as we saw, what made this possible was a conversation and a set of processes that helped the hotel staff resolve missteps and identify successes.

In this spirit, we embarked on defining the centerpiece of this book: the FIT Teaching Growth and Leadership Tool, which harnesses the FIT Teaching process and presents a detailed continuum of teacher growth and leadership. We offer it to teachers as guidance they can use to self-assess and chart a path forward. We also share this with those who support and lead teachers as a way to highlight the effectiveness of teachers' work and ground conversations in helping teachers achieve even greater success. After all, teachers are lifelong learners, dedicated to continually improving their craft.

What Is FIT Teaching?

The Framework for Intentional and Targeted Teaching®, or FIT Teaching®, is a process that evolved over the past 15 years. It began as a way of identifying the fundamental components that make up a productive educational environment for facilitating literacy development. We wanted to know: What did the most effective teachers do in order to promote successful learning? How did they plan, how did they instruct, how did they assess? What specific practices could we isolate as making the most difference?

Let's start with the words we selected as the name for this approach. The first is *framework*. We do not believe that exceedingly scripted or highly prescriptive approaches are the way to go, because they de-skill the teacher and assume that a curriculum can teach. They typically leave little room for differentiation or adjustment to the learning environment as teachers march through lessons one after another. We remember meeting a teacher who got a red card from her principal for not being on the same page in the textbook as the other 4th grade teachers. As she explained it, "We have fidelity checks every few days, and if we're behind, we're in trouble. But I had to stop because the lesson was confusing and my students didn't get it. There just isn't much wiggle room, and the district requires us to move on, even if some students don't get it."

Having said that, we're not advocating for an "anything goes" approach to curriculum and instruction. We do believe that teachers should have a *framework* for their lessons. As you will read in the chapters ahead, we are interested in instructional approaches that shift the responsibility for learning from teachers to students in an ongoing and iterative cycle. The framework we propose includes clear learning intentions, teacher modeling, guided instruction, collaborative learning, and independent learning tasks. Importantly, teachers mix and match these components in an instructional sequence designed to impact learning. They may model several times in a given lesson, or they may start a lesson with collaborative learning and then move on to modeling. The order doesn't matter, but the components of the framework do. We see a difference between teachers internalizing a framework for their lessons and them being told what to teach every minute of the day.

Intentional is the second word in this model, and we selected it because teachers' actions matter. The planning teachers do as well as the instructional decisions they make should be purposeful. High-quality instruction starts with knowing what students need to learn, then moves on to creating a wide range of learning situations in which students can engage. *Intentional* says that teachers are deliberate and that learning is expected.

Targeted, the third word, is there to stress that teachers must consider the current performance of students as well as how these students respond to the instruction. There is no reason to teach things students already know. At the same time, it's important to monitor students' learning to determine if the class needs to accelerate or slow down. When teaching is *targeted,* that means teachers are working to close the gap between what students already know and what they are expected to learn.

Two of us (Doug and Nancy) are teachers and leaders, researchers and practitioners, and we subjected the components of FIT Teaching to the best test we know: teaching them in our own classrooms and collaborating with talented colleagues in their classrooms. The framework developed further through trial and revision. As we learned more about what worked and what didn't, we honed and improved the components until they defined a coherent process that includes the essentials of effective teaching while avoiding a restrictive prescription or formula. After all, a healthy organization must be free to adapt processes to meet the needs of its particular context.

As FIT Teaching evolved, it became clear that these components can have great value to both individual teachers and teams of teachers, particularly in organizations that are inundated with multiple (and often competing) initiatives. The overarching philosophy of FIT Teaching is that it is *not* "one more thing" for teachers and leaders to do but a method for creating coherence and improvements to the complex jobs that schools undertake. Together, purposeful planning, a well-designed assessment system, and strong instruction make a difference.

Overall, FIT Teaching is a process that organizes and refines the hard work of professional growth that school leaders and dedicated teachers already seek. We all know that we can get better, no matter how good our lessons already are. As we have noted many times in our careers, there is no perfect lesson, and there is no one "right way" to teach. (There are wrong ways, but not one right way.) The FIT Teaching model is designed to keep student learning central while ensuring that teachers are empowered to make professional decisions in the best interests of their students.

The Five Interrelated Components of the FIT Teaching Tool

The FIT Teaching Growth and Leadership Tool—the FIT Teaching Tool, for short—is based on decades of research and practice. It relies on a thoughtful and intentional implementation of the work of teachers and of students, as well as the collaborative work necessary for deep learning. The instructional process it captures represents the tangible interactions of teachers and students in their learning environment, whether it consists of brick-and-mortar classrooms, a blend of virtual and face-to-face instruction, or instruction offered completely online. Irrespective of the instructional mode, teachers should plan lessons, create a productive learning climate, provide learning opportunities, assess student performance, and monitor student learning. These five components are illustrated in Figure I.1.

Figure I.1 | Components of the FIT Teaching Tool

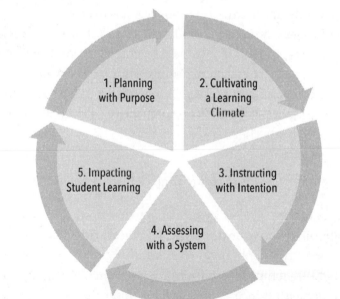

The first component, *Planning with Purpose*, highlights the work that teachers do to prepare lessons as they analyze the standards for their grade level or content area, identify learning targets and success criteria, and sequence learning. *Cultivating a Learning Climate* involves creating a welcoming classroom that also is efficient and allows for students' continuous growth and development. *Instructing with Intention* highlights the experiences that students have in the classroom as they learn. The fourth component, *Assessing with a System*, targets the formative assessment work that teachers do as they collect information about students' understandings and then take action to close any gaps that exist. And finally, the fifth component, *Impacting Student Learning*, focuses on the short- and long-term outcomes from the instruction—namely, whether or not students learned anything.

We include evidence of student learning in the FIT Teaching Tool because we think that it is important to recognize that teachers' efforts should have an influence on students' understanding. As we explain further in Chapter 5, with our tool, "student performance" is not limited to results on standardized or standards-based formal assessments. It includes evidence of student learning in the short term—as might be the case when a group of kindergarten students have mastered naming all of the letters in the alphabet or students in a chemistry class can successfully balance molar equations—and evidence of student learning in the long term, which could be measured on formal assessments, including state exams or other end-of-course and end-of-semester measures. Teachers can assess students' long-term learning in a number of ways, so this aspect needs to be negotiated, at either the state, district, or site level, depending on where the FIT Teaching Tool is used. In other words, we should not be afraid of considering student performance—the impact or outcomes of teaching—as we learn and grow as teachers.

The Structure of the FIT Teaching Tool

The full FIT Teaching Tool is presented in this book's Appendix and is also available online at www.ascd.org/ASCD/pdf/books/FITTeachingTool.pdf. Each of the tool's five components includes a number of factors (see Figure I.2), and most of the factors include a number of ingredients. For components 1–4, we provide ingredient-level rubrics for teachers and others to use to identify areas of success and areas for growth. Component 5's rubrics focus on its two factors.

The preceding paragraph makes a point so important that we need to say it again. This tool is for identifying *areas of success as well as areas for growth*. If we, as teachers, don't highlight our successes, how will our administrators and colleagues know we're capable of providing mentoring support to our colleagues? If we don't seek frequent feedback, how will we know where to focus our future learning?

Figure I.2 | Components and Factors of the FIT Teaching Tool

1. Planning with Purpose
1.1: Learning Intentions and Progressions
1.2: Evidence of Learning
1.3: Meaningful Learning

2. Cultivating a Learning Climate
2.1: Welcoming
2.2: Growth Producing
2.3: Efficient

3. Instructing with Intention
3.1: Focused Instruction
3.2: Guided Instruction
3.3: Collaborative Learning

4. Assessing with a System
4.1: Assessment to Support Learners
4.2: Assessment to Monitor Learning
4.3: Assessment to Inform Learning

5. Impacting Student Learning
5.1: Short-Term Evidence of Learning
5.2: Long-Term Evidence of Learning

Using any tool for infrequent classroom observations and a once-a-year summative conference is woefully inadequate and will not likely provide the growth opportunities all teachers deserve. Imagine if we all ran our classrooms in a similar fashion, with a single hour of testing serving as the only guide we had to assess an entire year of learning. Yet, too often, the results of a single observation are the only information school leaders rely on to evaluate teachers, or worse, student performance on a summative test is the only thing used to determine the success of the teacher.

The Purpose of the FIT Teaching Tool

The FIT Teaching Tool is designed to foster discussion among educators about our practices and to strengthen those practices through collaborative interactions. It is meant to be used by teachers for self-assessment, by teachers' trusted peers for collegial feedback, and by instructional coaches and leaders to develop the skills teachers need both onstage and offstage. Formative assessment of teachers has a significant effect on student learning at .90. It's high on the list of Hattie's (2012) meta-analysis of effective practices, yet it is frequently overlooked in favor of other classroom teaching practices and behaviors.

We have identified key behaviors and practices that, collectively, are manageable without being reductive. After all, no one is going to use these criteria routinely if the instrument is too cumbersome. Many of the criteria require conversation and discussion. You won't find a checklist, as we have learned that checking off boxes limits the focus to obvious items while overlooking those that are better determined through discussion, such as what the teacher noticed about a specific student or how the teacher planned to modify learning for another student.

We think that the more often educators use and reference the tool—during professional learning, for coaching conversations, and in professional learning communities (PLCs)—the more likely it is that teachers will internalize the items within the tool and continue to grow and develop as professional educators. For example, a group of 4th grade teachers focused on one ingredient, checking for understanding. They read various articles and information on websites to find ideas, and they planned opportunities to integrate checking for understanding in their classrooms. They also observed one another and provided feedback about the ways in which checks for understanding were used. Over time, their repertoires of strategies and techniques for checking for understanding expanded significantly, and their principal noted that they had developed a level of expertise in this area.

Assumptions Underlying the FIT Teaching Tool

The most important assumption we made in creating the FIT Teaching Tool relates to the rating scale. The tool has four levels, with a *Not Applicable* option for those rare situations in which an indicator (which we call an ingredient) could not possibly be demonstrated by a given teacher. For example, one ingredient focuses on the classroom environment. Teachers who travel from room to room each period may not have an opportunity to influence the physical aspects of the various rooms they use throughout the day. Having said that, we realize that some traveling teachers have created amazing spaces for their students' learning. For example, a fitness teacher we know brings her own supplies, including mats, battery-operated candles, and lavender spray, to create a conducive environment in any room she uses. We caution users of the FIT Teaching Tool to reserve *Not Applicable* for very rare situations.

The four growth levels are as follows:

• *Not Yet Apparent*—This level is indicated only when there is a *complete lack of evidence* that the teacher has considered a necessary aspect of instruction and incorporated it into practice. This level should be differentiated from *Not Applicable*, which indicates the very rare situation when the ingredient is not expected as part of the teacher's practice.

- *Developing*—Most typical with teachers new to the profession or new to a grade level, subject area, or curriculum implementation, this level is marked by inconsistency of practice. It is selected when it is clear that a teacher understands the criteria, but implementation is falling short of a desired level of success.

- *Teaching*—Most typical with teachers experienced in implementing criteria with fidelity, this level is selected when it is clear that the teacher's practice is intentional, solidly implemented, and resulting in success for students.

- *Leading*—Most typical with seasoned teachers, this level is selected for an individual who has embraced a particular aspect of the criterion at its highest level and is providing support, guidance, and resources for colleagues. *Leading* teachers develop learning opportunities for adults that respect individual levels of personal practice and focus on extending collective growth. Teachers at this level have classrooms with open doors and consider themselves continuous learners, thereby affecting classrooms outside their own.

We operate from an assumption that teachers show up to work every day intending to do the best that they know how to do. That does not mean we believe problematic classroom instruction or interactions are acceptable; it just means we believe that people have good intentions. In other words, we trust them. It is worth noting that trust is an important factor in teacher (and school) improvement efforts (Tschannen-Moran, 2014). When an organization has high levels of trust, people feel comfortable taking risks and stretching their practices. Without trust, people play it safe and avoid situations that may expose their misunderstandings. As Tschannen-Moran notes, when "well-intentioned principals fail to earn the trust of their faculty and their larger school community, their vision is doomed to frustration and failure" (2014, p. 1).

The language in the FIT Teaching Tool reflects these positive presuppositions about teachers and teaching. As noted, the tool includes a rating of *Not Yet Apparent* based on the assumption that the aspect of instruction in question is not yet happening because the person is not clear about expectations or needs support, in the form of coaching or professional learning, to start developing a given habit.

For example, one of the indicators that we look for, referred to as 3.1b in the tool, states that "relevance is established and maintained throughout the lesson as students are reminded about why they are learning the specific content." We assume that teachers want their instruction to be relevant. We also assume that relevance can be lost in the details of the tasks that students complete, which requires teachers to remind students of it regularly.

If a given teacher is observed not ensuring that the instruction is relevant, the teacher him- or herself can reflect on that, or an observer should ask about that. When there is no agreed-upon understanding of the importance of relevance, the conversation goes one way. If a concern emerges about how to make content relevant, the conversation goes another way. And if there is a misunderstanding about the need to remind students about relevance, the conversation goes yet another way. The positive presupposition is that the teacher who did not make learning relevant is trying his or her best and needs support to develop this habit. Having honest, open, humane, and growth-producing conversations about this will help more than punishing, berating, or humiliating someone. And talking about it with colleagues and coaches is more likely to result in change, compared with an administrator circling a low score on an annual evaluation and then moving on.

Having said that, we recognize that a small number of people may refuse to change, even with excellent coaching and support. In these cases, we still assume that they are doing their best but, for whatever reason, are not interested in the agreed-upon practices in the school or district. We recommend spending some time talking with these people to figure out why, exploring beliefs and experiences that may be influencing practices.

In addition, we assume that all teachers are leaders—leaders of classrooms and leaders of learning. In creating the FIT Teaching Growth and Leadership Tool, we wanted to recognize this fact about teachers and teaching, and thus we reserve the highest level for teachers who lead their peers. This feature makes the FIT Teaching Tool unique, because it recognizes the value of collaboration. Rather than include a single indicator on collaboration or leadership, every indicator in this tool recognizes teacher leadership. It is important to note that teachers can be leaders on some indicators and perform at the *Teaching* level on others. There is nothing wrong with being a great teacher.

We also assume that teachers are reflective about their practices. In fact, we take this as a given and do not include a factor about reflection in the FIT Teaching Tool. We all think about our work lives (and every other aspect of our lives) and make decisions about what could improve the quality of our lives. Naturally, this assumption is related to the positive presuppositions that drive our work. But realistically, we cannot imagine scaling reflections. We are not sure that there are "exceptional" versus "good" versus "adequate" reflections, in part because they are very personal and in part because reflection is best facilitated in collaboration with others. We do not think it is fair to evaluate a teacher's personal reflections or to evaluate performance based on the quality of interactions afforded to that person by peers and administrators. Thus we have chosen to assume that teachers are reflective and that the people around a given teacher will provide honest, growth-producing feedback on which the person can reflect.

Another assumption we make relates to teachers' own learning. We do not include an ingredient for professional development because the very nature of the FIT Teaching Tool requires learning. Teachers who are performing at the *Not Yet Apparent* level will have to learn something in order to improve. Teachers who are performing at the *Developing* level need to learn to refine a practice or increase their consistency in using the practice. Teachers who are performing at the *Teaching* level—again, the level we expect from everyone involved with providing learning opportunities for students—can learn to engage their colleagues. We agree with the notion that you really know something when you can teach it to another person; this is why we advocate for collaborative learning in the classroom and why we believe that the highest level should be reserved for people who can teach what they know to others. And those who are performing at the *Leading* level already know that learning is lifelong. Thus, we do not think it is necessary to include an indicator about lifelong learning.

A Note About Teacher Evaluation

Teaching is a complicated business. It requires passion and perseverance, expertise and effort. There is no one right way to ensure that all students learn. Not all instructional strategies are effective with all students. In fact, most expert teachers we know adjust their instructional repertoires as they encounter students who learn faster, or slower, than students those teachers worked with in the past.

These facts make deciding "how good" a teacher is right now—whether it's the teacher doing so for the purpose of pursuing improvement or a supervisor or coach doing it as part of an informal or formal evaluation process—complicated and tricky. So many questions need to be considered to evaluate the performance of a person tasked with changing the lives of so many. It is much easier, we think, to evaluate profit and loss or the number of cases won or lost or the percentage of satisfied customers.

As Darling-Hammond (2013) notes, "Existing systems rarely help teachers improve or clearly distinguish those who are succeeding from those who are struggling" (p. 1). Enter the FIT Teaching Tool. It's designed for teacher growth and teacher leadership, not summative evaluations. Still, we have correlated the FIT Teaching Tool with several of the major summative evaluation tools available, including

- Danielson Framework for Teaching (Danielson, 2007)
- Marshall Teacher Evaluation Rubrics (Marshall, 2011)
- Marzano Teacher Evaluation Model (Marzano, 2013)
- McREL Teacher Evaluation System (Davis, 2013)
- Strong Teacher Effectiveness Performance Evaluation System (Stronge & Tucker, 2003)

See www.ascd.org/ASCD/pdf/books/FITTeachingAlignment.pdf for these correlations.

Along with these five major models, there are state-specific criteria, home-grown rubrics developed by individual districts, and hybrid approaches, particularly in schools that provide blended and fully online options for their students. No matter the model selected, however, there are significant commonalities around teaching expectations. Thus, if teachers need to grow in a specific area of one of the above named summative evaluation tools, they can use the correlations to learn how FIT Teaching supports teachers to improve their practice.

Having acknowledged that teacher evaluation is complicated, we return to the point that we all know that we can get better at our jobs. And getting better requires identifying strengths and areas that need development. Unfortunately, in too many places, formative and summative teacher evaluation tools and "effectiveness models" have been used punitively, resulting in insecurity and fear. We believe these tools should be welcomed, because they provide growth opportunities for the very people charged with leading learning—teachers!

A Caution Before Continuing

As we have noted, the FIT Teaching Tool is designed to encourage teacher collaboration. Darling-Hammond (2013) states that good evaluation systems "must be designed so that teachers are not discouraged from collaborating with one another or from teaching the students who have the greatest educational needs" (p. 87). We designed this tool to meet that goal. Remember, the tool's highest level describes teachers who collaborate and share with their colleagues. Too many of the current effectiveness models and evaluation tools force teachers into competitive roles, because a given teacher's success depends in part on the failure of others. When this situation occurs, our profession suffers. There is simply too much evidence that teacher collaboration is powerful; in fact, it is probably the most powerful predictor of improved student achievement over time (Darling-Hammond, 2013). Competitive teacher evaluations reinforce a hoarding mentality the prevents teachers from sharing lesson ideas with one another, providing honest feedback to their colleagues, and engaging in professional dialogues about ways to respond to groups of students who do, or do not, demonstrate mastery.

Even worse, competitive teacher evaluation tools undermine professional learning communities (PLCs), the very communities that we have worked so hard to establish because they are highly effective in responding to students' learning needs. As Marzano notes, school and district-level PLCs are "probably the most influential movement with regards to actually changing practices in schools" (DuFour & Marzano, 2011, p. x).

We recognize that teachers need to be evaluated, fairly and honestly. We believe that they deserve to be evaluated so that they can receive appropriate coaching and support. But teacher evaluation in the absence of forums for collaboration will not achieve breakthrough results. Investing in collaborative planning teams that discuss high-quality instruction can lead to improved student achievement. We purposefully included ingredients that can be discussed in the context of a collaborative planning team or an entire professional learning community. The examples we provide in this book often note the ways in which groups of teachers engage with their colleagues, discussing the four essential questions of a PLC (DuFour, DuFour, & Eaker, 2008):

- What is it we expect our students to learn?
- How will we know when they have learned it?
- How will we respond when some students do not learn?
- How will we respond when some students already know it?

Our hope is that the necessary teacher evaluation process becomes integrated into the professional learning that all teachers do. We encourage teachers to share their best ideas with one another because every child deserves an amazing education. We want teachers to understand that they operate in a microcosm, as their actions and interactions have ripple effects on entire schools, districts, and communities. And we look forward to a time when teachers can engage in honest conversations with their colleagues about providing the very best learning opportunities for students. When that happens, perhaps formal evaluations will no longer be necessary, and teachers will lead their own learning and that of their peers, striving for excellence for every student.

1
Planning with Purpose

Did you know that a disproportionate number of skiing accidents happen during the fourth, fifth, or sixth time a person goes skiing? When we first heard this, we were surprised, as we thought more injuries would occur during a novice skier's initial outings. Alternatively, we could see how experienced skiers might get hurt more frequently because they are taking on challenging slopes. But the ski instructor who told us this explained that novice skiers with a handful of trips under their belt know just enough to get themselves hurt . . . and not enough to prevent it.

As novice teachers, we have all had a similar moment of reckoning. Perhaps it occurred during your second or third year in the profession. The daily jitters from constantly feeling unsure had faded, and you had begun to amass a string of successes. And then you got a bit reckless. You were confident you could wing it and decided not to devote quite as much time to planning as you had previously. After all, you had taught this content once or twice before, and the experience had left you feeling more surefooted.

And then it happened. You tried to teach the lesson, but your students were unclear about the content and began asking questions you were unable to answer. Or you had difficulty linking the new information to the unit of study, and students grew restless. Or the principal came into your classroom during a learning walk and asked you about your formative assessment plan. Whatever the particular circumstances on your day of reckoning, you learned a vital lesson: planning is critical to the success of a lesson. That humbling moment reminded you that you didn't know nearly as much about teaching as you thought you did.

Expert educators have learned that careful planning is key to advancing student learning. For this reason, we begin our focus on high-quality teaching by discussing **Planning with Purpose**, the first component in the FIT Teaching Tool. To paraphrase the Cheshire Cat in *Alice in Wonderland*, if you don't know where you are going, any road will take you there. Without a clear plan, teachers and students may get somewhere, but it may not be where they needed to go.

Planning with Purpose begins with intentionality. By that we mean that unit design should provide students with the necessary frame to link what they are learning to existing and new knowledge. It should promote transfer. This intentionality is represented in the FIT Teaching Tool as the first factor of the Planning with Purpose component: *Learning Intentions and Progressions*. A second factor in this component is the teacher's ability to identify short-term success criteria and to plan strategically for how evidence of progress will be collected: *Evidence of Learning*. Rounding out the planning component is attention to planning learning experiences that will be worthwhile and coherent for learners: *Meaningful Learning*. We begin with the first factor, *Learning Intentions and Progressions*.

Factor 1.1: Learning Intentions and Progressions

Planning begins with identifying the learning intentions of the unit under study and then continues with creating a series of lessons that will ensure that students develop proficiency in the content being investigated. In this chapter, we focus on the planning that teachers do to ensure that students achieve high levels of success. In subsequent chapters, we focus on the enactment of the plans as well as the ways in which these plans are modified as students respond, or fail to respond, to the instruction. Remember, hope is not a plan. Students deserve well-planned and sequenced lessons that build on their strengths and address their needs. To our thinking, the *Learning Intentions and Progressions* factor includes identifying transfer goals, building schema through links to important themes or problems, and crafting content and language learning intentions that are lesson specific.

The following discussions of each of these ingredients include the corresponding rubrics that are part of the FIT Teaching Tool and that describe the four levels of teacher growth—*Not Yet Apparent (NYA)*, *Developing*, *Teaching*, and *Leading*—explained in the Introduction. (Similar discussions and rubrics appear in Chapters 2 through 5, which cover the other four components of the tool.)

1.1a: Identifying transfer goals

NYA	Developing	Teaching	Leading
The teacher does not consider transfer goals during planning.	The teacher identifies transfer goals but does not use them to align plans for student application and assessment.	The teacher plans with grade- or course-appropriate transfer goals in mind, and uses them to align activities and assessments.	The teacher supports colleagues in their ability to plan with grade- or course-appropriate transfer goals in mind and use them to align activities and assessments.

Learning intentions are foundational to everything teachers do with students. The work of planning begins not with listing the isolated facts and skills that students should know but with determining the major conceptual processes that lie at the core of a unit of study. These enduring understandings go well beyond skills (Wiggins & McTighe, 2005). For example, learning the Toulmin method for constructing a written argument is a skill; understanding that these elements frame logical and reasoned argument throughout society is an enduring understanding. McTighe (personal communication, 4/13/15) says that teachers know that they are working on a transfer goal when they can complete this sentence: "Students will be able to independently use their learning to. . . ."

Enduring understandings are put into operation through identification of transfer goals. Think of transfer goals as what one does with enduring understandings in novel situations. In other words, they are the expression of understanding. To extend the example from the last paragraph, a transfer goal is that students will be able to write cogent arguments to support claims using formal reasoning and evidence. Learners should be able to do this in a variety of settings. For instance, students may construct a formal argumentation essay in their English class and then use similar features to write an analysis of a document-based prompt in their history course.

Transfer goals are identified through analysis of the standards. If you live in a place where the Common Core State Standards are relevant, some transfer goals are identified through grade-level outcomes. For instance, in 6th grade, students are explaining the relationship between claims and reasons; by 8th grade, this outcome has expanded to include counterclaims and evidence, as well as claims and reasons. McTighe (2014) explains that transfer goals possess the following characteristics:

- They are long-term in nature; i.e., they develop and deepen over time.
- They are performance based; i.e., they require application (not simply recall).
- The application occurs in new situations, not ones previously taught or encountered; i.e., the task cannot be accomplished as a result of rote learning.
- The transfer requires a thoughtful assessment of which prior learning applies here; i.e., some strategic thinking is required (not simply "plugging in" skill and facts).
- The learners must apply their learning autonomously, without coaching or excessive hand-holding by a teacher.
- Transfer calls for the use of habits of mind; i.e., good judgment, self-regulation, persistence along with academic understanding, knowledge and skill. (p. 1)

As you examine your standards documents, keep these features in mind.

We especially appreciate McTighe's advice concerning "excessive hand-holding" as it speaks to the long-term nature of transfer. It's a lot easier and faster to learn discrete skills than it is to learn how to transfer that knowledge across situations. For example, we might introduce 6th grade students to writing for argument through intentional instruction, including extensive scaffolding in the form of paragraph frames, essay templates, and so on. However, those 6th graders will need much more than a single short unit on argumentative writing to craft strong written and spoken arguments in other disciplines and situations. Transfer goals require an investment of time to create opportunities throughout the year for students to apply this knowledge. It is for this reason that Wiggins and McTighe (2005) advise that transfer goals consist only of those that will be assessed. Although argumentative writing involves lots of important skills and information, not all of these need to be assessed.

A group of 11th grade teachers kept these characteristics of transfer goals in mind as they planned an interdisciplinary unit on writing for argument. English teacher MaryAnn Gates, chemistry teacher Christina Hobson, and history teacher Antoni Caro used the standards in their content areas to identify argumentative writing as a transfer goal common to their disciplines. To foster transfer, they planned a two-week unit in September to expose their students to the use of argument in each content area, and they created assignments to promote application. Ms. Gates taught elements of argumentation in her

English class, while Mr. Caro focused on the use of argument in excerpts from U.S. Supreme Court decisions. Ms. Hobson used science articles to analyze evidence that supported and refuted claims. In each course, students wrote short argumentative essays that aligned with the content they were learning. It is important to note that the team understood that this unit alone would not be sufficient, so they mapped out a series of competencies throughout the year that would continue to press students to use formal reasoning in their writing.

This example is an excellent illustration of a *Teaching* level of growth for the ingredient of *identifying transfer goals*. However, the three teachers advanced to a *Leading* level through Doug's support. With his encouragement, they individually shared their processes with other faculty at the school, using short videos they each made to capture their instruction. They also discussed their efforts and success at a professional learning session, where they spoke to the rest of the faculty about their work and their students' progress. We note this to reiterate that achieving *Leading* levels is not dependent on job title, and that sharing experiences with an eye toward developing the capacity of others is within the reach of any skilled teacher.

A teacher at the *Developing* level of growth is applying knowledge of transfer goals but is not yet sustaining attention to them systematically. George Diaz was developing his ability to use transfer goals. He attended a summer institute on curriculum development after his first year as a kindergarten teacher. "I can see now how transfer goals are essential in learning how to read," he told his induction coach. He abandoned the "letter of the week" approach he had used the previous year because he realized that it sacrificed transfer in favor of discrete skills. After reexamining the kindergarten expectations, he identified using letter-sound relationships to decode unfamiliar words as an important transfer goal. Near the end of the first quarter, he met again with the induction coach, who asked him about how he was assessing his students on their progress toward this transfer goal. Mr. Diaz acknowledged that although he had completed several screening assessments during the first weeks of school, he had not yet revisited them. "I realize I should," he said. "I said this was important, but then that means I also have to monitor [it]." He and his coach scheduled several assessments to administer during the second quarter so Mr. Diaz would have a better sense of his students' progress. "I can't do a great job planning if I don't know how they're doing," he said.

Unfortunately, not all teachers have identified transfer goals, and some simply teach individual lessons. Marco Parma was one such teacher. Despite having taught for several years, he had never considered transfer goals and thus regularly performed at the *Not Yet Apparent* level. Talking with a colleague who had focused on transfer goals piqued Mr. Parma's interest. This colleague regularly brought examples of student work to their collaborative planning team meetings, and the work was far superior to that of Mr. Parma's students. This colleague did not brag about her students' performance; instead, she engaged in reflective conversations about their learning. Mr. Parma planned a time to talk with her further about implementing transfer goals so that he could determine what he wanted his students to know and be able to do in unique situations.

1.1b: Linking to theme, problem, project, or question

NYA	Developing	Teaching	Leading
The teacher does not link learning intentions to themes, problems, projects, or questions.	The teacher identifies learning intentions that are minimally linked to themes, problems, projects, or questions.	The teacher identifies learning intentions that are linked to themes, problems, projects, or questions.	The teacher supports colleagues in their ability to identify learning intentions that are linked to themes, problems, projects, or questions.

Themes, problems, projects, and questions can make the learning journey as interesting as the destination. They are used to foster inquiry and curiosity about the unit of study. The use of such devices builds schemas to transform isolated bits of information into a unified and flexible whole.

Themes, problems, projects, and questions work like a magnet to draw information together in ways that build schemas. Students might have an array of isolated facts about a topic but no real way of gathering them together. Think of a bunch of paper clips scattered across a desktop. If you wave a large magnet near them, the paper clips form a unified whole. Suddenly, what seemed like a disordered mess is transformed. Using themes, problems, projects, and questions as inquiry approaches serves as an important way to gather daily learning intentions into schemas that move students closer to attaining enduring understandings, which, in turn, form the basis for transfer goals (see Figure 1.1).

The professional learning communities at Grant Middle School were studying the importance of oral language in learning, and they decided to base their discussion on an issue of *Educational Leadership* focused on talking and listening. The mathematics department selected an article titled "Talking About

Figure 1.1 | A Focus on Learning

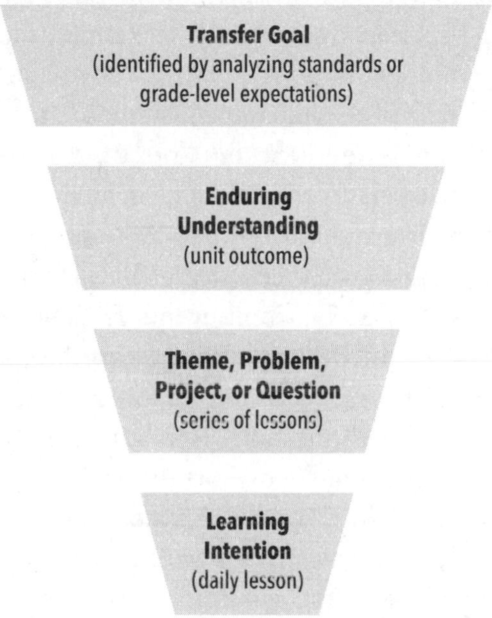

Transfer Goal
(identified by analyzing standards or
grade-level expectations)

**Enduring
Understanding**
(unit outcome)

**Theme, Problem,
Project, or Question**
(series of lessons)

**Learning
Intention**
(daily lesson)

Math" (Hintz & Kazemi, 2014) for their discussion. The PLC members took turns leading, and this time it was Kathy Ellington's turn. A few days before the meeting, she had sent copies of the issue to her colleagues, along with two sets of questions to spur their thinking as they read:

1. The authors state that "[d]ifferent discussions serve different purposes, and the discussion goal acts as a compass as teachers navigate classroom talk" (p. 37). How do you match discussion protocols/routines with your learning intentions? How do you know you got it right? How do you know when there's a mismatch?

2. "The ways teachers and students talk with one another is crucial to what students learn about mathematics and about themselves as doers of mathematics" (p. 40). What do you observe among your own students? Do they see themselves as "doers of mathematics"?

Ms. Ellington's use of questions helped her colleagues organize their thinking beyond simply summarizing the article. By planning thought-provoking questions for a collegial conversation, she set the stage for a discussion of the link between content knowledge and students' use of language and demonstrated her *Leading* level of growth for this ingredient. Later in the year, when Ms. Ellington met with a supervisor, she used this example as an artifact of her work leading colleagues.

Another member of Ms. Ellington's school, 7th grade social studies teacher Lyn Jeffries, was at the *Teaching* level of growth. Her students were studying Islamic civilizations in the Middle Ages. She identified an enduring understanding that human migratory patterns ensure that a culture spreads rapidly throughout a region. Her transfer goal was for her students to see patterns between historical and current events as they relate to the impact of human movement. She planned a unit of instruction designed to ensure that her students would reach this understanding by organizing learning experiences around a thought-provoking question. Her students engaged in an online investigation using the question "How did the Hajj pilgrimage shape politics in places like Spain and Timbuktu?" Over the course of two days, students worked collaboratively in small groups to address the question and share information with their peers. The question was posted in a prominent place in the classroom. In addition, students saw the question on their course home page each time they logged into the learning management system. To foster transfer, Ms. Jeffries asked her students to identify a current event in which human movement was affecting a society. When she prepared her midyear self-reflection of her professional growth for her PLC, she used this unit as evidence of her *Teaching* level of growth for this ingredient.

Down the hall, 6th grade music teacher Nate Wilcox was at the *Developing* level of growth for this ingredient. An experienced music educator, Mr. Wilcox had joined the school earlier in the year after moving into the area from another part of the state. He was new to the practice of using themes, problems, projects, and questions in his teaching. As the only music teacher in the school, he didn't have content-alike colleagues to consult, although the instructional coach helped him build a general level of knowledge. Mr. Wilcox wrote an e-mail to several music educators he knew around the state and asked them how they used themes, problems, projects, and questions in their classes to facilitate deeper learning. The responses he received ranged from planning a project (a public performance), to a theme (music expresses human experiences and values), to a question (How does culture affect music?). Thrilled with these ideas, Mr. Wilcox began his journey to ensure that students developed enduring understandings, rather than only skills, in his classes. He used these ideas to plan a series of lessons for his students focused on the question "How do music and history influence each other?" The instructional coach used the FIT Teaching Tool to spark Mr. Wilcox's reflections on his professional growth since arriving at the school. Mr. Wilcox placed himself in the *Developing* category, because he had done this kind of planning only once so far, whereas his earlier units had mostly been skills-driven.

Next door to Mr. Wilcox's classroom was Gary Hines's technology classroom. During one observation, Mr. Hines administered an online test to his students for the entire period and therefore did not pose a question for them. During another observation, the students worked independently on updating their websites. Having noticed the lack of a theme or an essential question on at least four different occasions, a trusted colleague met with Mr. Hines to discuss the fact that his efforts in this area were *Not Yet Apparent*. When asked about this, Mr. Hines said, "As I circulated around the room, I wondered whether it might not be useful to let them know why we were learning all of this. I could have easily let them know the question we've been working on, but I thought it would be obvious. It's part of my lesson plan. See, it's written right here [pointing to his plan book]: *How can technology be used productively to solve social problems?* Did you think I didn't have one? Wow! If you didn't get it, then how would my students ever get it? These lessons must have made no sense to them. I gotta go back and fix this. We've done all of this work to figure out how to solve social problems. Will you excuse me? I have some planning to do!"

1.1c: Identifying lesson-specific learning intentions

NYA	Developing	Teaching	Leading
The teacher does not identify lesson-specific learning intentions.	The teacher identifies learning intentions that may be too broad to accomplish during a specific lesson.	The teacher identifies learning intentions that are achievable during a specific lesson.	The teacher supports colleagues in their ability to identify learning intentions that are achievable during a specific lesson.

The third ingredient in this factor is keeping the daily learning intention just that—*daily*. As we discussed in previous sections, enduring understandings capture the big ideas that will linger long after a unit of study is over, and the theme, problem, project, or question fosters inquiry across several lessons. However, the lesson-specificity aspect of the learning intention anchors students in today's work. Together, daily learning intentions and larger units of study allow students to consider what it is they are learning at the macro and micro levels. But this isn't possible if the teacher (1) is not aware of both levels or (2) can't articulate these levels to students in developmentally appropriate ways.

Excellent teachers are able to analyze the standards to identify transfer goals; develop enduring understandings; express those in themes, problems, projects, or questions; and then distill the needed learning into daily targets. The evidence supporting the use of learning targets or learning intentions has grown substantially in the learning sciences, as these expectations direct students' attention to what they will be learning and what it is they will be doing with this knowledge. It is important to note that these daily learning intentions form the basis for how the teacher will formatively assess learning (Chappuis, Stiggins, Chappuis, & Arter, 2012).

Sixth grade teacher Claudia Rowe was working on her lesson plans when she said, "I've got it! I want them to write a strong informative essay. So that's my learning intention, right? It might take them a few days, but is that what you're talking about?" Her colleagues, patient as ever, said, "Writing a strong informative essay is an outcome, but it's not what they will learn. What do you want your students to *learn* on the first day, and then the second, and so on until they show you they have learned it through the essay?"

Ms. Rowe responded, "I'm not sure. No, I really think that's it. I want them to write an informative essay. Why can't I just say that each day until they can do it?"

Matt Robenstein explained, "Because it's too broad. Take it in pieces. Could you see that students might learn to write a strong introduction on their topic on the first day? If that's a good starting place for you, then it helps you decide what to teach and what evidence you are looking for from students."

Jessica Andrews added, "And if those introductions aren't as strong as you want and don't meet our 6th grade expectations, then you'll know what you need to teach to which kids. If they get it, then the learning intention on your second day might be for them to learn how to cite evidence for their paper. You could do a whole lesson on that and then get them started. You'll want to collect their work to see if the lesson worked. Is that making sense? We have to take it apart and decide what they need to learn each day, not just have a statement up on the wall, like wallpaper, for days and weeks on end. It's about understanding the content so well that we know what students have to learn each day, and to notice who does and does not learn it."

Ms. Rowe, reflecting, said, "Those first two days would be excellent. I could really see how to use class time to accomplish that. But then, I was thinking that the third day could focus on explaining why the evidence was important. Do you think that would work? I mean that they would learn how to explain to their reader why the evidence was important and how it was linked to their claim from the introduction. Am I getting it? And once this is all done, they will have amazing papers. And then, sometime in the future, can I assign this again to see if it stuck?"

Ms. Andrews responded, "Yes, I think we're all getting it. It's about making sure our students know what they're supposed to learn and then figuring out if they learned it. And I really like the idea of cycling back to make sure it sticks."

High school teacher Paula Evans is an interesting case in point. She was in the early stages of using clear, lesson-specific learning intentions in her planning but was still not sure when and how best to implement them. She met with her induction coach, Sam Carter, to discuss the use of daily learning intentions in her lessons. Mr. Carter had shadowed Ms. Evans earlier in the day, and now they were debriefing. Her coach asked about her first-period earth science class, and Ms. Evans said, "I didn't need a learning intention because it was a review day for them. They're taking a test in two days."

Mr. Carter didn't address this comment immediately but instead asked about Ms. Evans's planning process for her second-period class, which was environmental science. Unlike those in the first-period class, these students were learning new content. Ms. Evans explained how the specificity of the lesson's learning intention—to analyze data on declining monarch butterfly populations and decreased forest acreage—related to the course content standards. Mr. Carter followed with questions about how she had formatively assessed her students. "The kids worked in small groups and had to use a couple of different data sources to draw conclusions and develop hypotheses," she explained. "Each group submitted their findings on [the course learning management system], which allowed them to meet their language learning intention, which was focused on a language function: to draw conclusions. I'll be reviewing those tonight to decide what I need to review or clarify tomorrow."

"That's great," said the induction program coach. "Now I'd like you to think further about your use of a lesson-specific learning intention in both periods. You said you didn't need one for first period [*Not Yet Apparent* level of growth] because students were reviewing for the test. But you clearly used one effectively in second period [*Teaching* level of growth]. In both cases, aren't you looking for evidence of what students know and don't know, so you can plan future instruction?" Ms. Evans nodded in agreement and said, "I see what you're saying, but I still don't know what my learning intention would be in a test review lesson. Can we talk about that?"

At the same high school, seasoned English teacher Dave Franklin used the FIT Teaching Tool in partnership with colleague Mai Lam. Although Mr. Franklin had taught for many years, his experience was largely with 9th graders. Conversely, Ms. Lam, although she had fewer overall years in the profession, had spent most of them teaching American literature to 11th and 12th graders—levels that were new to Mr. Franklin this year. Ms. Lam and Mr. Franklin planned together and observed in each other's classes when possible. The day after Mr. Franklin's lesson-specific learning intention was determining the usefulness of research sources for a literary analysis paper his students were developing, Ms. Lam pointed out that, although it was precise, the learning intention was not content-appropriate for 11th grade students. "This is definitely a good learning intention for 9th graders, but by the time they get to their junior year, we're raising the bar. When I'm teaching this content, I'm challenging students to determine the limitations of the source as it relates to their essay. It's a subtle difference but an important one," she said. Mr. Franklin agreed. "It's really pushing them to see the nuances across sources and how one source might be better than another for their research," he said. "I'm not sure what I would have done without your help in planning. It's really valuable, and I hope I can pay you back sometime." In this discussion, Mr. Franklin was at the *Developing* level of growth because his learning intentions were not fully aligned with the course expectations, whereas Ms. Lam's support of Mr. Franklin placed her at the *Leading* level of growth.

1.1d: Identifying content learning intentions

NYA	Developing	Teaching	Leading
The teacher does not identify content learning intentions.	The teacher identifies content learning intentions that may be vague or not grade- or content-appropriate or are primarily centered around isolated activities or tasks rather than on learning targets or enduring understandings.	The teacher identifies content learning intentions that are clearly stated and grade- or course-appropriate and are related to learning targets and enduring understandings rather than tasks or activities.	The teacher supports colleagues in their ability to identify content learning intentions that are clearly stated and grade- or course-appropriate and are related to learning targets and enduring understandings rather than tasks or activities.

Understanding the content is foundational to planning effective and responsive lessons. It is hard to teach something you don't know very well.

Understanding the content well allows us to identify appropriate early lessons versus those that are built on prior foundations. As part of the planning process, be sure to sequence a number of lessons, with each building on the previously mastered content. These content learning intentions can be assessed for the progression, as well as for their match with grade-level and content-area expectations. An amazing content learning intention statement for 4th graders that is based on 2nd grade standards will not result in high levels of achievement.

Daily content learning intentions are distilled from the standards for the course, and they describe the range of declarative (factual), procedural (application), and conditional (judgment) knowledge (Brown, 1987) expected of students at that grade or in that course. The content is what students are expected to *learn*, not what they are expected to *do*. This is an important distinction that will play out in the other aspects of the FIT Teaching Tool. We have to know what we want students to learn if we are going to be effective in aligning instructional minutes to that expectation and in designing appropriate assessments to identify which students learned the content and which still need additional instruction.

A teacher at the *Not Yet Apparent* level has done nothing to establish a content learning intention for the class. When principal May Yoon visited a series of classrooms, she discovered the children in one classroom playing a word game on the board during math time. "I figured we would be going out to recess in about 15 minutes" was the teacher's reasoning for the complete absence of any content learning intention. No learning intention was apparent for this lesson, even though students seemed to enjoy the task at hand.

After recess, Ms. Yoon visited the same teacher again and discovered that the learning intention that was posted was not appropriate for the content. The students were working collaboratively on a PowerPoint presentation about a person who made a difference, but the content learning intention indicated that students would be journaling about their recent trip to the zoo. Ms. Yoon met with the teacher to talk about the content expectations, noting that the students deserved to know what they were expected to learn. When Ms. Yoon asked to see her plans, this teacher confessed that she wasn't sure how to design lessons that met the standards because her role in the past was to implement a curriculum that had been developed for her. She asked for help, and Ms. Yoon scheduled some time for them to meet to plan a lesson together.

Later, Ms. Yoon observed in the classroom of Vanessa Artiles, a first-year teacher who had invited her to watch her teach. Ms. Artiles told her students that their learning intention was to "successfully and accurately complete the mathematics problems on page 43 of your workbook." When the two debriefed the lesson, Ms. Yoon asked her colleague to examine the rubric and invited her to self-assess. "I'd have to say I'm at the *Developing* level," said Ms. Artiles. "I wanted them to complete a task, but I really don't know how to take it to a higher level. I'm mean, that's what I want them to *do*." Ms. Yoon asked, "Yes, but what do you want them to *learn*?" Within a few minutes, the two had polished a learning target that Ms. Artiles planned to use in the next lesson: "I can read a series of fractions and put them in order from smallest to largest."

Meanwhile, in a classroom nearby, Frank Desiderio was using the tool to self-assess in preparation for a meeting he would be having with the principal. Ms. Yoon had conducted a teaching observation the previous day, and Mr. Desiderio was reflecting on his lesson. He identified at the *Teaching* level of growth because he had explicitly linked the learning target for the lesson ("to describe to a partner the characteristics of yellow dwarf and red dwarf stars") to the science unit's enduring understanding ("stars form and change over time in predictable ways"). He planned to bring his unit of study to their discussion so that he and his principal could talk about the lesson she observed and how that content fit into a larger overall unit.

Later the same day, Ms. Yoon met with another teacher, Avery Lincoln, to discuss her supportive work with Ms. Artiles, the first-year teacher. "I appreciate the way you're *Leading* learning with her," said the principal. "Your conversations are supportive but also clear and informative. You have really helped her with her planning by dissecting the standard and pacing it out over several lessons. I suspect in no time Ms. Artiles will easily recognize the difference between a learning target focused on activities and one focused on enduring understandings. What can I do to support your work with her in the future?"

1.1e: Identifying language learning intentions

NYA	Developing	Teaching	Leading
The teacher does not identify language learning intentions.	The teacher identifies language learning intentions that may be vague or not grade- or content-appropriate.	The teacher identifies language learning intentions that are clearly stated; focused on vocabulary, structure, or function; and grade- or content-appropriate.	The teacher supports colleagues in their ability to identify language learning intentions that are clearly stated; focused on vocabulary, structure, or function; and grade- or content-appropriate.

Language development is another ingredient in learning progressions. Content and language learning intentions are really two sides of the same coin, with the content element outlining what students will learn and the language element defining how students might use that information or demonstrate their understanding of the content (the success criteria). The language learning intention can encompass the reading, writing, speaking, listening, and thinking that students do. This intention is also vital for assessment purposes because it signals how learning can be measured. In other words, if the language learning intention is "to use the technical vocabulary of the stages of meiosis in a written explanation," then the formative assessment should be exactly that. A language learning intention is easiest when considered in terms of tangible products but more challenging when one is considering listening and thinking.

The language demands required to learn content are an important consideration no matter what grade level you teach. If students don't understand key vocabulary in science, history, mathematics, art, and so on, it's hard to argue that they are proficient in that subject. Humans think in terms of language, and we expect all our students to be thinking about the course content. Accordingly, then, we need to ensure that students have developed the language of the discipline. And this language is not just vocabulary that students need to learn. They also need to develop their understanding of *language structure* and *language functions* within the discipline (Fisher & Frey, 2010b). In general, the language learning intention relates to one of the following:

- *Vocabulary*—the general academic or domain-specific words that students need to know to be proficient in the content area. Sometimes the focus is on general academic terms that have specific meanings in a given discipline, such as *prime* or *expel*. Other times, the focus is on domain-specific terms that are unique to a discipline, such as *rhombus* or *stoichiometry*.
- *Language structures*—the formal grammar and syntax that users of academic language employ. An important point is that different disciplines have different conventions for the language structures commonly used. For example, science uses passive voice more frequently than other subjects.
- *Language functions*—the various reasons we use language, such as to debate, describe, explain, inform, persuade, or entertain, to name a few. Often, as students get older and have more knowledge in a discipline, the language learning intention focuses on the function that language is serving for the user.

Figure 1.2 contains sample language learning intention statements in different content areas.

Preschool lead teacher Arlette Jackson saw her own practice develop during her two decades in the profession, and she modeled and engaged in a think-aloud about her reflective practice during a professional learning session she led with her colleagues. She selected the language learning intention portion of the FIT Teaching Tool because this was a current area of study at her school. "When I first started teaching preschool in the late 1980s, nobody thought about learning intentions," she said. "I just did what everyone did in those days. I used an agenda to help the children organize their time and anticipate transitions, but I didn't share the learning intention for anything we did. In those days, I'd have been a *Not Yet Apparent* on the scale," she chuckled.

Ms. Jackson continued:

As our profession turned to DAP [Developmentally Appropriate Practices], I saw that I had a learning curve. We all know that language is everything in our classrooms, and I'd encourage language use, but not always as well as I could have. It took me a while to get a better sense of the language progressions of young children and how to be more specific with them so that I could add to the challenge as needed. Initially, I would describe myself as being at the *Developing* level of growth. My plans were vague, and I wasn't always sure that they were age-appropriate. With time and practice, I got better at thinking through these progressions and using them in my planning. Now, I would say that my language learning intention statements are directly connected with the assessments I use. I'll share one I used the other day in my small groups. I think it might help my colleagues understand why this is an important aspect of planning and teaching. [*Leading* level of growth]

I'm being more intentional about teaching and assessing listening skills. So I told the children that our language learning intention was to listen to details of a weather report to decide what to wear. I recorded myself reading some simple weather reports and then played them back. The children selected outerwear and put them on the boy and girl figures on the felt board. When they disagreed, I played the weather reports again for them.

Figure 1.2 | Examples of Language Learning Intention Statements

Content Area	Vocabulary	Structure	Function
Mathematics	Use *less than, equal to,* or *greater than* to compare groups or numbers.	Highlight addition signal words in a word problem.	Describe the relationship between numbers in expanded form and standard form.
Social Studies	Name the routes and explorers who used them on a map.	Sequence the steps of food production using the signal words *first, then, next,* and *finally.*	Justify in a paragraph the ways fire was used for hunting, cooking, and warmth by citing three examples.
Language Arts	Use *who, what,* and *why* to ask a question of your partner.	Identify the verb tenses used in the reading to explain what happened long ago and what will happen in the future.	Explain what organizational pattern was used by the writer and critique its adequacy.
Science	Label a diagram of the digestive system (*teeth, mouth, esophagus, stomach, small intestine, large intestine, colon*).	Using the sentence frame "On the one hand, _____. On the other hand, _____," students will demonstrate their knowledge of the Earth's layers.	Inform your team members about three ways that an environment can change.
Art	Use visual analysis terminology (*line, color, balance, form, shape*) to describe a painting.	Use a museum-exhibition label form to cite a displayed work of art.	Compare and contrast two paintings from the same time period in a written critique.
Physical Education	Identify body movements used in soccer (*scissor, drag and push, cuts, dribble*).	Use language frames to signal teammates about changing game conditions (e.g., calling for the ball, letting a team member know when there is pressure from an opposing player, signaling encouragement).	Participate in a postgame discussion of successes, challenges, and action steps.

Source: From "Unpacking the Language Purpose: Vocabulary, Structure, and Function," by D. Fisher & N. Frey, 2010, *TESOL Journal, 1*(3), pp. 315–337. Copyright 2010 by TESOL. Adapted with permission.

One colleague asked Ms. Jackson why she had bothered to record the weather reports, when she just could have read the examples to the children. Here's how she replied:

> That's a great question, and for a long time that's exactly what I did. But it dawned on me that it wasn't purely listening, because they could watch my facial expressions and gestures. I changed my lesson so that it lined up better with my language learning intention, which was to listen, not listen and watch. I feel like these plans have better addressed the language that I was focused on with my students. I think that planning this out made me a better teacher because I had the chance to think about the language that I wanted students to learn. [*Teaching* level of growth]

High school chemistry teacher David Flores was observed on several occasions by his principal, Brianna Adams, who noticed that Mr. Flores never posted a language learning intention and students did not know what the language expectations of the class were. When Ms. Adams met with Mr. Flores, she asked him about his plans for language learning intentions. Mr. Flores responded, "Yeah, I don't really do that. By the time they are juniors or seniors, their language should already be developed enough to succeed in my class. If it's not, it's not my job to go back and fix it. That should be taken care of by the English department." Mr. Flores was clearly at the *Not Yet Apparent* level of growth and did not see a need to change.

Ms. Adams invited Mr. Flores to observe a physics class in a nearby high school. She offered to cover his class for the day so that he could observe all of the classes taught by the other teacher. In addition, she asked Mr. Flores to watch a video clip from a genetics class at a nearby magnet school in which the teacher focused on key terminology that students must learn. Ms. Adams ended their conversation saying, "I so appreciate you watching that clip with me and your open mind during our visit to the physics class. I look forward to talking with you and seeing where your thinking is after some of these experiences."

Several weeks later, following a very productive visit by Mr. Flores to the other school and a great conversation about the value of language in science, Ms. Adams had an opportunity to observe him again, and she noted that he had moved to the *Developing* level. The lesson plan lying on the desk identified key vocabulary terms, and Mr. Flores reminded students several times to practice their vocabulary. Ms. Adams knew that this teacher had made progress and that the chemistry students were better off as a result.

Factor 1.2: Evidence of Learning

The second factor of Planning with Purpose relates to the evidence of learning that teachers *plan* to collect as part of their lessons. Of course, during classroom instruction, teachers are regularly, even continuously, collecting information about students' understanding. Teachers also know what it is that students should learn as an outcome from the lesson and unit. That last point is a critical aspect of Instructing with Intention, which we will explore further in Chapter 3, and Assessing with a System, which we will discuss in Chapter 4. For now, let's focus on the plans that teachers develop to gauge student learning and the opportunities they create to collect evidence about students' learning.

1.2a: Identifying success criteria

NYA	Developing	Teaching	Leading
The teacher does not design summative assessments related to the lesson's learning intentions.	The teacher designs summative assessments that indirectly relate to the lesson's established learning intentions, permit limited application opportunities to foster transfer, or yield inconclusive data around student understanding.	The teacher collaborates with students to design summative assessments that relate directly to the lesson's established learning intentions and permit students the opportunity to demonstrate their understanding in order to foster long-term transfer.	The teacher supports colleagues in their ability to collaborate with students to design summative assessments that relate directly to the lesson's established learning intentions and permit students the opportunity to demonstrate their understanding in order to foster long-term transfer.

As we have noted, learning intentions provide students with information about what they will learn. Students also need to know how they are expected to demonstrate that learning and, even more critically, how they, themselves, will know if they have learned the content. Often this aspect is called the *success criteria*, which detail the performance expectations for students. The New Zealand Ministry of Education (n.d.) provides this definition:

> Success criteria describe how students will go about achieving a learning intention or how they will know when they have learnt it. The purpose of creating success criteria is to ensure students understand the teacher's criteria for making judgments about their work, and so that they gain an "anatomy of quality" for that particular piece of work. If students have been involved in the creation of success criteria they are more likely to take more ownership of their learning, be self-evaluative as they are working,

and question the assessed work as it evolves. Measuring whether a single learning intention has been met may involve co-constructing several success criteria. (para. 1)

Clear success criteria ensure not only that students take ownership of their learning but also that teachers have defensible data for grading and other summative evaluation tasks. Further, clearly articulated success criteria allow you to engage in backward planning (Wiggins & McTighe, 2005), which results in stronger lessons with greater internal cohesion.

Success criteria provide students and their teachers with a clear understanding of what is to be assessed as well as how it will be assessed. These criteria can be relatively simple and designed for student self-evaluation, such as when they are crafted in the form of statements that are oriented to the student (e.g., "You will write a 150-word summary of the article, using the correct terminology, and cite paraphrased evidence from the text to support the article's thesis"). Success criteria are also needed when the assessed assignment or project is more complex. In these cases, a rubric is an ideal means for conveying the success criteria. Rubrics may be co-constructed with learners, although the teacher has significant input into the design and the criteria. Rubrics include a range of performance levels and give students clear measures of how they will be assessed and graded. These rubrics are even more effective for conveying success criteria when students have a chance to view a range of quality work samples, from inadequate to excellent.

Teacher Matthew Bradley refrained from designing any assessments until the end of the unit. As he said, "I like to see what I really taught, not just what I thought I would teach, before I think about how I will assess students." As a result, Mr. Bradley's students experienced a hit-or-miss approach to learning. Because Mr. Bradley did not know what he wanted his students to learn and failed to identify clear success criteria, his students often did not master the content standards, and their performance on common formative assessments, designed by his colleagues, was below par. Mr. Bradley was at the *Not Yet Apparent* level of growth—and he was a source of frustration for his collaborative planning team.

The other members of his 7th grade social studies team were at the *Teaching* level. For each unit of study, they identified success criteria and created common formative assessments, as well as summative performance tasks that allowed students to demonstrate their mastery. The team liked to provide students with choices, and they regularly created several different performance tasks from which students could choose. As the teachers noted, "It's important that each choice maintain the rigor of the class."

The daily assessments might or might not include choice. For example, on one day during the unit of study on Islamic civilization, the students in Ms. Jeffries's class were asked to respond to the following prompt: "The Qur'an and the Sunnah greatly influence the lives of Muslims. Explain what the Qur'an and the Sunnah are, why they are significant, and how they influence the daily lives of Muslims." Toward the end of the unit, Ms. Jeffries provided the students with several quotes from the Qur'an and the Sunnah and asked them to select specific quotes that they wanted to explain. All students had to include at least four quotes, but the quotes they selected were their choice. They also had to include clear explanations of the meaning of the quotes and answer two questions: (1) What would a person say if he or she held this belief? (2) What actions would a person take if he or she held this belief? At the end of the unit, students were asked to select two aspects of social studies (geography, religion, achievements, politics, economics, or social structures) and produce a report with information about a medieval country or group that they had studied.

As part of their collaboration with students, this teaching team increased student choice. Another aspect of their collaboration with students involved surveying students about their preferred performance tasks. When the teachers learned that students wanted to engage in debates, they revised a few of the daily lessons to include debates as a way for students to demonstrate success. They also learned that students wanted to create digital products, so they added a creative component to the final paper in which students selected a visual way to demonstrate their understanding. Some students created short videos, others wrote song lyrics, others created digital posters, and still others used animation tools to inform their audience.

It is interesting to note that the science teachers in the same school were consistently performing at the *Developing* level of growth because they never collaborated with their students in the development of success criteria, and their use of generic assessment items sometimes resulted in inconclusive results. The science teachers used the generic assessments for grading but could not agree on their use to guide instruction or intervention. An area of strength for the science team was their use of interactive notebooks, in which students maintained notes, lab reports, vocabulary learning, and ideas for experiments. This tool provided the science team with an opportunity to determine if individual students were understanding the content.

Tina Setain, a math teacher at the same school, regularly engaged her colleagues in conversations about success criteria and how to plan backward from the learning outcomes to individual lessons. She also created a number of survey tools that her colleagues could use to invite students to share their thinking about success criteria and developed a feedback system for students to share their thinking about how future assessments could be developed. As she said, "I got a really interesting idea from students about our assessments. Several kids commented that they were getting tired of exit slips and suggested that teachers use the polling system a few days a week." In the past, the math department had used PollEverywhere.com to check students' responses via their mobile phones. They had implemented exit slips to encourage students to write more frequently about their understanding.

Ms. Setain asked her colleagues, "Could we try some polls every few days? I would be willing to develop the first set of questions and share them, and then we could meet to compare the results and then develop future polling questions collaboratively. This could even replace our next common formative assessment, and we could analyze student responses for our reteaching time." Ms. Setain's behavior is an example of the *Leading* level of growth.

1.2b: Designing evidence-collection opportunities

NYA	Developing	Teaching	Leading
The teacher does not plan to collect evidence of student understanding.	The teacher plans to infrequently collect evidence of student understanding or relies solely on summative assessment data.	The teacher has a clear plan for consistently collecting evidence of student understanding related to established learning intentions.	The teacher supports colleagues in their ability to develop a clear plan for consistently collecting evidence of student understanding related to established learning intentions.

As we have noted, summative assessment is important, but it's not sufficient to guide students' understanding. Teachers need systemic ways to check for understanding, collecting evidence as the lesson progresses. There are so many ways to do this, ranging from asking compelling questions to inviting students to write. (We will explore more about procedures for checking for understanding in Chapter 4's look at Assessing with a System.) In the planning phase, it is important to remember that systematic collection of evidence cannot be left to chance. Effective planning includes specific opportunities for collecting evidence of student learning.

Cheryl Whitehurst was an expert at this. As her team planned history lessons, they included options that they could use to collect data about students' understanding. It is important to note that Ms. Whitehurst did not simply tell her team members how to collect evidence. They talked about options at major transition points in their lessons. As Ms. Whitehurst told them, "I think we should always try to include at least one oral language task in each lesson so that we can hear students thinking. I see an opportunity to use Numbered Heads Together when we move from the think-aloud to the group work. But I also think that there are other ways to check for understanding there. Let's identify a few different ways so that people don't feel constrained by the lesson." Ms. Whitehurst's guidance of her team members demonstrated her *Leading* level of growth.

At another school, Margo Caldera's lesson plans consistently required students to produce an exit slip after each lesson. In addition, Ms. Caldera wrote probing questions into the margins of the texts she used so that she could collect evidence about student understanding. Further, her students practiced a number of nonverbal responses that Ms. Caldera taught them. A quick look at her lesson plan indicated several places where she would ask students to reflect on their understanding. For example, she said to her students, "Give me Fist to Five. Remember, a closed fist indicates you have no idea what we're talking about. Holding one finger up shows me that you have a little bit of understanding; two fingers means more. That goes all the way to five fingers, which means you totally get this and you could teach it to another person." Ms. Caldera had a clear plan for checking students' understanding, which allowed her to respond to students, making real-time adjustments in the lesson. As she said, "My students hold up their fingers truthfully because they know I use that information to make adjustments in the lesson." Ms. Caldera was operating at the *Teaching* level of growth.

Brian Thibodeaux used the same method for collecting evidence for each lesson: directing students to write a summary of what they learned. Over time, the effectiveness of this approach waned because students grew tired of it and used fewer and fewer words in their responses. As a result, Mr. Thibodeaux considered focusing his efforts on summative plans, rather than asking his students to continue to write summaries. He was demonstrating the *Developing* level of growth.

Natalie Manchester had no plan for collecting evidence. Instead, she explained, "I watch my students and make adjustments to the lesson based on what I see." This was a case of systematic evidence collection being *Not Yet Apparent*. Perhaps Ms. Manchester was very good at catching student confusion, misconceptions, and errors, but her students deserve a more purposeful approach. Simply including a few ideas for how she would check for understanding in her lesson plans would have allowed Ms. Manchester to share them with others or obtain feedback about more effective ways to determine success.

Factor 1.3: Meaningful Learning

Another factor necessary when Planning with Purpose is to create meaningful learning experiences that resonate with and engage students. One aspect of this factor is relevance. Keep in mind that relevance doesn't mean we have to tie a lesson to world peace; it just needs to be meaningful today and in the near term. Relevance increases when several processes are in place, including interactions with peers and materials, differentiated instruction, and opportunities to inquire and apply knowledge and skills. Relevance also increases when students understand why they are asked to learn something. It is about utility and making things interesting.

This conclusion was borne out in an analysis of classroom and schoolwide conditions in middle school science classrooms in New York State. Oliveira and colleagues (2013) used data from Regents exam results across several years to identify demographically similar schools that performed well above the average. The researchers then identified demographically similar schools that posted average results. They studied the conditions that were common in the high-performing schools but infrequent in the average-performing middle schools. Guess what? The conditions that set the two groups apart were making science curriculum relevant, fostering collaborative learning and inquiry, and differentiating instruction. It is important to point out that the authors noted that these results were not specific to a single classroom but were aligned to school and district initiatives, as well as associated with administrative support, making decisions supported by data analyses, and a school culture that values collegiality and communication among the adults. In other words, planning with meaningful experiences in mind is intertwined with schoolwide systems.

1.3a: Designing aligned experiences

NYA	Developing	Teaching	Leading
The teacher does not design aligned learning experiences.	The teacher designs experiences that are minimally linked to the learning intentions. Activities rarely require students to construct meaning through interaction with the teacher, the content materials, and each other. Instead, they rely on replication rather than innovation.	The teacher designs experiences that are clearly aligned to the established learning intentions and require students to experiment with concepts and actively construct meaning through interaction with the teacher, the content materials, and each other.	The teacher supports colleagues in their ability to design experiences that are clearly aligned to the established learning intentions and require students to experiment with concepts and actively construct meaning through interaction with the teacher, the content materials, and each other.

Until now, we have downplayed task design in order to examine the purposes for learning. Now it is time to foreground the activities that constitute so much of our instructional time.

Nancy recalls believing, as a novice teacher, that teaching was mostly about having as many activities as possible so that students would stay busy. In retrospect, this was the "camp counselor" approach to teaching—hands on, even if it meant "minds off." In those days, Nancy's lesson plans included a lot of worksheets, finger painting, art projects, and read-alouds. If you dropped by her room, you'd think she and her students were doing fine. But there was no link from these activities to anything beyond the letter of the week and the monthly theme (apples, bears, dinosaurs, outer space, and so on). At that time in her career, Nancy was definitely at the *Not Yet Apparent* level of growth in terms of designing aligned experiences. Fortunately, she had an experienced and generous colleague who guided her development, and within a few months, Nancy's activities were a bit more coherent. Her young students had occasional, but inconsistent, opportunities to construct meaning. One example was when a disastrous field trip resulted in a revised plan for the following day. Nancy's 1st graders wrote about their trip, using Judith Viorst's classic *Alexander and the Terrible, Horrible, No Good, Very Bad Day* as a mentor text. However, experiences such as this were only occasionally related to the transfer goals she should have been fostering. In reflection, she describes herself at the *Developing* level of growth at that time.

Fast-forward several years to when Nancy's ability to design meaningful tasks had become more consistent. She considered the complexity of the task to determine whether a given activity might be better suited for independent rather than collaborative learning. Many of us have had similar experiences. We design a small-group task, only to see some students divide the duties, go their separate ways, and then meet up again near the end for final assembly. That task, for those students, was simply not complex enough. As a new teacher, Nancy would have seen that experience as a success. After all, shouldn't group tasks be simple enough that success is ensured? Several years later, however, she knew better. If a learning experience is not complex enough, students don't have much reason to talk with one another. Her ability to raise the level of complexity grew, and she would describe herself as being at the *Teaching* level of growth in these instances.

Nancy had the opportunity to repay her mentor when she welcomed teachers new to the grade level. Whether her role was a formal one (grade-level chair or support provider for the induction program) or an informal one (as a grade-level colleague), Nancy met and planned with fellow teachers. One memorable example of her *Leading* level of growth was when the school engaged in a curriculum-mapping process to implement a new reading program the district had purchased. She and her colleagues noted when and where meaningful experiences and interactions were in evidence and created additional Specially Designed Academic Instruction in English opportunities with the school's English language learners in mind.

An important consideration for this ingredient of the growth tool is the expectation for interaction. The meaningful experiences that teachers plan should involve some type of interaction. Students can interact with each other, the teacher, or the content, and a host of instructional routines are useful for this. We do not prescribe any particular routines. Some teachers like to use reciprocal teaching and book clubs. Others like cognitively guided instruction, whereas others prefer inquiry approaches. The key is that students are actively constructing meaning through their interactions. These experiences become meaningful when they support the transfer goals that have been identified.

This situation was not the case in Brad Farragut's classroom. He routinely asked his students to read chapters of their textbook and then answer questions at the back of the book. Mr. Farragut argued that his students were interacting with the content materials, which was partly true. But if they could essentially teach the content to themselves using this approach, it was probably not appropriately complex and likely not very meaningful. It's not that independent tasks are inappropriate, but students need a range of experiences so that they learn at high levels. The plans that teachers develop should include opportunities for student interaction with content and peers in order to support transfer goals.

Shawna Cartwright designed tasks that were linked to the learning intentions but required limited interactions. For example, she always had a listening station in her class. Listening stations can be a great learning experience for students—or not. In Ms. Cartwright's class, the content of the listening station was linked with the learning intention for the day, but students were not expected to talk with one another as part of this experience. What could be a great learning opportunity was instead a passive experience in which some students learned and others did not. Ms. Cartwright was at the *Developing* level. Her teaching partner, Bonnie Schindler, also used a listening station with the same content, but she invited her students to pause the digital or video recording to talk about their responses. Ms. Schindler's students asked each other a lot of questions and, compared with Ms. Cartwright's students, took much better notes during their listening-station time, which resulted in improved understanding of the content. Ms. Schindler was at the *Teaching* level. Designing aligned experiences has less to do with the activity itself than it does with the interaction planned to accompany the activity.

1.3b: Planning for differentiation

NYA	Developing	Teaching	Leading
The teacher does not differentiate instruction.	The teacher has a limited differentiation repertoire or provides differentiation that is only loosely based on formative assessment data.	The teacher designs for differentiated instruction based on formative assessment data, using flexible grouping and providing a variety of experiences that meet student needs or interests.	The teacher supports colleagues in their ability to design for differentiated instruction based on formative assessment data, using flexible grouping and providing a variety of experiences that meet student needs or interests.

Differentiating instruction to meet the needs of individual students has been firmly established as wise practice for several decades (Tomlinson & Imbeau, 2010). Rooted in gifted education, the intention of differentiation is to ensure that students achieving above, at, and below grade level have an opportunity to access content and advance their learning. Differentiation is often delegated to the instructional dimension of teacher evaluation systems. In our growth tool, we have placed it within the planning phase, because differentiation should be proactive, not strictly reactive. Tomlinson (2015), in her study of effective mixed-ability classrooms, found that

> teachers in [effective] schools typically "teach up," planning first for advanced learners, then scaffolding instruction to enable less advanced students to access those rich learning experiences. Further, they extend the initial learning opportunities when they are not sufficiently challenging for highly advanced learners. In those schools, achievement for the full spectrum of learners—including advanced learners—rose markedly when compared to peer schools where this approach was not pervasive. (p. 26)

As Tomlinson (2000) notes, teachers can differentiate at least four classroom elements based on student readiness, interest, or learning profile:

• *Content*—what the student needs to learn or how the student will get access to the information

• *Process*—activities in which the student engages in order to make sense of or master the content

• *Products*—culminating projects that ask the student to rehearse, apply, and extend what he or she has learned in a unit

• *Learning environment*—the way the classroom works and feels

Accordingly, teachers should consider a range of options that demonstrate their differentiation across these dimensions. In other words, effective teaching is more than altering an assignment for a given student.

Some teachers, including Amanda Stark, don't "believe" in differentiating instruction. She said, "Students have to demonstrate mastery in my class if they want a grade." Other teachers, including Arnold Tillman, are not sure how to differentiate. As he said, "I am not sure what I'm allowed to do and still give students a grade for the class. I mean, I want to support my students, but I am not sure how far is too far."

Both of these teachers are at the *Not Yet Apparent* level of growth, but for different reasons. Both of them need to develop their skills in planning for all students, including plans for differentiation. The path to get there will likely be different. Ms. Stark first needs help to confront her beliefs and values, whereas Mr. Tillman needs additional professional development.

Effective differentiation is based on formative assessment. Teachers use hard and soft data to construct flexible groups and design appropriate tasks that move students' learning forward. As part of a department meeting, visual arts teacher Pam Unger started the conversation by saying, "I'm going to describe my current practice right now at *Not Yet Apparent*. It's not that I don't differentiate. I do. But I've always relied on interest rather than any kind of information." She showed a recent digital design assignment she gave students and explained, "I always structure assignments based on choice. I'm not sure how I could formatively assess students based on their choices."

Daniella Smithson, a newer colleague to the department, offered a suggestion. "Let me show you what I've been doing," she said. "Whenever I start a new unit, I have students complete a short online quiz and a survey of interest." She was at the *Leading* level of growth and regularly offered support like this to her colleagues.

Musical director Walter Yates said, "For me, formative assessment is part and parcel of what I do, although I hadn't thought of it in those terms before we started studying it more closely." He continued, "I put myself at the *Teaching* level of growth here, because I have students audition regularly to determine their position in the orchestra. Based on their seating, I do lots of small-group instruction. I also make sure that the first chairs in each section are coteaching with me."

Responding to Mr. Yates's comments, dance teacher Trina Knox said, "Wow, I hadn't thought about auditions as part of my formative assessment. I don't think I do it enough. I originally put myself in the *Teaching* category, but now I'm going to change that to the *Developing* level of growth. I used tryouts at the beginning of the school year, but those groups have remained the same since then, and now it's December. And truthfully, the groups are all doing the same thing," she confessed. "I need to rethink how I'm using formative assessment in my classes."

Summing Up

The first component of the FIT Teaching Tool focuses on the backstage planning processes that teachers use to guide student learning. Evidence for this component, and each of the factors that make up the component, can include documents and interviews, as well as observations. As we have noted throughout this chapter, teachers who plan collaboratively with their peers are more likely to develop stronger lessons and end up at the *Leading* level. As Darling-Hammond (2013) notes, "Peer learning among small groups of teachers was the most powerful predictor of improved student achievement over time" (p. 60). Simply said, we're better when we collaborate with others, which is why our highest level of growth is reserved for teachers who lead the learning of peers.

In addition to the planning that teachers engage in, some of the ingredients discussed in this chapter require that teachers invite students into learning. Effective teachers know what they want students to learn, and why, and explain that in such a way that students understand it. They also align the meaningful experiences students have and identify ways that students will demonstrate their understanding. Student performance on each success criterion should be used formatively to influence future instructional planning.

2
Cultivating a Learning Climate

We selected the word *cultivating* quite intentionally for this component of the FIT Teaching Tool because it captures two essential truths: (1) a positive classroom climate requires careful preparation; and (2) that kind of classroom climate requires regular tending. Even the most knowledgeable teacher cannot perform at optimum levels without developing positive student-teacher relationships, considering the growth of the whole child (and not just progress in academic performance), and providing a safe and efficient environment in which students can work, take risks, engage in productive struggle, and find success.

The social health of the school and its classrooms is affected by the relationships between adults and students, not to mention the welcoming environment extended to families. Unfortunately, these conditions are sometimes viewed as being "soft" and not worthy of the same level of attention (and resources) dedicated to test scores and teacher quality. Although these climate-related elements alone will not directly change student achievement, their absence renders other initiatives ineffective. The Consortium on Chicago School Research followed schools in their district of more than 400,000 students for 20 years, beginning in 1988. They identified 100 elementary schools that met with success and 100 that did not. The Chicago group found that socioeconomic status, mobility, and neighborhood crime were not predictive, as schools that succeeded and those that didn't often shared similar circumstances. However, the researchers (Bryk, Sebring, Allensworth, Luppescu, & Easton, 2010) found five conditions present in the successful schools:

- A welcoming environment for all stakeholders
- A safe and stimulating classroom climate
- Quality instruction
- An emphasis on developing the professional capacity of all educators
- Strong principal leadership

Although these findings are not startling, it is the internal relationship among the five conditions that proved to be critical. The researchers found that "a material weakness in any one ingredient means that a school is very unlikely to improve" (Bryk, quoted in Viadero, 2010, p. 1). Too often, our society hopes that a single factor—a magic bullet—will move the needle, and we devote human and fiscal resources toward making it happen. Yet the Consortium on Chicago School Research's findings challenge this assumption and provide strong counterevidence that a sustained and comprehensive approach, which includes unswerving attention to climate, instruction, and the development of the leadership of teachers and administrators, is what matters.

It is this intertwined relationship that underpins the design of the FIT Teaching Tool. The previous and upcoming chapters focus on aspects of quality instruction, including planning and assessment. Each factor positions teacher leadership as the highest expression of professional excellence. In this chapter, we turn our attention to the learning climate in order to examine two of the five factors identified by the researchers: creating an environment that is welcoming for all and is safe and stimulating. In the Cultivating a Learning Climate component of the tool, we have recast these qualities across three factors. The first is *Welcoming* (2.1), expressed in the way the classroom environment is constructed and through investment in relationships with students and families. The second factor is *Growth Producing* (2.2), as teachers use their interactions to build their students' agency and identity, encourage academic risk taking, and repair harm. The final factor in this component is *Efficient* (2.3), which is key to creating an orderly and stimulating environment. We have included record keeping as an ingredient in this component, because so much of the information that students, colleagues, and families need begins with the teacher's ability to organize and furnish this information in a timely and accurate way. Even in otherwise welcoming and nurturing classrooms, poor organization undermines these important relationships and stunts student growth, family support, and teacher collaboration.

Factor 2.1: Welcoming

Think back to an occasion when you felt welcomed. Maybe you were greeted with a smile, asked about your personal state, offered something pleasing, and guided to your next destination. Regardless of the circumstances (arriving home after work, entering a department store, or arriving at a professional conference), the positive way that others reacted to your presence allowed you to set aside other concerns. Most important, you felt that you belonged.

Now contrast this with a time you felt unwelcome. If you've ever hosted a teenager's sleepover, you'll understand what we mean. If you're not bringing cold drinks and treats, you're likely to be greeted with exasperation, if you're greeted at all. Any answers to your questions are short and blunt. The unspoken message: *You don't belong. When are you leaving?*

Belongingness at school is linked to both learning outcomes and motivation to learn in elementary (e.g., McMahon, Wernsman, & Rose, 2009) and secondary (e.g., Goodenow, 1993) classrooms. Membership alone does not automatically result in a sense of belonging (the slumber party example comes to mind; you *know* you don't belong, even though it's your house!). Similarly, the presence of a child's name on the class roster doesn't mean that child will feel she belongs. The teacher's disposition to build and establish a positive relationship with the child is a key way to signal belonging to the rest of the group. We call this disposition *positive regard*—the first ingredient of the *Welcoming* factor. The classroom's *physical environment*—the second ingredient—further enhances the teacher's intentions for providing a safe, orderly, and welcoming space for learning. The third ingredient is the *community building* that occurs as the teacher develops relationships inside the classroom and with each child's family.

2.1a: Positive regard

NYA	Developing	Teaching	Leading
The teacher has strained relationships with students or does not hold students in high esteem.	The teacher exhibits positive regard but has limited interactions with more challenging students.	The teacher actively seeks to establish and maintain positive relationships with all students by showing interest in their academic lives, interests, and aspirations.	The teacher supports colleagues in their ability to establish and maintain positive relationships with all students by showing interest in their academic lives, interests, and aspirations.

Positive regard encompasses a collection of attitudes and behaviors that effective teachers exhibit toward their students. These include greeting students, using their names, and demonstrating interest in them as people. We hear these expressions of positive regard in the halls of the school where we work every day. As students return from their internship experiences, one of our colleagues always asks, "How did you make a difference today?" Our principal greets students every morning with the words, "Welcome home." An English teacher stands in the doorway of her classroom during passing period and says hello to each student, often adding the reminder, "Your future is waiting for you right in here." All of us can come up with dozens of examples of ways in which we demonstrate positive regard for students.

But these practices are more difficult to apply with students who struggle behaviorally. Although the expectation is that we treat all students equally, in practice, teachers often do not. We behave differently with students who are more challenging. We stand farther away from them, talk with them less, make less eye contact, call on them less during class, and hold lower expectations for them (Good & Brophy, 2007). What's more, students pick up on these differential expectations, which leads to an even wider achievement gap within the class as the year progresses (Brattesani, Weinstein, & Marshall, 1984).

Teachers at Prendergast High School turned their attention to positive regard as a means to address differential teacher expectations. The school adopted several practices that communicated a higher degree of positive regard to all students, with special attention devoted to more challenging learners. Each cycle of their professional learning included a specific set of teacher behaviors. For example, the planning week session was dedicated to back-to-school topics and included positive regard practices such as standing at the doorway of the classroom to greet students, as well as methods for learning students' names.

Another session a few weeks later concerned developing student profiles and asked teachers to assess whether they had conducted at least one short conference with each student. Sgt. Kendra Garvey, a JROTC instructor at the school, adopted a number of practices to increase her ability to exhibit positive regard for her cadets. "Lots of people think that [JROTC] is all about barking at kids and treating them like they're in boot camp," she chuckled. "Too many movies." Although her program emphasized personal discipline and professional behaviors, Sgt. Garvey recognized that these need to be taught. "I want cadets to see that the procedures we utilize come from somewhere," she said.

Noting that some of her students initially lacked self-discipline, she used positive statements to instill a sense of camaraderie and teamwork. When she met with her assistant principal, Owen Patrick, to debrief after an observation, he asked her for information about a quiet discussion she had with three male cadets near the end of class. Sgt. Garvey explained that the students were considering getting tattoos. She explained the pertinent U.S. Army regulations and then asked the cadets to discuss why they wanted to get tattoos. "Now, I don't approve," she said, "but it's important that I hear them out and that they don't feel like there's all this disapproval coming from me."

Sgt. Garvey told Mr. Patrick that the boys had explained that all the male members of their families had tattoos and that they wanted to get them too. "These boys' families are from Fiji and Tonga, and tattoos play a ritualistic and spiritual role in their lives," she said. "If I hadn't taken the time to listen, I would have just assumed that they wanted them for the usual teenage reasons. The real reason they were asking was because they wanted to honor their families but also adhere to the U.S. Army regulations. So I contacted a friend of mine at the local recruiting office who is of Samoan descent, and he's going to meet with the boys to discuss this. I'm going to sit in on this conversation so I can learn, too." Sgt. Garvey, at the *Teaching* growth level, is displaying the personal regard she has for her cadets by approaching them with positive presumptions, listening to their concerns, and seizing opportunities to become more culturally competent.

Several weeks into the school year, chemistry teacher Martin Scott was transferred to Prendergast from another high school. A veteran teacher, Mr. Scott had taught at a number of schools, and he anticipated that Prendergast would be similar to the others. Therefore, he was surprised when Mr. Patrick met with him during his first week at the school to review both the FIT Teaching Tool and the school's focus on creating a welcoming environment. During the next quarter, Mr. Scott was observed twice, and he and Mr. Patrick met after each observation to debrief. Although Mr. Scott's planning and instruction were solid, his performance on positive regard was lacking. "I noticed that you rarely talked with students before the bell rang or after class," the assistant principal commented. "When you did talk to Ricardo, it was to give a short answer to his question about homework, but nothing else. I'm interested in your thoughts," Mr. Patrick continued. "How do you believe you're exhibiting positive regard?"

What followed was an extended conversation about building relationships with students. The teacher didn't hold much stock in it, reminding the administrator that his focus was on the content. "That kind of relationship building won't happen to them in college," Mr. Scott pointed out. "I'm getting them ready for the classes they'll need to take." Mr. Patrick reminded him that building relationships with students would help him tailor his chemistry instruction so that it would resonate more with his students. "For instance, I wonder if you know that two of the students in the class I sat in on, Ken and Travis, are members of the school's rocket club. They could have contributed to today's discussion about chemical combustion," Mr. Patrick noted. The assistant principal cited several other connections to specific students that might have enriched the lesson. "I know you're still new here, and it's a big school, but your outreach to students can make a difference," said Mr. Patrick. The chemistry teacher agreed that he was at the *Not Yet Apparent* growth level when it came to positive regard and expressed interest in developing his skills in this area. "I'd like to arrange time for you to work with Ms. Leung, the instructional coach for science," the administrator said. "I appreciate your willingness to get better at this."

Mimi Leung met with Mr. Scott and also with Ulysses Robertson, an earth science teacher previously identified as being at the *Developing* growth level. Mr. Robertson had consistently struggled throughout his four years at Prendergast to form positive relationships with some of his students, especially those with more challenging behavior. Determined to improve his ability to reduce problematic behaviors in his class, Mr. Robertson had been collaborating with the instructional coach to proactively develop relationships with students who challenged him. With Ms. Leung's guidance, Mr. Robertson identified four students in two periods and was targeting them for his positive regard efforts. For the previous two weeks, he had made it a point to stand closer to these students as he taught, call on them more frequently, and add positive statements to his replies.

In the three-way meeting with Mr. Robertson and Mr. Scott, Ms. Leung began by asking the earth science teacher to talk about his student observation efforts. "I like to call it my campaign," Mr. Robertson said. "I have to say I didn't expect much, but there's been a real reduction in the disruptive behaviors from these four students." The instructional coach pressed him for evidence, and he showed her the tally sheet he had developed. "I tried to keep track of the number of times I'd have to reprimand them, and I also compared it to students in my other periods whom I didn't target but would have," he said. "I like data."

This information captured the interest of Mr. Scott, the chemistry teacher. "Can you give me some examples of what you did?" he asked. "These numbers are impressive." The earth science teacher shared several strategies but noted that the most effective one was the 2 x 10 method: spend 2 minutes a day, for 10 consecutive school days, talking to the targeted students about anything but school. "The kids were kind of suspicious at first, but I've learned a lot about them. For instance, I found out that Yessenia [a targeted student] is the oldest of five and gets up at 3:30 a.m. to get the little ones ready. Her mom works the night shift, so Yessenia needs to be there for them. No wonder she's so tired in my class." Ms. Leung asked the earth science teacher about his next steps. He didn't hesitate. "I'm going to do the same thing in my other periods." Mr. Scott indicated that he'd like to do something similar. "We have lunch at the same time, Ulysses. Can I talk with you about some of these ideas?"

Ms. Leung, the instructional coach, was released two periods each day to work with her colleagues in the science department. She was collecting information about successes to profile in the next professional learning session that she and other part-time instructional coaches from different disciplines were organizing. Her plan was to recruit Mr. Robertson and others who were experiencing success to share their insights. "We want to share these success stories, but we'll also want to make time for all of us to talk about the continued struggles they're having. I'll have the room set up so we can sit by departments, and each coach will sit with his or her team to facilitate the conversation," Ms. Leung explained. "We're not going to grow as a school if we don't acknowledge and address the difficulties." At the *Leading* growth level for this ingredient, Mimi Leung was engaged in building the capacity of her departmental colleagues.

2.1b: Physical environment

NYA	Developing	Teaching	Leading
The classroom is disorganized, cluttered, or dirty and negatively affects student learning.	The teacher has designed but has difficulty maintaining an inviting classroom environment that will support student learning and movement.	The teacher designs and maintains an inviting classroom environment that supports student learning and movement.	The teacher supports colleagues in their ability to design and maintain an inviting classroom environment that supports student learning and movement.

The learning environment lies at the nexus of two aspects: the social aspect and the physical layout (Lippman, 2013). The classroom's physical spaces convey a welcoming atmosphere when they are designed with learners' usage and interactions in mind. Although the practice is commonplace now, schools did not outfit classrooms specifically for children until the 20th century, when educator Maria Montessori introduced furniture scaled to the size of her young students. Beyond furniture, the bulletin boards, signage, and organization of materials all signal to students how they will be working throughout the period or day. These touches should be developmentally appropriate, to be sure, but learners of any age appreciate when their names are displayed. Evidence of student work further communicates that the people in the classroom are valued. Finally, the room should be clean and tidy; a dirty or chaotic environment interferes with the efficiency of the work and telegraphs a general disregard for the room and for its occupants. A study of the perception of secondary students on the condition of their physical environment found that their negative perceptions were associated with higher rates of absenteeism and lower reported levels of motivation and participation (Asiyai, 2014).

We don't mean that rooms must be as neat as a pin at all times, or that the décor needs to be particularly fashionable. But rooms that are dirty, disheveled, and lacking in any kind of acknowledgment of the people who spend hundreds of hours there each year can inhibit learning. Although the overall design of the room and the quality of its furnishings are outside the direct influence of the teacher, other elements, such as the following, are not:

- *Movement and circulation patterns* can be established to facilitate access to materials and one another.
- *Common and individual spaces* can promote community while preserving ownership of place.
- *Arrangements* of furniture that can be easily reconfigured for small-group learning can promote collaboration among students.
- *Pleasing colors* can be used to stimulate and organize.

These elements can assist or hinder a teacher's work as well. When teachers have difficulty moving around the room, or when it is too much trouble to reconfigure the furniture for collaborative learning, they are forced to teach with fewer tools. Middle school instructional coach Sue McIntyre worked with Ashira Abbott during planning week on classroom reconfiguration. During the previous school year, Ms. Abbott had garnered a *Not Yet Apparent* growth level for this ingredient on her summative evaluation. She and her administrator had agreed that a goal for the next school year was to change the physical environment. A veteran teacher, Ms. Abbott had a reputation for maintaining a classroom packed with books and other materials. Previous observations had noted that a significant number of instructional minutes were routinely lost as she looked for items. And although she was a caring and involved teacher, Ms. Abbott was impeded from making contact with students because it was too difficult to move about the room.

"But I love all my books! I'm an English teacher!" she had protested. However, she admitted that students and colleagues had complained over the years and that an infestation of silverfish in the papers and books made students reluctant to handle materials. Over the summer, the facilities manager worked with her to move unnecessary items out of the classroom and had the room professionally treated by district personnel. Ms. McIntyre, the instructional coach, was paid for a day during the summer to help Ms. Abbott sort through items and donate or dispose of those she didn't need. The teacher was pleased with the progress she was seeing and spent an additional day covering bulletin boards with fresh paper so she could display student work. During planning week, she and Ms. McIntyre rearranged furniture to promote table discussions and placed smaller but more cohesive book sets on the shelves.

The teacher and the coach met again after the first week of classes to discuss the changes. "The first thing I noticed is that I'm spending more time in different places in the room. I've always used a seating chart, but the extra space has made it easier to circulate," Ms. Abbott said. Both women did a prearranged "ghost walk" (our term for visiting empty classrooms) to get more ideas for further personalizing the room. Ms. Abbott took notes about using student names and displaying student work. The instructional coach suggested that the English teacher put reminders on her smartphone so that she would remember to change the work regularly. "Last year on my evaluation the principal wrote that I had student work from October still hanging up in May. That was embarrassing," Ms. Abbott confessed.

When Ms. Abbott was visited a few weeks later, she was tagged at the *Developing* level for this ingredient. "It's starting to get cluttered in here again, but I'm on it," she said. "I don't want to fall back into my old ways." She added that at the last post-observation debriefing, she decided to collect circulation data in the second quarter to track which books were being selected more often than others.

Middle school mathematics teacher Luis Calderón transformed his classroom each fall into a physical environment where students were invested in taking ownership. During the first week, he took a photograph of each student and created a wall display, organized by period, of the names and interests of each student. "I load these photos into my digital attendance and seating charts, so that I can learn everyone's names. Later in the year, when I have a substitute, they can use the same tools to manage the class a bit better," he said. Because he taught six periods a day, he couldn't have everyone's work on display at the same time, so he rotated students' work. Every two weeks, he changed a bulletin board titled "Spotlight on Period ___ Mathematicians" to feature their written work. For open house and family math nights, he had his students make a short video of themselves talking about an aspect of mathematics and assigned a QR (Quick Response) code for each so that families could view their own children discussing their learning. Mr. Calderón's classroom had stations highlighting historical figures in mathematics and a popular one about mathematical failures that led to other inventions. "The one I've got up right now is about how a failed formula for an adhesive at 3M led to the development of their Post-it notes products," he said. With Mr. Calderón at the *Teaching* level, his students entered a classroom each day that was tailored to the needs of young adolescents to explore and to see themselves as mathematicians.

Another middle school educator, social studies teacher Leticia Rogers, sat on the advisory board of her district's induction program. She had a particular interest and skill in setting up classrooms, especially in terms of how the physical environment, rules and procedures, and record keeping can support new teachers. "I wish I'd had a program like this when I was a new teacher 23 years ago," she said. Ms. Rogers developed an online module for new teachers on physical environment, including photographs of classrooms all over the district. "The induction support providers access these materials as well and can make suggestions using these items while they're meeting in the teacher's classroom," she said. She explained that a goal of the district induction program was to develop a complete set of online tools aligned to each of the factors in the FIT Teaching Tool. At the *Leading* level for this criterion, Ms. Rogers was using her experience to shape the practices of new teachers in her district.

2.1c: Community building

NYA	Developing	Teaching	Leading
The teacher rarely creates opportunities for students to build relationships with one another and communicates with families only when there is a problem.	The teacher occasionally engages in relationship building between and among students or has limited contact with families.	The teacher strengthens the social fabric of the classroom by building relationships between and among students and their families in order to foster a positive community of learners.	The teacher supports colleagues in their ability to strengthen the social fabric of the classroom by building relationships among students and their families in order to foster a positive community of learners.

Community drives each of us as humans. We look to our communities to understand our identities, seek reaffirmation, solve problems, and celebrate achievements. Each classroom is a collection of individuals; the teacher builds a sense of community by building relationships among its members. This effort is deepened when the classroom community is nested within the larger communities of school, family, and neighborhood. Block (2008) describes the act of community building across three dimensions:

- Build the social fabric and transform the isolation within our communities into connectedness and caring for the whole.
- Shift our conversations from the problems of community to the possibility of community.
- Commit to create a future distinct from the past. (p. 177)

Many teachers, especially those at the elementary level, routinely schedule class meetings, morning circles, and end-of-week gatherings to discuss the learning lives of the class members. These events are marked with discussion about recent and upcoming events, routines that allow children to know one another better, and ways the group can address problems they are facing. However, these meetings are far less common at the middle and high school levels, perhaps because of time constraints and a higher number of students on the roster. A damaging assumption that some teachers make, however, is that someone else will take care of the community building. Unfortunately, that is rarely the case.

A growing number of elementary and secondary schools are using elements of restorative practices to address the importance of classroom community building. Although more readily associated with discipline issues (discussed later in this chapter), the process rests on the proactive measures teachers take to build a strong classroom community that can weather problems that arise. Class meetings are times when the class addresses issues faced by the students, which can include low-level problems, such as equitable distribution of playground equipment at recess or how the art room is reset near the end of the class period. Formal class meetings follow an agenda, such as the one in Figure 2.1. Over time, the agenda is increasingly student-driven. First-year teacher Shannon Potter studied the effects of implementing class meetings three times per week for eight weeks in her 5th and 6th grade multi-age classroom and reported "increased students' skills in relation to listening attentively, complimenting and appreciating others, showing respect for others, and building a sense of community" (Potter & Davis, 2003, p. 88).

Figure 2.1 | Sample Meeting Agenda

I. Call the Meeting to Order
II. Encouragement Circle
III. Old Business
IV. New Business
V. Shout-Outs
VI. Close Meeting

Source: From Better Than Carrots or Sticks: Restorative Practices for Positive Classroom Management (p. 91), by D. Smith, D. Fisher, & N. Frey, 2015, Alexandria, VA: ASCD. Copyright 2015 by ASCD.

Another approach for community building in the classroom is circles. These events are held with students either sitting in chairs or standing in a circle. Students speak one at a time, holding a talking piece to signal their intention to do so, and have an opportunity to pass if desired. Topics of circles at the school where we work have addressed test anxiety, strategies for dealing with difficulties during collaborative learning, and processing emotions after a visit to the Museum of Tolerance in Los Angeles. These circles further build relationships as students learn about shared and unique perspectives of others. Teachers can use a number of ways to build community in the classroom; meetings and circles are just two of them.

Community exists outside the classroom as well, and teachers play an integral part in this outreach. Families are critical partners in the learning lives of their children, but some don't feel welcomed into the classroom or may be reluctant or unable to come to the school because of work or transportation issues. The National Network of Partnership Schools at Johns Hopkins University has studied successful family partnership practices (Epstein et al., 2009) and recommends these six practices:

• Make the school a place where parents can learn skills to support their children academically and emotionally (e.g., parent academies, literacy and math nights).

• Provide regular communication to families about the classroom and their own children (e.g., phone calls, personal letters, and newsletters).

• Extend volunteer opportunities in the classroom and remotely to families who are interested and able.

• Create homework assignments that allow children to involve their families (e.g., interviewing a family member about a historical event).

- Involve families in decision making (e.g., governance, classroom surveys).
- Invite community collaboration (e.g., coordination with other service providers, community service projects).

Many of these practices have school and classroom implications. Although some involve the entire school (e.g., literacy night), they can begin with a grade level hosting an event. Some community service projects are quite large and complex but can begin as a classroom effort, such as cleaning the school grounds. In other words, we firmly believe that community building with families should not be dismissed because there is no current school initiative to do so. It begins with individual teachers who signal their understanding of the mutual benefits derived from such efforts.

Unfortunately, Donovan Bradshaw did not believe that it was his responsibility to build community in his middle school social studies classroom. As he said, "Look, I keep it safe in here, but I'm not all touchy-feely. I think that students need to know how to behave and that there are consequences for when they don't." When disputes arose in his classroom, Mr. Bradshaw sent students to the office to be dealt with. His principal, Marcia Layne, had visited his classroom on several occasions and had engaged in a number of conversations with Mr. Bradshaw about community building. She told him, "Donovan, you're a generally strong teacher. Last year when we met and reviewed the year and your artifacts, we agreed that you consistently performed at the *Teaching* level, which is totally fine. I asked about your desire to move to the *Leading* level, but you didn't seem interested in that. A major area that is still *Not Yet Apparent* in your classroom is community building. I have never seen anything that allows students in your class to feel connected with each other or with you. This year, as I have visited, I have been asking students if they feel valued in your classroom, and they generally don't. Only 3 of the 27 students I've asked in the past few weeks said 'kinda'; all of the others said no. Is there anything that I can do to help you build a stronger learning community?"

Mr. Bradshaw asked if he could have a couple of days to think about this and get back to her. When he did, this is what he said: "Look, I've been burned so many times. I got close to some students, and then they broke my heart. So I guess that I keep my distance now. You're the first one to really call me out on this. I've had a lot of administrators over the years, and you're the first to really notice this and then offer help. I'm willing to give this a try, but only if you understand that I may backslide a bit. I talked with my wife, and she reminded me about when I became a teacher and my passion for the classroom. Where do we start?"

In a neighboring school in the same district, a group of teachers redesigned their community-building activities. As part of their commitment, they decided to visit other classrooms to observe the community-building activities that other teachers used. Kimberly Knox, a 6th grade teacher, was the first to invite others to her classroom. Her students had been working on providing help to one another. Ms. Knox noted, "I think that helping other people is an important way to build community, so I started teaching my students how to do this and not just give away the answer."

A large poster in Ms. Knox's classroom included the following questions:

- Have you asked for help today when you needed it?
- Have you offered help to another when you recognized the need for it?
- Did you accept help when it was offered?
- If you wanted to continue to try on your own, did you politely decline help?

When asked about this effort, Ms. Knox responded, "I remember back in my credential program years ago being introduced to this idea in a book [Sapon-Shevin, 1998]. I just thought I'd try it to see if it builds community, and I'm amazed. My students don't just tell each other the answer anymore. They actually offer help and then talk about why the answer is correct. It's been great for building community between students and with me."

The visitors watched Ms. Knox's students work collaboratively. In one group, they heard a student ask, "How did you know that was the right answer?" Another replied, "Well, it's because you have to remember that you reverse the inequality symbol when you multiply by a negative number." The first student then responded, "Oh, I forgot that. Thank you for reminding me."

In another group, Marco completed his problem set, looked around at the other members of his group, and asked, "Does anyone need help? I'm finished, and I think I understand it pretty well." Fredley responded, "Maybe, but can you give me a sec? I think I almost got it," and Jacobson said, "I'll take some help on number 9. I think that you color in the circle on the number line because the symbol is less than or equal to, but I could be wrong." Marco said, "Does anyone else want to jump in?" None of the others did, so Marco continued, "When you shade, that means that the number is included. Let's put the number in the equation and see if this is right."

Following their visit, Ms. Knox offered to provide the visitors with the sentence frames she used to introduce the helping curriculum. She loaned one of the visitors the book she had used and offered to meet again after that person had read the relevant chapter. She also offered to visit their classrooms, saying, "This isn't the only way to build the learning community, and I'd like to see what you all are trying in your classroom." Ms. Knox was *Leading* on this indicator.

When she had a chance to visit the classroom of the 8th grade teacher who had borrowed her book, she noted that the students were involved in a class meeting. An agenda was posted on the board, and a student was leading the discussion, which focused on the results of a recent test. The students were deciding what to do about the fact that many of them had not done well on the assessment. Samuel said, "Maybe we could learn from this and try again. But is that fair to the people who did a good job already?" Kerri responded, "I was one who didn't do so hot, but I don't think it's fair because it would waste time for people who really studied." Maria added, "I agree with Kerri because it's our own fault, and Mr. Handler shouldn't have to do more work."

Mr. Handler remained quiet as his students discussed the situation. Another student, Brad, spoke. "I got an *A*. But I know that everyone can get an *A*. What if we took a day and did our own review so that Mr. Handler didn't have extra work? And then we could teach each other the information. Mr. Handler could just check us, and then we could all try again and the best out of two would be our grades."

When Ms. Knox discussed this exchange with Mr. Handler, she noted the students' skill in communication and their trust in each other. She commented that Mr. Handler was clearly at the *Teaching* level of growth. He disagreed, saying, "I appreciate that, but this is new to me. I've only had about three formal class meetings. I feel like I'm still at the *Developing* level and want to know more ways to build community. I'm enjoying it because I like to see students take on more responsibility."

They discussed this further and decided to visit another teacher at their school, Susan Stramburg. They asked if they could observe a lesson, and Ms. Stramburg agreed reluctantly. When they entered the classroom, the students were engaged in various learning tasks. Some were working on computers; others were at desks in groups. Ms. Stramburg was meeting with a small group of students. A poster on the wall identified specific actions that groups of students should engage in: attentive listening, appreciation/no put-downs, mutual respect, and the right to pass.

When talking with a group of students, Mr. Handler asked about the poster and learned that the class worked in "Tribes," a kind of learning community (see tribes.com), and that students knew that they were part of a community that is designed to be collaborative and supportive. One of the students commented, "Ms. Stramburg makes sure that we know that we are all important in this class. Everyone has something to offer." Another student added, "When we meet our goals, we celebrate as a whole class."

As Mr. Handler and Ms. Knox noted, Ms. Stramburg was at the *Teaching* level. When asked why she was reluctant to host visitors, Ms. Stramburg said, "I have invested a lot in Tribes, but some people don't value it, and I guess I don't want to be judged. I'm proud of the learning community I've built, and I'm willing to share, but I don't go out of my way to promote social and emotional stuff because it can put other people off."

In response, Ms. Knox said, "I would love to collaborate with you to learn more about this. I have been sharing a lot of my experiences in building community, and I learned a lot more today. I hope you'll join our team. We're going to change our school, and we need you!"

Factor 2.2: Growth Producing

Students thrive in an atmosphere where learning is valued above all else. We can't imagine a school that wouldn't agree with that statement, but it is much more difficult to practice it consistently. Without intending to, students can receive mixed and unintended messages from schools about learning. Here are a few that might ring a bell:

- There are "good kids" and "bad kids."
- There are "smart kids" and "dumb kids."
- It's better to be right the first time than to learn from a mistake.
- Compliance is more important than competence.
- Grades are more important than learning.
- I have to look out for myself, because no one else will.

The difference between a school's culture and its climate is this: the culture rests on what we do and don't do; the climate is how it feels. And unfortunately, although teachers never set out to teach these ideas, many students leave at the end of the day believing such statements are true. But if the climate is a response to our actions, then we need to alter those actions in order to send different messages, such as

- School is a place to grow as a person and as a learner.
- School is a place where errors are celebrated.
- School is a place to take academic risks.
- My competence grows each day.
- My school values my learning.
- We take care of each other.

The factor of the FIT Teaching Tool that we call *Growth Producing* is directly influenced by the attitudes and actions of the teacher. The first ingredient is *builds agency and identity*, meaning that deliberate actions are taken to help students see how they are growing personally and academically. Most of all, it consists of the many opportunities we are given to link students' performance with their efforts. The second ingredient, *encourages academic risk taking*, contributes to children's growth by encouraging them to experiment, to try something new, and to fail forward into new learning. The third ingredient in this factor is *repairs harm*, which goes beyond traditional classroom management. When we repair harm, we actively seek ways not only to reach resolution but also to equip students with the tools they need to resolve disputes and use prosocial responses that preserve the classroom community.

2.2a: Builds agency and identity

NYA	Developing	Teaching	Leading
The teacher belittles, shames, or humiliates students or uses sarcasm, diminishing student agency and identity.	The teacher often uses language that contributes to students' learned helplessness and, more rarely, builds resilience and persistence.	The teacher frames language so that students develop a sense of resilience and persistence in their learning lives.	The teacher supports colleagues in their ability to frame language so that students develop a sense of resilience and persistence in their learning lives.

Learning is underpinned by beliefs that learners hold about themselves in relation to the demands of a task and their ability to act upon the task, especially when such ability doesn't come readily. *Identity* is the development of a unique personality that is based on a person's interaction with the environment and the people in that environment. Johnston (2004) notes that "building an identity means coming to see in ourselves the characteristics of particular categories (and roles) of people and developing a sense of what it feels like to be that sort of person and belong in certain social spaces" (p. 23). Consider the following statements and how they contribute to the learner's identity.

- *"How are you thinking like a historian today?"* This question invites students to assume the role of a historian and think about what it means to do this type of work. It carries a clearly communicated assumption that the student knows how historians think and can assume this identity.

- *"Your opening line reminds me of something that other authors do. As a reader, I enjoy openings with a startling statement, and you really captured that here."* This comment suggests to the adolescent writer that he has engaged in writerly behaviors and that the reader enjoyed the approach. This builds the writer's identity, communicating that the writing was effective and that the writer should continue in this vein.

- *"There are so many ways to solve this problem, and I see that you solved it two different ways. I know that mathematicians often solve problems several different ways to check their findings. I'd bet it was fun to see it work out both ways."* This commentary communicates that the student is thinking like a mathematician and has solved the problem in ways that were effective. It also helps the student develop an identity as a problem solver who enjoys working through complex situations.

People with a strong sense of *agency* believe that their efforts and accomplishments are linked. As Johnston (2004) notes, some students understand that "if they act, and act strategically, they can accomplish their goals" (p. 29). Other students, those who do not have a strong sense of agency, think that their efforts will likely be ineffective; if they do succeed, it's probably because they were lucky this time, and that luck won't hold. In other words, "To be an agent is to intentionally make things happen by one's actions. . . . The core features of agency enable people to play a part in their self-development, adaptation, and self-renewal with changing times" (Bandura, 2001, p. 2). Teachers can foster students' agency through careful use of language that builds "bridges between action and consequence" and helps students see their role in the outcome (Johnston, 2004, p. 30). For example, here are two questions and a statement that can do a lot to build a learner's agency:

- *"Why?"* is probably one of the most effective ways for building agency, because reflecting on this question helps students understand the processes and procedures they use to accomplish things. As Johnston (2004) points out, "Asking why children do or say the things they do helps them develop the consciousness and hence ownership of their choices" (p. 37).

- *"What might you do next?"* helps students plan actions that they believe will result in success. When students learn to verbalize their plans, they have concrete examples of their actions that were or were not effective. This statement also communicates to students that the teacher believes that the student knows what to do next. This is in contrast to situations in which the teacher takes back responsibility and tells the student what to do next. Agency is built when the teacher assumes competence and guides the student to perform.

- *"You did it, but tell me how. I'm particularly interested in efforts that were and were not helpful."* This statement communicates to students that they were successful and that some of their efforts were useful and others were not. It gives students an opportunity to reflect on their actions and to determine which of those actions were useful and should be implemented again.

These two constructs—identity and agency—are integral to teaching, as adults are able to profoundly influence both of them as students grow and develop. The language that teachers use in their interactions with students can build or stunt. We want to teach our students to persevere and to rise to challenges rather than avoid them. But we also need to teach them resilience, especially how to dust themselves off when they fail so that they can try again. A child who is not resilient will be easily defeated and give up too early. Persistence and resilience are positively correlated with one another and are predictive of school enjoyment, class participation, and self-esteem (Martin & Marsh, 2006).

Identity and agency factor into problematic behaviors as well. Individuals who lack agency are more likely to be angry and immobilized, to blame others, and even to lash out. Contrast these two exchanges. Guess which one would provoke an angry response from the student.

Scenario #1. Teacher: "What you just said to her was wrong. You need to apologize."

Scenario #2. Teacher: "What you just said to her was hurtful. *You're better than that.* Do you think you need to apologize? *How can I help?*"

The first scenario might provoke an angry exchange with the teacher, and, more important, divert attention from the real problem, which is the relationship with a peer. The second exchange actually happened after Nancy overheard a comment a 10th grade student uttered about a female classmate. She spoke quietly to the male student, putting her hand on his shoulder, and uttered those four sentences. The boy spoke to the girl after class and apologized to her. The interjection of those two sentences made a difference. When you say, "You're better than that," you build the student's identity at a time when he is less than his best. That statement reminds him that his lapse in behavior doesn't represent who he wants to be. The question "How can I help?" reaffirms his agency and his ability to repair a relationship, even with help from another.

Statements that contribute to students' sense of identity help them tell stories about themselves and to themselves. We might call a talented writer a poet to remind her how much her words mean or tell another student that his kindness toward another classmate is an indicator of his empathy toward others. But is this done routinely and for all students? We don't mean teachers ought to build a false and inflated sense of self-esteem in every child—that approach encourages arrogant and self-centered young people. But teachers should be diligent in calling out those times when students exemplify the traits we want them to develop further. These "identify statements" should allow students to see how their actions played a role in the accomplishment. When we say, "I'll bet you're proud of yourself. This was a tough problem to solve. Can you tell me how you did it?" we signal the accomplishment (solving the problem) and link it to students' actions (asking how they did it). Through brief but frequent exchanges such as this, we build their identity ("I am a problem solver") and agency ("I did it by trying different strategies until I found one that worked").

When a teacher uses sarcasm with students, agency and identity are stunted. In fact, we believe that sarcasm should not be used when there are power differentials, as is the case in the classroom. In addition, the vast majority of children and youth do not understand the sophisticated humor that may be part of sarcasm; they just think that some of their teachers are mean. When a teacher uses sarcasm, the ingredient of building agency and identity is *Not Yet Apparent*. In addition, when teachers belittle, humiliate, shame, dishonor, demean, or chastise a student, this ingredient is *Not Yet Apparent*. That's not to say that the teacher has to be a pushover.

Max Doyle was at the *Developing* level in terms of building agency and identity with his students. As he says, "I'm not always sure what to do, so a lot of times, I don't say anything." When being observed by colleagues or his principal, Mr. Doyle was kind and supportive, but he did not seize the opportunity to build students' agency and identity. For example, during an observation of his small-group, needs-based instruction, Mr. Doyle said, "Well done. That's what good mathematicians do to solve problems." This statement won't cause harm to students, but a student who did not do what Mr. Doyle just reinforced might think she is a bad mathematician. Another time, Mr. Doyle said, "I see conflict here in the group. I need you to work this out so that you can get back to work." In this case, Mr. Doyle noticed the problem rather than asking students to identify what was wrong. He also expected students to comply so that they could get back to work. What if they didn't want to work? And could some students comply with his request simply because he said he needed them to do so?

Again, this kind of practice is not causing harm, but it misses opportunities to facilitate student growth. It would help if he rephrased his last comment to something like this: "Is there something wrong in the group? Can you name your feelings or experience? How does that feel? How would you like to work?" With this kind of guidance, students are encouraged to reflect on their actions and interactions, slowly growing and developing into collaborative learners.

Heidi Miller had engaged in a lot of professional learning about the language that teachers use to build students' sense of self. She had read *The Power of Our Words* (Denton, 2007) and had specifically requested coaching on her ability to engage students in growth-producing interactions. For example, she asked students a lot of open-ended questions as well as questions that allowed them to reflect on what their classmates said, including whether or not they agreed. One day, while walking around the classroom as her students engaged in a reciprocal teaching event (see Palincsar & Brown, 1984), she leaned over to Justin and said, "I see you wrote the main ideas down in your own words. How do you think that will help you when you share with your peers?" In another group, Ms. Miller smiled at Carmen and said, "Your questions sound a lot like a reporter's. Tell me about the kinds of answers you are getting in return." Ms. Miller's focus on agency and identity resulted in her attaining a *Teaching* level of growth.

Special educator Charles Shaginaw provided regular feedback and coaching on agency and identity for the general educators on his grade-level team. He noted, "I think it's my job to make sure that students are feeling good about themselves as they learn. I have direct responsibility for students with disabilities, but I like to think that I have indirect responsibilities for all students, and my contributions are about the language we use with them to help them grow." Mr. Shaginaw had the interpersonal skills and positive relationships with teachers to talk with them in an authentic, nonthreatening way about how they used language in their classrooms.

For example, he observed a teacher comment to a student during class, "Now why would you want to do that?" After class, Mr. Shaginaw asked the teacher about that comment, noting that it could have been interpreted as sarcastic. As part of their conversation, Mr. Shaginaw said, "You know I'm not the keeper of this, right? I just have the chance to hear things from our kids' perspective."

The teacher responded, "Yeah, no—I like when you have time to visit and ask me about these things. It makes me better, and it helps students learn. I hope that Brian didn't think I was being sarcastic. I wanted him to process through his thinking, so I was asking about the next step. But I see that it could seem like I wasn't being as respectful as I could have been. How could I say it?" Mr. Shaginaw responded, "Let's see. Again, I'm no expert, but I was thinking that you might want to say something like, 'I think I see where you're going, but it might help us all if you could explain your process a bit more.'" These two continued their conversation about language as Mr. Shaginaw demonstrated his *Leading* level of growth.

2.2b: Encourages academic risk taking

NYA	Developing	Teaching	Leading
The teacher does not encourage risk taking and potential failure, instead valuing student comfort and contentment over challenge.	The teacher values accuracy over potential growth and only occasionally challenges students to extend their thinking, even if it means initial failure.	The teacher fosters a growth mindset for students by creating a safe and respectful environment where failure is not ridiculed but considered an important component of the learning process.	The teacher supports colleagues in their ability to foster a growth mindset for students by creating a safe and respectful environment where failure is not ridiculed but considered an important component of the learning process.

Carol Dweck (2006) has written extensively about the role of a growth mindset in learner success. People with a growth mindset presume that it's effort, instruction, and persistence—not innate traits, such as intelligence and heredity—that alter one's abilities. More important, well-meaning praise, when offered for the wrong reason, can actually decrease motivation, as when a child's intelligence is the focus. "You're so smart," we say, and the child's motivation to expend effort decreases just a bit. After several years of marinating in this sauce, students begin to encounter more academic challenges, but they haven't appreciated the effort that others expend. Many students begin to choose less-demanding coursework because they fear failure and are not entirely sure they are willing to put forth effort.

We had a spirit week not too long ago at the middle school where two of us work, and one day's theme was "Dress to Impress." There was a dance scheduled for the afternoon, and many students came to school dressed in suits, ties, and dresses. We chose to wear our doctoral garb, telling students, "It's not what you have. It's what you do." That's the message we want to send students every day. When we share our accomplishments—and make sure that we don't leave out the parts of our stories when things got more difficult—we help students to see that academic risk taking is part of the learning process.

In the classroom, academic risk taking means that grades are earned through competence, not compliance. To put it differently, students have an opportunity to try again when they don't do well the first time on a homework assignment, a project, or a test. Importantly, these same students are not penalized for their practice in getting the learning down, which means they're not penalized with point deductions for not being academically successful on the first attempt (Fisher, Frey, & Pumpian, 2011). Dweck (2006) reminds us that challenge lies at the heart of learning:

> Speed and perfection are the enemy of difficult learning: "If you think I'm smart when I'm fast and perfect, I better not take on anything challenging." So what *should* we say when children complete a task—say, math problems—quickly and perfectly? Should we deny them the praise they have earned? Yes. When this happens, I say, "Whoops. I guess that was too easy. I apologize for wasting your time. Let's do something you can really learn from!" (p. 179)

Fifth grade teacher Monica Ritter and her fellow team members were discussing students who were not making progress. In response to a suggestion from another teacher, Alicia Olivera, Ms. Ritter said, "I really don't know if that will work to close the gap, but I think it's worth a try." Ms. Olivera had developed a rather elaborate intervention schedule that included scheduled times when the academic coach could oversee the classroom for a few minutes while the teacher engaged in a private conversation with students who continued to struggle. Ms. Olivera said, "I've been thinking about this a lot and have piloted this in my classroom. I'm now confident enough to share. I think a lot of our students have acquired learned helplessness, and our interventions are not getting through because they do not see themselves working hard and then being successful. So I asked Beth [the academic coach] to come into the class and essentially supervise while the students worked independently or collaboratively. During those times, I met with Brandee and Chad individually. It wasn't the intervention time, so I wasn't focused on their skills. I just had a chat with them about their efforts and what I saw paying off. It's been amazing, and I was hoping that we could try this as a grade level. I have developed a schedule that I think can work. And I'll do all of the work in writing out these statements to build students' growth mindset. I have to admit that I wasn't really into this part of the growth tool until I saw Monica teach. She always encourages risk taking, so I thought to myself, I can too." Alicia Olivera had moved into the *Leading* level, while Monica Ritter was at the *Teaching* level.

A visit to Ms. Ritter's classroom clearly confirmed her comfort with encouraging her students to take risks. The students even talked this way to their peers, having heard their teacher model this for them over the course of the school year. On one particular visit, Ms. Ritter was interacting with a small group of students who had completed their assigned task. Joining their group, she said, "You've been focused on this for several minutes, and I see that you have completed the task. But I'm wondering something. How could you change this to make it more complex for each other? Could you rewrite the problems and questions and then trade papers? Go ahead. Take a risk and see what else you can learn."

First grade teacher Jesse Hernandez was performing at the *Developing* level. He provided students with a lot of praise, but it was not specific, and students were not routinely encouraged to try things that would stretch their abilities. Nevertheless, Mr. Hernandez did focus on each student's individual efforts and had regular individual conferences to talk with children about their work habits. For example, Mr. Hernandez met with Andrew to review his writing, asking him to describe how he decided what to write. Andrew responded, "I just know what I wanna write." Mr. Hernandez said, "I bet you do, but can you tell me how you think about it when you write? I'm interested in how you work to get things done."

Andrew thought about this for several seconds and then said, "It just pops in my head. But sometimes it goes away again. I make it into a picture so that I can remember. And then I write about the picture. Do you think that's good, to make pictures to remember?" In response, Mr. Hernandez said, "Yes, as long as it works for you and helps you keep focused on your writing."

This approach differed from that of Janelle Black, who was at the *Not Yet Apparent* level of growth. She avoided risk taking herself and regularly told her peers, "I want my students to be successful. In fact, I plan for them to succeed on their work. I hate seeing them struggle. I don't see any reason to harass a 1st grader. Their day should be fun and easy." It would likely take a number of conversations with her peers, and perhaps even her administrator, for Ms. Black to reconsider the value of risk taking in the classroom.

2.2c: Repairs harm

NYA	Developing	Teaching	Leading
The teacher does not address disruptions and misbehavior or routinely has others outside the classroom address behavior issues.	The teacher's responses to disruptions and misbehavior are primarily respectful but reactive, and the return to productive learning is often delayed.	The teacher expects, plans for, and responds to disruptions or misbehavior in a manner that respects students and focuses on a return to productive learning.	The teacher supports colleagues in their ability to expect, plan for, and respond to disruptions or misbehavior in a manner that respects students and focuses on a return to productive learning.

Earlier in this chapter we discussed restorative practices. In the section on ingredient 2.1c, we described the importance of community building in the classroom, especially through techniques such as class meetings and informal circles. These peace-building efforts form a foundation for the group to stand on when problems arise. Ingredient 2.2c describes the peacemaking efforts to repair harm when it occurs. The teacher typically facilitates these discussions so that affected students not only resolve the problem at hand but also leave the exchange more skilled in responding to problems in preparation for the next time.

Any number of incidents might occur to cause harm: a teacher has money stolen from her purse; two former friends are threatening one another; a student has sold copies of an exam; a teacher humiliates a student in front of others. The conventional response for the first three incidents is to identify the perpetrators and dole out suspensions. In the last case, unfortunately, reparations are unlikely.

Bullying is another form of harm. Despite heightened attention to the problem, children routinely report that their teachers are either unaware of bullying that is going on or unwilling to intervene in many instances of bullying (e.g., Veenstra, Lindenberg, Huitsing, Sainio, & Salmivalli, 2014). Although physical aggressions are usually met with swift action, more subtle relational problems, whether in face-to-face interactions or in cyberspace, often go unaddressed. Children use unkind actions and words against one another, and an unkind act is not necessarily bullying. Bullying involves a differential distribution of power, which can manifest itself in a number of ways (size, ability, number, or social capital). But it also involves others, not just the victim and the aggressor. Bystanders, friends of those directly involved, and the classroom community are all involved (Olweus, 2003). Whether the harm that is done is through unkind interactions or because of bullying, effective teachers know how to notice and respond to these incidences.

Regardless of the type of harm done, teachers need to work to repair the harm so that learning can continue to occur. We use the principles of restorative practices outlined by Costello, Wachtel, and Wachtel (2009):

- Try to foster understanding of the impact of the behavior
- Seek to repair the harm that was done to people and relationships
- Attend to the needs of victims and others in the school
- Avoid imposing on students intentional pain, embarrassment and discomfort
- Actively involve others as much as possible. (p. 52)

Of course, there are many other ways, both formal and informal, to address and repair harm. Tribes, a formal program, was cited earlier in the chapter. Various character education programs feature the language and practices of expressing remorse, accepting apologies, and restoring relationships. The common thread in all of these approaches is that the teacher notices when the social fabric of the classroom has been disrupted and takes steps to repair the harm and restore the learning environment.

Fourth grade teacher Amanda Payne used a peace table in her classroom to ensure that her students had a physical place to resolve conflicts and repair harm. The peace table, inspired by Montessori educational approaches, always had a timer and a "peace item" sitting on it; there were two chairs at the table as well. Ms. Payne used a sand timer, and a jewelry box contained the peace item, a small rock shaped like a heart. She let the students know that her husband gave her the heart-shaped rock so that she would always know she was loved and could love others.

Ms. Payne talked about the challenges of establishing the peace table at the beginning of each year: "Every year, it seems like a lot of work. I have to mediate a lot of the conversations at the table, providing students with language frames and support to repair the harm that is done. But then an event occurs and a student will ask to meet with another student at the table, and I won't have to offer any support. It's magical, and it happens every year."

On one visit to her classroom, Principal Leigh Corbin observed Mark ask Zach to meet at the peace table. Mark turned the timer over, signaling that they both should remain quiet for two minutes while the sand ran through the hourglass. When the time was up, Mark held the rock and said, "I didn't like it when you took my stuff."

Zach responded, "What stuff? When did I take something of yours?"

"Yeah. You took the book I was reading, and then last week you took my fidget toy."

"I didn't know they were yours. You shoulda told me. I'm sorry. Do you want the book to read? I could get a different one."

"My feelings were hurt, but I guess that I don't need that book. You can read it and then give it to me after, OK?"

This conversation may not seem like much, but it established a habit for students to identify when they had been hurt and needed to have the harm repaired. This interaction was over a fairly minor situation, but the habit that Ms. Payne was developing in her students would allow them to address much bigger issues when they arose.

When asked about more significant issues and events, Ms. Payne related a story about two students who got into a fight at recess. They could not even remember why they got into the fight, but clearly harm had been done and feelings were hurt. At that point, neither of the students was ready to learn. Ms. Payne said, "I talked with Ms. Corbin, and we decided to notify the parents but not send [the students] home. We decided to let them try to work it out at the peace table and see what happened. If they couldn't do that, then we'd have to do something more formal. Of course, I was right near the table, just in case, observing and every once in a while interjecting. They did such a good job. It made me really proud that these students could repair the harm that was done, take ownership, and understand that they hurt another person. And you know what? They have never done this again." On this ingredient, Ms. Payne was performing at the *Teaching* level.

Ms. Payne's approach differed significantly from the actions taken by Elizabeth Lewis, who sent students to the office each time there was an infraction. She said, "It's really not my responsibility to figure out the discipline. I'm here to teach, and I appreciate the support from my admin, who talks with students about their behavior and how to correct it." On the ingredient of *repairs harm*, Ms. Lewis is *Not Yet Apparent*. Interestingly in this case, the administrators are enabling her and actually preventing her from assuming responsibility for repairing harm. Of course, some situations are beyond teachers' control, and counselors and school leaders should be involved in supporting teachers and classrooms. Having said that, we believe that teachers should have a role in creating and maintaining the learning community, and doing so requires addressing harm when it occurs.

High school biology teacher Madison Henry had experienced a great deal of success in developing relationships with students and holding them accountable for their academics, attendance, and citizenship. When harm was done, she met with students to ensure that it was repaired. Ms. Henry worked at a school with a fairly traditional discipline policy in terms of referrals, in-school suspensions, out-of-school suspensions, and expulsions. However, as she noted, there was still a need to repair the harm done when students returned to class.

Ms. Henry was so effective at this that the school social worker asked her to support other members of the science department as they worked to improve in this area. Ms. Henry provided her colleagues with examples of the questions she used in different situations. As she explained, "I have different scripts based on what happened, so that I can follow the same line of questions. These have really helped me more quickly and efficiently repair harm and reestablish relationships." Sample questions from Ms. Henry appear in Figure 2.2.

Ms. Henry captured on video several interactions she had with students and shared the clips with her colleagues, saying, "I hope you can give me feedback about which questions worked and which you think fell flat." Together, they viewed the clips and discussed what they saw.

Michael Davies said, "This is all fairly new to me. I try to do this, but I'm not sure that I'm very effective—yet. But what I noticed in the clips is that you have conversations with students who are doing really well, both academically and behaviorally. I hadn't thought about that, but I bet it makes

Figure 2.2 | Sample Prompts for Repairing Harm and Reestablishing Relationships

For meetings with individual students who are struggling behaviorally or academically:
- How do you describe yourself?
- How do other people describe you?
- What assumptions do teachers make about you that are not true?
- How would you like others to describe you?
- Let's make a plan to get you where you want to be. . . .

For meetings with individual students who are doing well:
- How do you describe yourself?
- What assumptions do teachers make about you that are not true?
- What are we doing that is helping you reach your goals?
- What should we be doing more or less of to help you reach your goals?
- Let's make a plan to get you where you want to be. . . .

the conversations easier when there is something that goes wrong." Mr. Davies was at the *Developing* level of growth and was clearly interested in growing in this area. Ms. Henry was at the *Leading* level on this indicator, yet she was still questioning the most effective ways to meet student needs.

Factor 2.3: Efficient

A lack of organizational skills that keep the learners moving forward without excessive disruptions can undermine an otherwise effective teacher. Although such skills may not be obvious in an efficient classroom, their absence is certainly noticeable in classrooms without them or in those where the teacher struggles to prioritize. Often referred to as classroom management, these practices contribute to the learning momentum. Well-paced and efficient managers do the following:

- Establish rules for how the class functions.
- Have routines and procedures in place for tasks.
- Smoothly transition students from one task to another.
- Use time wisely to maximize instruction.
- Maintain necessary records such that colleagues, families, and students are kept apprised of learning.

In this third factor of Cultivating a Learning Climate, we further discuss the teaching behaviors that align to these practices. The first ingredient describes qualities of *rules, routines, and procedures* that ensure the classroom runs efficiently. The second ingredient, *record keeping*, allows teachers to organize data that benefit students and other stakeholders.

2.3a: Rules, routines, and procedures

NYA	Developing	Teaching	Leading
The teacher does not establish rules, routines, and procedures, resulting in a confusing learning environment.	The teacher establishes some rules, routines, and procedures, but they are used inconsistently or do not anticipate common situations, resulting in needless learning interruptions.	The teacher proactively establishes and maintains rules, routines, and procedures that enable students to self-regulate, resulting in smooth classroom operations that maximize learning.	The teacher supports colleagues in their ability to proactively establish and maintain rules, routines, and procedures that enable students to self-regulate, resulting in smooth classroom operations that maximize learning.

Cultivating a learning climate requires strong, positive student-teacher relationships and a focus on fostering the growth of the whole child. These factors should be aligned with the rules, routines, and procedures that make communication and collaboration possible. We define these elements as follows:

- *Rules* comprise a set of expectations that govern the ways people work together.
- *Routines* describe the daily or weekly systems that govern the learning day.
- *Procedures* are aligned to the spirit of the rules and put the routines into operation.

Most classroom management researchers recommend that there be three to five positively stated rules and that they be posted and revisited regularly (Good & Brophy, 2007). Some educators, especially those working with younger children, make the rules concrete and specific (e.g., "Keep hands and feet quiet," "Raise your hand before speaking," etc.). Secondary educators tend to design broader rules that convey a set of classroom values (e.g., "Take care of yourself, each other, and this place"). Whether broad or specific, the rules are usually an amalgam of classroom etiquette and values in support of a group's prosocial development. Some educators codevelop rules with their students, whereas others present them as fully formed and complete. Valid arguments support both methods.

Routines are used regularly and provide structure to the learner's day. For instance, primary educators often begin the day with an extended calendar routine, hold a classroom circle on the carpet just after lunch, and end the week with a class meeting. Middle and high school educators have a much shorter time with students each day but rely on their own routines, such as posting bell work on the board for students to complete in the first minutes of class or giving short, low-stakes quizzes so that students can measure their learning progress. Like all humans, our students rely on routines that allow them to develop a sense of the flow of the day or the class period. We aren't suggesting for a moment that each day should look exactly the same as the previous or the next. However, a lack of expected routines can have a destabilizing effect on learners (Good & Brophy, 2007). As with rules, the details of these routines should be taught and revisited, especially after school breaks.

Procedures, the third facet of this ingredient, are used to teach students how the classroom community works together. The best procedures anticipate common situations, such as these:

- Sharpening pencils or locating a writing instrument
- Checking laptops and tablets out of the classroom recharging cart
- Using the restroom
- Marking attendance
- Storing belongings and materials
- Lining up for recess, lunch, and dismissal
- Turning in papers and digital assignments

This list could be much longer, but we hope you get the idea: procedures teach students how to make decisions without consulting the teacher each time. In other words, procedures should build students' independence and provide them with structures to self-regulate rather than relying on others to make these decisions.

A team of 10th grade teachers representing all subject matters met to examine the rules, routines, and procedures used in their classrooms. They chose to do so because they had noticed quite a bit of unevenness regarding student performance across the day. Students who were reported by some to be reliable in one class were described as being disruptive in others. The teachers speculated that their expectations varied widely and that students responded differently to each context.

The team first toured each other's classrooms to determine what visual markers people were using to guide student decisions. Only three of the seven classrooms had rules posted, and despite many similarities, there were some variances. Joel Mullins, a geography teacher, explained that he didn't post the rules because "students should know by now how to act. They're 15." Two others said that their rules were written on the syllabus they distributed at the beginning of the year. "How do students who enroll later in the year know the rules?" asked Travis Hardy, the geometry teacher. "Some of the students we identified as having problems in some classes came after the school year began. I keep my rules posted in a prominent place and revisit them each quarter. When I get new students, I supply a welcome packet for them that includes the rules and procedures and review the material with them."

The 10th grade team reconvened, this time to chart the routines they used. Again, despite many similarities, the specific procedures varied widely, especially in the use of personal technology and leaving class to visit the restroom. Mr. Mullins let students use the restroom at any time, regardless of how many students were gone, resulting in many of his students roaming the halls at any given time. English teacher Samantha Reynolds kept a small whiteboard next to the door for students to log their names, and she limited restroom visits to one boy and one girl at any time. This procedure sparked minor conflict in her classroom, as students complained and pointed out that "Mr. Mullins doesn't care when we go."

Use of personal technology always seemed to be a struggle, but the entire team liked the approach that geometry teacher Travis Hardy used. He made a poster using an old smartphone case and a set of earbuds, with the words *Plugged In* and *Unplugged*. Mr. Hardy plugged and unplugged the earbuds throughout the class to signal when it was OK to listen to music (e.g., independent learning time) and when everyone should be unplugged (e.g., during focused instruction, guided instruction, and collaborative learning). "It's really worked for me this year, and it's helped me be more consistent in my message to the kids on this subject," he said.

The 10th grade team agreed that the use of consistent procedures would help all of them, especially by reducing incongruent or conflicting procedures that caused disruptions. Mr. Mullins, at the *Not Yet Apparent* growth level for this ingredient, admitted that his laissez-faire approach contributed to ongoing behavior problems in his class. On the other hand, Mr. Hardy, at the *Teaching* growth level, had far fewer interruptions to his instruction. Ms. Reynolds, at the *Developing* level, used a generally effective procedure for students requesting to use the restroom but also struggled with behavior. She decided to post her rules and design a welcome packet like Mr. Hardy's.

Several months later, as the end of the school year approached, the team asked Mr. Hardy to coordinate an effort to formalize rules and procedures so that the entire grade level would hold consistent expectations for next year's students. Over the summer, Mr. Hardy wrote a short insert that the team could use in their syllabi that explained the rules, routines, and procedures. Mr. Hardy's efforts demonstrated his transition from the *Teaching* level to the *Leading* level for this ingredient.

2.3b: Record keeping

NYA	Developing	Teaching	Leading
The teacher's instructional and noninstructional records are consistently incomplete, delayed, not secured, or missing.	The teacher maintains instructional and noninstructional records, but these are sometimes delayed or incomplete, making them less useful to students, families, and colleagues.	The teacher maintains both instructional and noninstructional records so that data are immediately available for planning and to inform students, families, and colleagues.	The teacher supports colleagues in their ability to maintain both instructional and noninstructional records so that data are immediately available for planning and to inform students, families, and colleagues.

We identified *record keeping* as an ingredient in the Cultivating a Learning Climate component because it affects so many other aspects of the FIT Teaching Tool. Specifically, the ability to organize student information, handle papers, grade and return student work, and communicate student progress to colleagues and families is necessary to do the following:

- Identify transfer goals (1.1a)
- Identify success criteria (1.2a)
- Plan for differentiation (1.3b)
- Organize the physical environment (2.1b)
- Scaffold support (3.2b)
- Provide differentiated language support (3.3c)
- Check for understanding (4.2a)
- Analyze errors (4.2b)
- Deliver needs-based instruction (4.3c)
- Monitor student progress in both the short and long term (5.1 and 5.2)

Although information management is critical, it rarely receives much attention until it is a problem. Anyone who has spent time in meetings between educators and family members can attest to the genuine frustration that occurs when multiple students claim that a particular teacher routinely loses their work and then gives them failing grades. Parents rightly protest when they are contacted late in the year about their child's academic struggles, when little previous information has been relayed. "If this is a problem, why didn't I know about it sooner?" they ask, and they're right. A third circumstance, one not readily apparent, is when a child fails to make progress. How often do we dig deeper to find out if the student has had the formative assessment experiences, scaffolded supports, and needs-based instruction she really requires? A final example of the deleterious effects of poor record keeping involves communication with colleagues.

Student study teams and professional learning communities operate on the basis of current information about student performance. The data management clerk needs grades to be submitted on time in order to run report cards. Special educators require up-to-date information about student progress in order to develop meaningful statements on present levels of performance and annual goals for individualized education programs. The district's administrator of the student information system needs electronic records to be stored securely so that student privacy is not compromised. And let's not forget about students whose teachers use digital grade books so that students can assume responsibility for checking their own progress. If work is not promptly graded, returned, and recorded, the information is far less useful. Many a student can attest to parental displeasure when viewing the electronic grade book and finding "missing" assignments that were submitted on time but not recorded by the teacher.

Marcus Woo had found himself overwhelmed by record keeping problems before. The previous year, at his summative evaluation, he received a *Not Yet Apparent* designation for this ingredient. A veteran teacher with more than 30 years of experience, Mr. Woo had resisted using the district's learning management system (LMS), which included an electronic grade book that students and parents could access. Instead, he continued using the same paper grade book he had used for decades. The inability to retrieve grading information had negatively affected the special education support provider who worked with several children in Mr. Woo's 5th grade classroom. Because Mr. Woo didn't use the district's system, she was unable to retrieve information about students' progress, which compromised her ability to effectively complete her job responsibilities.

Based on this review, Mr. Woo attended two district-sponsored workshops during the summer to overcome his reluctance and build his skills. He met with a 5th grade teacher during planning week to set up his grade book. Hilary Estes had served on the district's technology committee to evaluate several LMSs two years earlier, and she received additional training on the implementation of the tool. During the first quarter, Ms. Estes met with Mr. Woo at lunch every Wednesday to look at his grade book. Initially, he needed some assistance inputting grades, but he soon got the hang of it with Ms. Estes there to guide him. As the end of the first quarter approached, he had new questions about weighting assignments and reporting progress on annual goals for his students with disabilities. Ms. Estes's work with her colleague was evidence of her *Leading* growth level on this criterion, while Mr. Woo had progressed to the *Developing* growth level.

As Idrina Duque, another member of the same 5th grade team, prepared for a summative meeting using the FIT Teaching Tool, she assembled artifacts for the Cultivating a Learning Climate component. The evidence she brought for the *record keeping* ingredient included the binder she kept for logging her anecdotal notes as well as her telephone log of calls made to families to report student progress. Ms. Duque noted that she had phoned each family at least twice during the first nine weeks of school. These short conversations included a welcome, a positive story about their child, and a discussion of the child's academic progress. She and the administrator agreed that she was performing at the *Teaching* growth level at this time.

Summing Up

We have a positive presupposition when it comes to students. We believe that students want to develop healthy relationships with their teachers and expect to be treated with respect and fairness. Further, we think that students respond best when the rules, procedures, and expectations are clear and are implemented consistently. Unfortunately, clear and consistent expectations are not always the case, which is why the same student behaves (and learns) differently with and from different adults.

The learning climate takes time and investment to nurture and can be easily disrupted throughout the year. For this reason alone, it is worth regularly checking in with students, family members, and colleagues. Adjustments to the climate can be made at any time. If students aren't following the rules and procedures set for them, then they need to be taught again. If students feel disrespected, the rules and procedures will likely not matter to them. Data about this component can be obtained through self-assessments and grade-level discussions, as well as meetings with instructional coaches and administrators. The climate of the classroom is fragile, and adjustments to procedures and the physical environment can transform the classroom and give it new energy.

3
Instructing with Intention

A teacher must possess two kinds of knowledge: content knowledge and instructional, or pedagogical, knowledge. Shulman (1987) calls this essential combination "pedagogical content knowledge" (PCK). In the words of Gess-Newsome (2013), PCK is "a unique knowledge base held by teachers that allows them to consider the structure and importance of an instructional topic, recognize the features that will make it more or less accessible to students, and justify the selection of teaching practices based on learning needs" (p. 257).

For more than a decade, much of our work has centered on the enactment of pedagogical content knowledge through quality instruction (Fisher & Frey, 2014a). We describe our instructional model as a gradual release of responsibility, implemented in four phases. Critically, implementing this model requires the teacher to understand not only the tools of teaching (pedagogy) but also how to make the content understandable to others who do not possess the same level of knowledge (content). Taken together, these instructional moves systematically advance student learning by gradually shifting the cognitive and metacognitive responsibility from teacher to students (see Figure 3.1). Here are the four phases of our instructional model:

• *Focused instruction*, during which the teacher establishes the learning intention and uses modeling and demonstrating to show how skills and concepts are utilized.

• *Guided instruction*, during which the teacher uses questions, prompts, and cues to scaffold student learning. This requires careful noticing of student

Figure 3.1 | Essential Components of the Gradual Release
of Responsibility Model

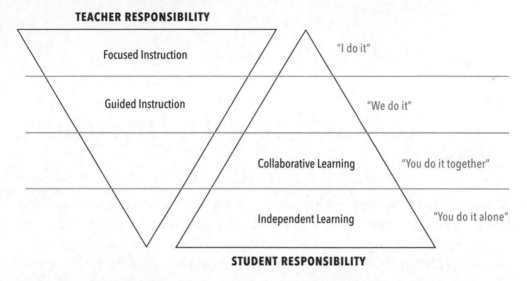

Source: From *Better Learning Through Structured Teaching: A Framework for the Gradual Release of Responsibility,* 2nd ed. (p. 3), by D. Fisher & N. Frey, 2014, Alexandria, VA: ASCD. Copyright 2014 by ASCD.

need and monitoring when they are integrating new knowledge, versus when they need more overt support.

• *Collaborative learning,* during which students work with peers to take on sufficiently complex tasks in order to consolidate understanding.

• *Independent learning,* during which students practice and apply what they have learned, now equipped with the cognitive resources they need to engage in self-directed tasks.

The first three of the four phrases of the gradual release of responsibility model make up the Instructing with Intention component, and the fourth, independent learning, is planned for in *identifying success criteria* (1.2a) and is evidenced in Assessing with a System (the topic of Chapter 4). Success in implementing a gradual release instructional framework requires knowledge not only of the content but also of the anticipated learning progression that will be necessary for students to learn the content. Skilled teachers are able to match these instructional moves to the learning progression.

In this chapter, we turn our attention to Instructing with Intention. The instructional moves outlined capture the actions of teachers who are applying pedagogical content knowledge to build student knowledge and then deepen it. These actions are described as *Focused Instruction* (3.1), *Guided Instruction* (3.2), and *Collaborative Learning* (3.3). We have deliberately not used the word *steps* as a synonym for these actions, as it falsely suggests that the complex science of teaching can be reduced to a recipe or that it is linear in nature. Each move is dynamic, as the teacher attends to a student's idea (noticing), frames the interaction ("What's going on right now?"), makes a decision based on personal PCK ("What shall I do in response?"), and then engages. This sequence occurs countless times throughout a lesson. An observer sitting in the back of the classroom can provide context but can't possibly be privy to the teacher's internal decision making. Therefore, as with all other factors of the FIT Teaching Tool, the discussion of these moments is vital. A checklist of boxes that state whether a teaching behavior occurred or did not occur would fail to fully capture the complexities of a teacher's pedagogical content knowledge and how the teacher applied it. So although classroom observation is an important step, it is by no means the only one. As we have noted in previous chapters, pre- and post-observation reflective discussions, as well as artifacts and evidence, are vital to construct a complete portrait of an educator's practice.

Factor 3.1: Focused Instruction

Sound instruction begins long before we step to the front of the classroom. It starts with planning. As we described in Chapter 1, Planning with Purpose sets the stage for what follows. But plans don't teach; *teachers* do. The ability to execute a well-designed plan is just as important as the plan itself. Numerous studies over the decades have cataloged the behaviors of effective teachers (e.g., Marzano, Pickering, & Pollock, 2001; Pianta, La Paro, & Hamre, 2008). All measure the quality of the instructional interactions between the teacher and the students. They show that effective teachers are able to set the learning intention, provide actionable feedback, make decisions about when and how to scaffold, and foster the use of academic language in the classroom.

Strong teachers establish the learning intention throughout every lesson, revisit the learning intention throughout the lesson to redirect, and use the learning intention to formatively assess students in order to make instructional decisions (Fisher & Frey, 2011). Establishing a learning intention requires ongoing investment in the students' understanding of what they are learning and what they will be doing with the knowledge. Notice that we use a gerund (*establishing*) because it is nonfinite; it indicates action that continually exists in the present tense. In other words, a learning intention isn't stated once and then never revisited. It is the ongoing act of making the learning meaningful and relevant to the student. Teachers can, and should, reestablish the learning intention multiple times during a given lesson, especially during transitions and when students need redirection.

3.1a: Clear learning intentions

NYA	Developing	Teaching	Leading
The teacher does not establish learning intentions with the students.	The teacher establishes the learning intentions with students at the beginning of the lesson segment but does not return to the learning intentions at any other time during the lesson.	The teacher uses the learning intentions to focus students throughout the lesson (such as during transitions and closure activities).	The teacher supports colleagues in their ability to use the learning intentions to focus students throughout the lesson (such as during transitions and closure activities).

The first ingredient in the Instructing with Intention component concerns the way content and language learning intentions are conveyed to students. These come in the form of statements that are delivered verbally, although many teachers, including ourselves, also write them on the board to keep the learning targets in front of students. The content learning intention describes what students will be learning about *today*. It is not the standard or the enduring understanding, which may take weeks or months to achieve. The language learning intention describes the reading, writing, speaking, listening, viewing, and thinking that students will use during the lesson. For example, a biology teacher posted her learning intention on the whiteboard and said, "Today you're going to learn about the stages of meiosis in cell division, and you'll use that vocabulary in your writing to explain each stage." Near the end of the lesson, she returned to this intention and used it to formatively assess her students' understanding and make decisions about the lesson for the following day.

Although the practice of posting and discussing learning intentions seems pretty straightforward to us, we have seen it being misused in a reductive way. Several years ago, Doug and Nancy worked with a large district that had enacted several initiatives to improve student achievement. Their community's majority language was not English, although the language of instruction was. Not surprisingly, the district's major focus targeted teaching and learning issues for English language learners. Among the practices they required was to clearly establish a learning intention for each lesson with students. We have written about this practice extensively, and it has been documented as an effective means for increasing the performance of English language learners (e.g., Echevarria, Short, & Powers, 2006). Yet resistance was high among teachers, who resented what they called "the clipboard police" who came into their classrooms and noted whether the learning intention was written on the whiteboard. Several teachers confided that they had trained their students to recite the learning intention when questioned so that they would get credit for the requirement that "students know the learning intention and can repeat it." You may be thinking, *OK, that's not that bad.* But here's the worst part. The learning intention written on the board often had nothing to do with what the lesson was about. When building or district administrators came into the room, the entire class would pretend the posted learning intention was what the lesson was about.

To be clear, these were not uncaring or uninformed teachers. But the power of the walk-through form trumped everything else, and its misuse as a crude yardstick to measure effective teaching created bitter feelings that overshadowed reasonable thought. Establishing clear learning intentions is a good initiative; reducing this complex practice to two checked boxes is wrongheaded. We raise this concern now because our experience has been that the importance of establishing learning intentions can be lost when a behavioristic approach supersedes teacher development. The form must never become a replacement for its function.

Although a teacher may be clear on what her intentions are when planning, the results are diminished considerably when learners remain unaware of them. "School's hard enough. I shouldn't have to guess what she wants me to learn," an 8th grader named Sharise once confessed to Doug. Clearly frustrated, she was feeling the strain of being lost in the midst of a complex topic her teacher was covering. Arms crossed and head down, she stood in the hallway outside of her classroom, which is where Doug first saw her. He felt for the student—and for her teacher, too.

As someone new to the school, Sharise's teacher, Kendra McGowan, was not practiced at establishing learning intentions with students. However, Sharise had come to expect a posted learning intention, because it was something her other middle school teachers had done daily. Doug met with Ms. McGowan later in the day to debrief the incident with Sharise, and he asked about the learning intention of the lesson. Ms. McGowan explained, "I was really excited about this lesson. They were going to be comparing the weight of objects on each of the planets in the solar system so they could see the effects of gravity on weight. But I don't know what went wrong with Sharise. She just got mad and stormed out of the room. That's when you saw her."

Doug explained, "Sharise told me she didn't know what she was supposed to learn. From your viewpoint, how do you believe you let her in on the learning intention?" Ms. McGowan thought for a moment and then said, "I had an agenda written on the board, and I told the kids that we would be studying weight and mass on different planets," she said. "Is it possible," Doug asked, "that Sharise is not understanding the difference between weight and mass, and she can't go forward until she does?" For the next few minutes, they discussed the challenges learners face when they're unsure about the content, and Ms. McGowan, who was at the *Not Yet Apparent* growth level, agreed that she needed more support. Doug made plans for her to accompany him on a learning walk through several classrooms the following day.

They met the next morning to discuss the problem of practice, which was to determine whether the learning intention was clear to students, and then agreed to talk with a sampling of students in each class. The two of them first stopped at a 6th grade social studies classroom, where Robin Ware was starting her lesson. Doug selected this classroom as the first destination so that Ms. McGowan could see an educator at the *Teaching* growth level. Ms. Ware displayed the content and language learning intentions on the document camera and took a few minutes to parse the statements for her students. For example, she said, "Let's take a closer look at the term *justify* in the language learning intention. Please talk to your partner about what it means to justify, and then put it into your own words." As students talked, Ms. Ware asked individuals about the learning intention. As Ms. McGowan listened to partner discussions, she saw that the students had written the learning intention in their notebooks and dated them.

"Why do you do that?" she asked one boy. "Ms. Ware has us check our notes at the end of class so we can highlight the things that helped us get to the learning intention," he said. He added, "It helps me know what questions to ask when I don't know something."

Next, Doug and Ms. McGowan entered Rich Donaldson's 8th grade math class about 30 minutes into the period. When queried, the students Doug and Ms. McGowan spoke to would point to the board and repeat the learning intention verbatim. However, the math teacher never returned to the learning intention, not even at the end of class. Doug pointed this fact out to Ms. McGowan, noting that although the students knew where the learning intention was posted, Mr. Donaldson, at the *Developing* growth level, was not yet leveraging the learning intention for maximum benefit. "The close of the lesson is a natural place to return to the learning intention," Doug said. "It allows students to do a bit of self-assessment."

After visiting three more classrooms, Doug asked Ms. McGowan what she saw. "I was surprised by the variance inside classrooms and across classrooms," she said. "In most of the rooms, the majority of kids I talked to could at least repeat the learning intention. But in some classrooms, the learning intention wasn't used again, at least from what I saw. I'm thinking about your point that the learning intention can be used in a variety of ways during the lesson." Doug then asked, "What classroom do you want to return to now that it's near the end of first period?" Ms. McGowan said she'd like to see what was happening in Ms. Ware's social studies classroom, because one of the students had told her how they used the learning intention at the end of the lesson. They returned just as the social studies teacher was wrapping up the lesson. "I'd like you to read the learning intention statements you wrote in your notebooks and check in. Use your partner to identify the notes you took that led to that learning intention," she continued. Ms. McGowan sat with the same boy she had visited earlier. "Show me how you do this," she said.

A few minutes later the bell rang, signaling the end of the period. As Ms. Ware approached, Ms. McGowan complimented her on how she made the learning intention clear. "I'm having trouble with that, and I'd like to get better," she said. Ms. Ware said, "Why don't we eat lunch in my room today, and we can talk about the lesson. I'd like your feedback, and perhaps I can help you as well." Ms. Ware's collegial support for using learning intentions in the classroom was a clear demonstration of a *Leading* growth level.

3.1b: Relevant learning intentions

NYA	Developing	Teaching	Leading
The teacher does not establish the relevance of the content.	The teacher loosely or vaguely establishes the relevance of the content to students. The relevance of the content is not revisited.	Relevance is established and maintained throughout the lesson as students are reminded about why they are learning the specific content.	The teacher supports colleagues in their ability to establish and maintain relevance throughout the lesson as students are reminded about why they are learning the specific content.

It is one thing to make the learning intentions clear to students; it is another to make the content relevant. By relevance, we don't mean that everything students learn has to be of world-changing importance. After all, lots of things we teach are pretty mundane, yet we all agree that they are critical. Take syllables, for example. We teach young children to hear and see the syllables that are present in the language because it helps them figure out how to decode longer words, pronounce them correctly, and spell them more accurately. So let's allow our students in on this secret. When we remind students *why* they are learning something (not just *what* they are learning), we appeal to a different part of their thinking. We tap into their motivation to learn. Relevance is simply addressing the question "Why are we learning this?" (Hint: The answer is not "Because it's on the test we're taking next Monday.") It is essential that students see the relevance of what they are learning in order to foster the kind of enduring understandings that will persist long after the course is finished.

We also do not subscribe to the notion that everything that is taught in school needs to be used in the "real world." In fact, we don't like the term "real world." Teachers don't simply prepare students for the real world; they prepare students for a better world. Relevance can be established when students know that they will use the content outside the classroom walls (or beyond the screen of their device). Importantly, relevance is also established when students get to understand themselves as learners, not to mention when they are afforded an opportunity to form opinions about the information.

Science instructional coach Meg Klein, at the *Leading* level of growth, does a great job helping colleagues locate the relevance in their content. "That's one thing our science teachers are really good at doing," she said. "But they're not as practiced at communicating that relevance to their students." She worked with the science teachers at two junior and senior high schools in her district to help them develop this practice. Teams of teachers worked together to augment their learning intention statements by adding a question: "Why is this important?" Working in course-alike groups, they developed relevance statements. Here are a few examples of their work:

- *High school earth science:* Today's learning intention is to identify the stages of the rock cycle, using the terms *sedimentary*, *igneous*, and *metamorphic* in a discussion with your peers. Why is the rock cycle important? When we know that rocks move throughout the layers of the

Earth to form and recycle, we understand that all this movement creates other disruptions, like earthquakes, volcanoes, and seafloor spreading.

• *Middle school physical science:* The learning intention today is to find out why Newton's first law of motion is sometimes called the *inertia law*. Why is this important? Because this law explains why doing tricks on your skateboard can be difficult.

• *High school biology:* Today's learning intention is for you to be able to demonstrate the transfer of energy through a food chain in an ecosystem, to explain why trophic levels vary throughout the food chain. Why is this important? Because when you know why these trophic levels vary, you understand that protecting the bottom of the food chain is critical in order to protect species at all levels.

Biology teacher Darcy Lazaroff used the last example with her own 10th grade students in a lesson about energy transfer. The lesson she taught was essentially the same as what she had taught in previous years, but with additional attention on the relevance of the topic. She began with students enacting the food chain, each representing a species such as a plant, an herbivore, or a predator. As in years past, the students learned that because some energy is lost at each phase, more plants are needed to sustain the herbivores and the predators. Soon students returned to their seats to learn about trophic levels and ecological pyramids. But the difference this year was in Ms. Lazaroff's being more intentional about building relevance. At several key points during the lesson, Ms. Lazaroff turned students' attention back to the critical issue of protecting grasslands and forests to preserve the habitat of ground squirrels and foxes. She spoke to the instructional coach, Ms. Klein, about the experience. "The quality of their exit tickets was much higher than those I collected last year," Ms. Lazaroff said. "I've done the lesson a number of times, and the kids always like it because they get to wear signs saying what species they represent, and there's a good deal of movement around the room as the ecological pyramids begin to form." The biology teacher continued, "But this time I had students writing about conservation efforts and the importance of national parks. I didn't explicitly teach this, but I was blown away by the connections they made between this content and other knowledge they had."

Debriefing after the lesson, the instructional coach asked the biology teacher to reflect on her processes using the FIT Teaching Tool. "I'm feeling very comfortable with placing myself at the *Teaching* level of growth for using clear learning intention statements," Ms. Lazaroff said. "I've been doing this consistently for over a year now. But when it comes to relevant learning intentions, I'd say I'm at a *Developing* level of growth. This is new to me, and I'm only just beginning to use it, but I'm already seeing how it is encouraging [my students] to think critically." After pausing, she said, "I think I'm going to add the question 'Why is this important?' to the section of the whiteboard where I post the daily learning intention. This will help remind me to make the case for relevance."

The instructional coach checked in with Dave Schultz, the middle school physical science teacher. Ms. Klein explained that Mr. Schultz was at the *Teaching* level of growth for this criterion, as he consistently linked his content to its relevance for his students. His classroom featured the question *WHY?* in large letters over the center of his whiteboard, and from the first day of school, he reminded his students to ask this question of him when they didn't see the relevance of what they were learning. "They keep me on my toes," he chuckled. "Nothing like a 12-year-old asking *why*? all the time." In fact, it was Mr. Schultz's expertise in this area that prompted Ms. Klein to bring the issue of relevancy to the science team. She asked the middle school science teacher to partner with her to design the professional learning session on the topic. Mr. Schultz used examples from his own practice, and he video-recorded several of his students explaining why an understanding of matter and its interactions, taught a few weeks earlier, was relevant to them. In addition, he showed the rest of the team how he started with disciplinary core ideas and crosscutting concepts to formulate transfer goals (Planning with Purpose 1.1a), and then he distilled the ideas into a series of relevant learning intention statements. When Mr. Schultz met with an administrator near the end of the year for a summative evaluation, he used this as an example of his *Leading* level of growth for this criterion.

First-year chemistry teacher Loren Owens left the science team meeting in what he later described to his induction coach as "a state of cognitive dissonance." He said, "It seriously never occurred to me that I should even be doing this. I don't remember my master teacher from last year ever talking about this. I just assumed the students would connect the dots. Dave's video [of his own students explaining the relevancy] shocked me. These were middle schoolers talking about atoms and molecules in ways my high school juniors can't." He and the induction coach discussed his next steps. "Well, up until now, I'd be at the *Not Yet Apparent* level of growth," he admitted. "Not on my radar at all. But that's going to change. If I can't make chemistry relevant to my students, I'm wasting their time and mine."

3.1c: Accurate representation of critical content

NYA	Developing	Teaching	Leading
The teacher does not provide accurate content.	The teacher provides accurate content that is loosely linked with learning intentions. The instruction prevents students from engaging in related tasks or fails to provide them with the appropriate foundation.	The teacher provides accurate content that is clearly linked with the learning intentions. The instruction ensures students have the foundation necessary for the tasks they will accomplish.	The teacher supports colleagues in their ability to provide accurate representations of critical content that are linked with the learning intentions and provide a foundation for related tasks.

Think about any academic or growth skill you've ever learned, and chances are good that it's something you first observed someone else doing. Perhaps you studied the stance of a favorite baseball player in order to improve your swing. Or you leaned in closer to the television when an actor you admired talked about how he prepared for a role. You witnessed someone more skilled or knowledgeable than you *doing something* with that skill or knowledge, *applying it*. Teachers are able to accomplish similar feats when they provide students with representations of the content under investigation—by modeling, thinking aloud, lecturing, presenting a video, staging a demonstration, and so on. Each of these instructional experiences is designed to develop students' cognitive and growth skills.

It's also true that modeling, lecturing, video viewing, and demonstrating can be overdone. Stream-of-consciousness ramblings can cause students to become more confused. We can all remember a very boring lecture, modeling that did not capture our interests, and video clips that were not relevant to our learning. Also note that think-alouds lose their power when too many skills or concepts are modeled all at once.

When done well, however, the representation of critical content provides students with information, strategies, ideas, and skills that they can and will use. Figure 3.2 lists common ways that teachers can represent critical content. Of course, this is not an exhaustive list, and there are other valuable ways to provide students with access to information and ideas.

April Mendoza, a special education support teacher, had been *Developing* her representation skills through modeling, but she had seen few results with

Figure 3.2 | Instructional Approaches for Representing Critical Content

Modeling—Providing students with an example of the thinking that the teacher does, as when a teacher thinks aloud to solve a math problem.

Lecture—Providing students with information about a specific topic, as when a teacher explains the process of mitosis.

Video viewing—Providing students with information using diverse media, as when a teacher shows students a clip of a historical reenactment.

Demonstration—Providing students with a direct experience that includes an explanation, as when a teacher shows students how to mold clay on a potter's wheel.

Read aloud—Providing students access to a text, as when a teacher reads a science picture book aloud to students.

her students. She asked a 2nd grade colleague, Susanna Estrada, to watch her as she modeled thinking aloud about a piece of informational text. Ms. Estrada audio-recorded Ms. Mendoza as she read aloud a passage about types of trees and then thought aloud:

> The first thing I noticed was that there were these illustrations on the side of the page of three different types of deciduous trees. But then I didn't know what that word meant, so I knew I had to read. I read the first sentence and saw there was an exclamation mark at the end. Why would the author put an exclamation mark there? So I read it again, because it didn't seem like a surprise to me. [Rereads sentence.] *There are more than a billion trees in the United States!* Oh, OK. Now I see it's not a surprise. The author was using an exclamation mark to emphasize a point. A billion is a big number. I have to stop and think about how many zeros I would need to make a billion.

Later, the two teachers ate lunch together in Ms. Mendoza's classroom. "I'm going to play back the recording of your think-aloud from this morning, but before I do, I'd like to hear your teaching point," said Ms. Estrada. Ms. Mendoza answered, "I wanted them to see how to use illustrations and text together." However, after listening to the recording, she said, "Boy, I'm all over the map in what, two minutes? I started talking about *deciduous*, but I got sidetracked with the exclamation point and the big number." Ms. Estrada nodded. "I have to agree with you. It would be hard for your students to follow, especially when they're not sure what they're listening for." She reached across the table to hand her colleague a planning sheet for a think-aloud (see Figure 3.3). "When I first

Figure 3.3 | Planning Sheet for Developing a Think-Aloud

1. Name the strategy, skill, or task. *Example:* "Today I am going to show you how to combine sentences to make more interesting and complex statements."	
2. State the purpose of the strategy, skill, or task. *Example:* "It's important as a writer to be able to construct sentences that aren't repetitive or choppy. Combining sentences is one way to make sure your sentences read more smoothly."	
3. Explain when the strategy or skill is used. *Example:* "After I have written a passage, I reread to see if I have choppy sentences or if I am repeating information unnecessarily. When I notice that's occurred, I look for ways to combine sentences."	
4. Use analogies to link prior knowledge to new learning. *Example:* "I like to think of this as making sure I am making a straight path for my reader to follow. When I eliminate choppy or redundant sentences, it's like making a straight path of ideas for them to follow."	
5. Demonstrate how the skill, strategy, or task is completed. *Example:* "I'm going to show you three short, choppy sentences. Let's look first at information that we can cross out because it is repetitive. Then I'm going to combine those three sentences into one longer and more interesting sentence."	
6. Alert learners to errors to avoid. *Example:* "I have to be careful not to cut out too much information so that I don't lose the meaning. I also need to watch out for sentences that become too long. A reader can lose the meaning of a sentence that's too long."	
7. Assess the use of the skill. *Example:* "Now I'm going to reread my new sentence to see if it makes sense."	

started developing my think-aloud skills, I used this to make notes about what I was going to say. I've got a structure to it now, but this helped me remember to do things like naming the strategy and using analogies. We've got a few more minutes. I can help you sketch one out for tomorrow," said Ms. Estrada, exhibiting a *Leading* growth level.

Instructional coach Daniel Min met with 4th grade teacher Hilda Salazar for a post-observation coaching conversation. The previous day, Mr. Min had observed in Ms. Salazar's mathematics class, and now they were debriefing the lesson. After reviewing the learning intention of the lesson and the formative assessment information that the mathematics teacher had gathered, the instructional coach turned his attention to a worked example Ms. Salazar had offered. "As you mentioned, your learning intention was to have students examine a worked example of a functions table, then use the same processes to complete their own functions," he said. "But I noticed that you gave them a direct explanation, rather than modeling and thinking aloud. Can you talk about why you did that?" Ms. Salazar explained that she had thought at the time that a direct explanation would be the best route. "They did simpler functions tables the previous two days, and I thought another explanation of the formula would be enough," she said. "It sounds like you're questioning your decision, Hilda. Why?" the instructional coach asked. Ms. Salazar replied, "When I checked in on the groups, I kept running into lots of confusion. I had to go to quite a bit of guided instruction to get them moving again. And I'm still not sure they're there yet." The coach saw this as an opportunity to advance the conversation, so he asked, "What's going to happen tomorrow? They'll still be confused." Ms. Salazar smiled. "I'm going to take a step back and model my thinking about how I complete a function table, and then I'll ask them to explain their thinking. I moved too fast. It's time to bring them back to the mathematical thinking, not just plugging numbers into a formula."

Although in this case Ms. Salazar's lesson featured no modeling or demonstrating, putting her at the *Not Yet Apparent* level for this criterion, it was clear from the coaching conversation that she knew the benefits of providing students with representations of content. She had erred in not including a representation of critical content in this lesson but in reflection saw that doing so might have been useful. All of us realize that there are times when we don't use the right tools for the job. However, Ms. Salazar's pedagogical content knowledge was solid, and the following day she invited Mr. Min to watch her as she modeled and thought aloud. She displayed a partially completed function table on the document camera and began:

> I'm going to talk about how I figure out a rule for completing a function table. The purpose of a function table is to complete the ordered pairs so that I can plot them correctly onto a graph. That word "pair" is important, because it reminds me that each pair has to match all the others, like the shoes in my closet. Each pair is different from the other, but they are all the same size. Ordered pairs in a function table look different from one another, but they all work with the same rule. But I don't want to just guess, because that might take a really long time, and there's a good chance that I'll be wrong. Instead, I am going to look at the number pattern for the input and output. [Pauses.] Because these output numbers get larger, I'm thinking that the pattern will be either an addition or a multiplication rule. I'll try addition first, because it is a small change. The output number is 4 more than the input number, so that might be the rule. When I look at the second ordered pair, the output is again 4 more than the input. Now I am considering whether +4 is the rule. When I think I have developed a rule, I need to recheck it to see if it always works. If it doesn't hold true, then I need to start again. But first I'll try +4 for all the ordered pairs to see if it works. [Calculates.] Yes, that works! So now I'll write +4 for the rule for this function table.

Mr. Min smiled as Ms. Salazar finished her think-aloud. On this day, her use of modeling and thinking aloud placed her at the *Teaching* level of growth. She transitioned students to guided instruction with another example and then had them work with partners to complete a more challenging one. This time, her students were more successful. She told Mr. Min later, "I had to smile when I heard one of the kids coaching her partner using some of the same language I had used during the think-aloud. I guess it worked!"

Factor 3.2: Guided Instruction

The ability to provide guided instruction to an individual student, a small group, or even a larger one comes with years of experience and experimentation. First and foremost, it requires that the teacher hold a firm understanding of the learning progression of novices as they acquire and master new knowledge. Second, the teacher needs to continually pose the same internal question: "What does this child's response tell me about what she knows and doesn't know?" Only then can the teacher provide the kinds of scaffolds needed to move the child's understanding forward.

The expert blind spot (Nathan & Petrosino, 2003) interferes with a teacher's ability to provide guided instruction, because the teacher's disciplinary knowledge obscures knowledge of students' developmental learning needs. Some teachers are able to reduce their expert blind spot rapidly; others never do. It seems that those with high levels of formal disciplinary knowledge but low levels of content pedagogical knowledge incorrectly emphasize the need to learn formal rules before students can learn real-world examples, when, in fact, the opposite is true (National Research Council, 2005). In other words, you need to know 10th graders, not just 10th grade geometry. With experience, and a willingness to explore student thinking, skilled teachers reduce this expert blind spot and become more adept at noticing student needs and scaffolding support based on student responses.

3.2a: Notices student needs

NYA	Developing	Teaching	Leading
The teacher does not notice students' misconceptions, errors, or confusions.	The teacher only occasionally notices students' misconceptions, errors, or confusions, as evidenced by minimal follow-up probes.	The teacher notices students' misconceptions, errors, or confusions by asking questions to probe their thinking, paying attention to nonverbal cues, or analyzing student work.	The teacher supports colleagues in their ability to notice students' misconceptions, errors, or confusions by asking questions to probe their thinking, paying attention to nonverbal cues, or analyzing student work.

The concept of teacher noticing has gained momentum in the last decade as a means for shifting instructional practices away from the "sage on the stage" to the "guide on the side." Van Es and Sherin (2002) describe noticing in three stages: "(a) identifying what is important or noteworthy about a classroom situation; (b) making connections between the specifics of classroom interactions and the broader principles of teaching and learning they represent; and (c) using what one knows about the context to reason about classroom interactions" (p. 573). This concept differs from "with-it-ness," which describes a teacher's ability to sense minute changes in the physical and emotional climate of the classroom. In fact, many teachers generally engage in noticing behaviors only intermittently, with more of their attention focused on classroom organization and management (Tekkumru Kisa & Stein, 2015).

In teacher noticing, the attention is focused on student thinking, as the teacher hypothesizes the student's current understanding and is able to respond with scaffolds that accelerate learning. High school administrator Winston James reviewed his first-semester observations of Hank Simmons, a physical education teacher. Mr. James wanted this first-semester debriefing to focus on guided instruction, and especially on noticing. In previous observations, Mr. James had noted that the PE teacher was growing in his ability to establish learning intentions, and he was becoming more adept at planning lessons across larger themes. However, a notable area for growth was teacher noticing. After reviewing Mr. Simmons's accomplishments during the first half of the year, Mr. James shifted the topic to noticing.

"I've been in your classroom and on the field with you three times so far this year, and I'd like to see you transfer what you're doing well on the field back into your classroom," the administrator began. "I've seen you really attuned to student needs on the field. For example, when you were teaching the volleyball unit, you closely observed their serves, and you stepped in to make corrections that seemed so small, yet even I could see they made a difference."

Mr. Simmons responded, "Thanks. I'm glad you saw that. It's really common for kids to pick their back foot up off the ground when they're serving instead of keeping their toes in contact with the floor." "And why is that a problem?" asked Mr. James. "Well," Mr. Simmons replied, "they end up launching the ball right into the net!" "That's a great example of your level of noticing," said Mr. James. "Right now, I would place you at the *Developing* level of growth, because you are definitely doing a lot of noticing on the field. But in your classroom, I've seen that you don't consistently respond with a follow-up probe when a student has an incorrect answer. You'll say something like 'I've got it here in my notes,' 'Can anyone help him?' or 'Who else can answer that?' Do you see why that would be a problem?"

Mr. Simmons thought for a moment and then said, "If I just said, 'Next' when a player didn't clear the top of the net, that player wouldn't know how to improve. She'd probably just keep making the same mistake again. It's the same effect when a student answers incorrectly and I move on to the next student. All that kid hears is the correct answer, but she doesn't know why hers was not correct." The administrator responded by saying, "I'd like you to sit in on the classroom portion of Marie Handler's PE class tomorrow, and then let's talk again. Use that time to script how she responds when a student has an incorrect response or has a misconception."

The following day, Mr. Simmons arrived a few minutes before Ms. Handler's class was to begin. Her students were studying the human circulatory system in order to relate it to their fitness levels. As she discussed key concepts with her students, she probed for common misconceptions. When she asked about the importance of the systemic and pulmonary circulatory systems, Jorge responded, "Well, the systemic system's more important, because if it stopped working, the heart wouldn't get any blood." In response to this incorrect answer, Ms. Handler said, "You've raised an interesting point. Can you talk more about your reasoning?" During the next several minutes, she and the class discussed his conclusion. The teacher then said, "Now let's consider what we know when somebody goes into shock. Think about the circulatory system. What's happening?" Jorge now realized his error. "When a person goes into shock, it's because the blood flow decreases to the limbs," he said. The teacher asked, "And where is the limited blood flow going?" Jorge responded, "Pulmonary."

The administrator and Mr. Simmons met up again during his planning period. "Tell me about your experience in Ms. Handler's room," said Mr. James. Mr. Simmons relayed the experience with Jorge concerning the circulatory system and listed several other responses Ms. Handler used, noting that she was at the *Teaching* level of growth. Mr. Simmons said, "I observed her really notice a lot of things, and she had ways to check out her assumptions, such as 'Tell me more about that' or 'Can you elaborate?' and 'Can you give me an example?'"

"These probes alone don't unpack student misunderstandings, but they certainly signal that the teacher is noticing something and wants to explore it further," said Mr. James. "Tell me your plan for integrating this into your classroom practice."

In an elementary school not far away, Marla Henderson was sharing a video collection of her lessons with a 3rd grade colleague, Isaac Serbin, who had asked for help with noticing. Mr. Serbin started the conversation by saying, "Patti [the instructional coach] has commented on my teaching several times, saying that I don't usually notice when students are confused or struggle. I think I follow the lesson plans we develop pretty carefully, but then my students don't do as well as the others on our benchmark assessments. I'm thinking that noticing may be something I need to be better at." Mr. Serbin is at the *Not Yet Apparent* level of growth and wants to improve in this area.

Ms. Henderson said, "I know that I've been teaching 3rd grade for several years, and my experience helps me notice students' understanding, but noticing is also something I've really worked on. I work hard to pay close attention to students when they're talking or thinking. I'm not perfect, and I'm sure I miss a lot, but if you're interested, we can watch some of my videos or Mr. Allen's [another member of the 3rd grade team] to see how we notice students' thinking and identify their misunderstandings." Ms. Henderson is at the *Leading* level of growth on this indicator. As they talk, she pauses the video for them to discuss her actions so that Mr. Serbin can identify specific teacher moves that relate to noticing.

3.2b: Scaffolds support

NYA	Developing	Teaching	Leading
The teacher does not scaffold support for students.	The teacher at times offers questions, prompts, and cues to scaffold support of student learning but at other times moves to direct explanations instead of scaffolding first.	The teacher scaffolds support for students using prompts and cues when student responses demonstrate incorrect or partial understanding, reserving direct explanations only for situations when prompts and cues are insufficient.	The teacher supports colleagues in their ability to scaffold support for students using prompts and cues when student responses demonstrate incorrect or partial understanding, reserving direct explanations only for situations when prompts and cues are insufficient.

After teacher noticing, then what? The key to guided instruction is the scaffolding that teachers provide as a catalyst to the learning process. These scaffolds, which come in the form of questions, prompts, and cues, provide just enough information to spark the learner. However, the skillful use of prompts and cues takes time to acquire and is often the line of demarcation between novice and skilled teachers (Frey & Fisher, 2010). A teacher with less experience at offering scaffolds is more likely to simply tell students the answer when they give an incorrect response rather than explore what they may already know. For instance, if a student reads "horse" instead of "house," several different hypotheses about the error can be formed (Fisher & Frey, 2014a):

- The child understands many consonant sounds.
- The child may not be attending closely to the word.
- The child may not yet be attending to the medial position in the word.
- The vowel combination may be unfamiliar.

That rapid formulation of a hypothesis must now be followed by a teacher response. The possibilities for responding to the error include the following:

- Tellling: "That word is 'house.' Read it again, please."
- Scaffolding: "Look again. Does that sound right?" [Not attending to print]
- Scaffolding: "You missed the middle sound. Look again at the middle letters and try it again." [Difficulty with medial positions]
- Scaffolding: "The letters 'ou' make the /ow/ sound. Try the word again using that sound." [Unfamiliar with this vowel combination]

A major drawback in telling the student the answer as a first response is that you never get to test your hypothesis. The first scaffolds we offer to students are designed to prompt them to consider previously learned but temporarily forgotten information. That's the nature of learning—it's the consolidation of isolated information that takes time. Prompts may be about any of the following:

- *Background knowledge*—This refers to content that the student already knows, has been taught, or has experienced but has temporarily forgotten or is not using correctly. (During a lesson about weather, the teacher says, "What do you remember about how clouds form?")
- *Process or procedure*—Established or generally agreed-upon rules or guidelines are not being followed, and a reminder will help resolve the error or misconception. (When a student incorrectly multiplies two fractions, the teacher says, "Look closely. Have you done the first step, which is to reduce the fractions?")
- *Reflection*—Asking students to be metacognitive and think about their thinking can then be used to determine next steps or the solution to a problem. ("Think back to our lesson's learning intention today. Have you accomplished that?")
- *Heuristics*—These informal problem-solving procedures are used to help learners develop their own way to solve problems. They do not have to be the same as others' heuristics, but they do need to work. ("What's a way you could rapidly count all those objects, without having to count out each one?")

Prompts such as these are often all that's needed to get student learning rolling again. But sometimes students need more overt cues that shift their attention to the salient information they need. Novice learners will sometimes perceive everything and nothing all at once. Either everything is equally important, or none of it is (many of us felt this way during our very first classroom experiences). Cues come in four different forms and are often paired with one another to strengthen the cue, as when combining a gestural cue with a verbal one:

- *Visual cues* focus student attention on a portion of text, such as when highlighting a sentence or circling a word.
- *Verbal cues* rely on both what is said and how it is said, such as slowing down a statement so that the child can complete it ("When two vowels go walking . . .").
- *Gestural cues* include body movements and motions, such as pointing, turning, or making hand motions to emphasize a phrase.
- *Environmental cues* are placed in the classroom to spur student thinking, such as a word wall or a language chart.

Fifth-grade chair Linda Matsushita was asked by her principal to support the teachers in her grade level as they expanded and deepened their use of scaffolds in student learning. Ms. Matsushita had been placed at the *Leading* level of growth for this criterion the previous year because of her professional development work on the topic with the entire school. Now she had been given release time to work with colleagues on their practice. Her first classroom stop was in Kathy Blake's social studies class. Ms. Blake had been anticipating her visit and had placed an extra chair for Ms. Matsushita to sit in while she met with a small group. "We're looking at documents about the Stamp Act," she explained. "Thanks for waiting," she said to her group. "Where were we?"

Jason replied, "We were talking about why the colonists were upset about the Stamp Act." His teacher asked, "And based on what we've read so far, what's your conclusion?"

"Oh, they were definitely upset," he said confidently.

"But why do you say that? Can you point to some evidence in the text?" He replied that one document said, "Awake, awake my countrymen and defeat those who want to enslave us." Ms. Blake asked, "Is there another document that holds a different perspective?" The children looked, and Ms. Blake slid the correct one to Ben, who was looking confused. Ben began reading silently and then said, "This one from the tax collector in Philadelphia is all about how bad the other colonists are, like that they're being disrespectful to the king of England." Over the next 10 minutes, Ms. Blake, at the *Teaching* growth level, offered several more scaffolds to her students, guiding their thinking but refraining from telling them the answers herself. As Ms. Matsushita excused herself, she thanked her colleague and made notes for use in their next team meeting.

Her next visit was with Sara Kitchener, who had already stated that she was at a loss for what guided instruction looks like in the math classroom. She had self-identified at the *Developing* level of growth. Ms. Matsushita came equipped with a sheet of prompts and cues that could be used for this purpose. The teachers had already agreed that Ms. Matsushita would meet with a small group of Ms. Kitchener's students, while Ms. Kitchener would watch the demonstration lesson. After the lesson, Ms. Matsushita and Ms. Kitchener discussed the prompts and cues Ms. Matsushita had used, and why. "It really turned out to be an incredibly valuable time for both of us," Ms. Matsushita said later. "Sara's questions really caused me to consider how I know when to deliver a prompt or offer a cue."

Later, she observed Brad Michael's classroom. The students in the class were working productively in groups, and Mr. Michael was meeting with students individually to conference with them about their writing. On this visit, Mr. Michael was rated as *Not Applicable* because the two individual meetings with students he had while being observed did not allow him to scaffold support. Both students expressed their ideas clearly and made a compelling case for their flow of ideas. Mr. Michael did not have the opportunity to scaffold at that time. Having said that, Ms. Matsushita had observed Mr. Michael using scaffolding with students numerous times and did not feel the need to talk with him about this aspect of his classroom.

Factor 3.3: Collaborative Learning

The merits of creating collaborative learning experiences are extensive. Benefits to students include academic achievement (Slavin, 1996), responsiveness to peers' needs (Ashman & Gillies, 1997), and transfer of learning (Pai, Sears, & Maeda, 2015) when compared to individualistic learning experiences. We regard this last point as especially compelling. A chief goal of learning is to promote transfer of knowledge such that learners can apply skills and concepts in new situations. Collaborative learning opportunities allow students to consolidate their learning through tasks that are novel and complex enough to promote interaction and interdependence (Fisher & Frey, 2014a). In fact, we feel so strongly about collaborative learning that our own school's goal is that approximately 50 percent of our instructional minutes are spent in student-to-student interactions. However, collaborative learning requires planning and instruction. Simply moving four desks together will not automatically result in consolidation and transfer. Collaborative learning requires establishing routines, an ability to construct sufficiently complex tasks, and provision of language supports to facilitate discourse and production.

3.3a: Interactive learning routines

NYA	Developing	Teaching	Leading
The teacher does not use collaborative learning routines.	The teacher uses collaborative learning routines but does not teach the processes and procedures necessary for students to maximize instructional time.	The teacher systematically teaches the process and procedural skills needed for collaborative learning routines that will be used throughout the unit or school year. This is apparent as students demonstrate clear understanding of collaborative learning routines in order to maximize instructional time.	The teacher supports colleagues in their ability to support students in acquiring the process and procedural skills needed to engage in collaborative learning routines in order to maximize instructional time.

Creating collaborative learning begins with establishing routines so that students can focus on the learning rather than the logistics. Most teachers have a few favorite arrangements that they like to use, but true collaborative learning (not just group activities) requires a thoughtful match between the students, the task, and the arrangement.

The roots of collaborative learning can be traced to the influential work of David W. Johnson and Roger T. Johnson, who developed the five conditions that are needed in order to develop positive social and academic interactions (Johnson, Johnson, & Smith, 1991):

• *Positive interdependence*—The first feature focuses on the interconnectedness of the learning situation. Each member of the group must be important for the overall success of the endeavor.

• *Face-to-face interaction*—In these interactions, students should teach each other, check each other's understanding, discuss concepts and ideas, and make connections between the content and their own lives.

• *Individual and group accountability*—Students must understand the products that are expected from the learning task and be held accountable for the overall result as well as their individual contributions.

• *Interpersonal and small-group skills*—For groups to work effectively and efficiently, each member must possess and use the requisite social skills. Often, specific skills such as those related to leadership, decision making, trust building, turn taking, active listening, and conflict management must be taught.

• *Group processing*—A final feature involves the group members themselves discussing their progress and what they might do to improve their productivity or working relationships.

To these conditions we add two important elements that elevate the learning that occurs. The first is that the task needs to be complex enough that students have reason to interact with one another. The second is that the teacher is an active presence in the learning. In traditional cooperative learning, the group is left to itself to resolve the problem, with the teacher providing minimal levels of support so as not to interfere with the group's processes. In collaborative learning, the teacher moves in and out of groups, often providing short guided instruction to move the group forward when it loses momentum.

However, the success of the group is influenced by the preparation of the teacher (and that's clearly related to Planning with Purpose). A good starting point is considering the necessary prerequisites for making collaborative learning a successful experience:

• *Plan for purposeful talk* by incorporating standards, establishing clear learning intentions, and identifying learning, language, and social objectives for lessons.

• *Create an environment that encourages academic discourse*, including the physical room arrangement, teaching the routines of talk, and scaffolding language.

• *Manage the academic discourse* through grouping and collaborative activities that increase confidence and provide students with ways to consolidate learning with their peers.

• *Assess language development* using practical tools for monitoring progress and identifying areas of need. (Fisher, Frey, & Rothenberg, 2008, p. 2)

This last element is crucial in collaborative learning, in that a major purpose is to foster the authentic use of academic language. This aspect can be especially challenging for English language learners, who may require more specialized supports in the form of language frames. We discuss this element later in the chapter, but for now we'll refer you to an extensive table of collaborative learning routines and linguistic frames for supporting students that we've gathered as an online resource at http://www.ascd.org/ASCD/pdf/books/CollaborativeLearningRoutines.pdf.

High school administrator Gwen Hayes just finished her third semester of using the FIT Teaching Tool to foster teacher growth. She observed teachers at the school multiple times a year, with pre- and post-conference meetings to discuss planning and debrief. The focus for her school district was collaborative conversations, and the staff had already attended several subject specific formal professional learning sessions. However, teachers varied widely in the extent to which they had adopted this instructional approach. At the high implementation end was Isla Peterson, an experienced mathematics teacher who used collaborative learning routines to increase the amount of mathematical discourse occurring in her room. Ms. Hayes reviewed the pre-conference notes she had collected when she met with Ms. Peterson and added information about Ms. Peterson's plan to conduct a learning walk with her professional learning community in two weeks. Later, after observing Ms. Peterson's class, Ms. Hayes read her field notes about the video-capture the teacher was doing with one group. As Ms. Peterson had explained to the administrator at the time, she planned to use the video to discuss how her students were using the Numbered Heads Together protocol she had introduced several weeks before. Her purpose was twofold, as she would first discuss the video with her own students and then use it later with her collaborative planning team. As Ms. Hayes reflected on the math teacher's growth level, she placed her in the *Leading* category.

She then turned her attention to the notes she collected for Don Veltri, a 9th grade algebra teacher. During their pre-conference, Mr. Veltri said that he was struggling to put collaborative learning routines in place. He had visited Ms. Peterson's class before but confessed to struggling with longer tasks. Ms. Hayes suggested that he scale back his efforts, as he had been trying several new routines each week. They agreed that he would focus on the Explorers and Settlers collaborative learning routine first, because he was feeling more successful with it. When Ms. Hayes observed in his classroom, he had a series of short algebra problems for students to work on together, although there was a bit of confusion at the start of the activity. Ms. Hayes made a note to discuss ways to make the directions clearer to students the next time and placed Mr. Veltri in the *Developing* category of the criterion.

Ms. Hayes conducted her third observation in Wendy Franklin's geometry class. Ms. Franklin spoke at length about the ways she used collaborative learning every day in her classroom and told Ms. Hayes that her students would be completing collaborative posters during the lesson. During the 30-minute observation, Ms. Franklin's students were engaged in extended small-group work as they determined geometric proofs. The members of each team were given different-colored markers and worked together to compose the correct proof. The teacher sat with each group to check for understanding and provide guided instruction as needed. Ms. Hayes took notes on the ease with which the teams got to work, and several students told her that they complete collaborative posters nearly every week. The administrator closed out her notes for the post-observation debriefing by placing Ms. Franklin at the *Teaching* level of growth.

While visiting Ms. Franklin's room, Ms. Hayes noticed a special education teacher working individually with a student who needed additional support to access the course materials. In this situation, the special education teacher's growth would be rated as *Not Applicable* because there was no need for her to engage in collaborative learning routines at that time.

Ms. Hayes saved her most difficult situation for last. Mike Switalski, a pre-calculus teacher, had made it clear in his pre-conference meeting that he did not subscribe to the notion that collaborative learning should occupy a significant portion of his instructional time. A veteran teacher with more than 20 years of experience, Mr. Switalski argued that higher-level mathematics courses like his did not function best with a group approach. "They aren't going to run into anything like this in college," he had said. True to form, he did not have any collaborative learning going on in his classroom when Ms. Hayes observed. Instead, he lectured while students took notes for 35 minutes, and then he assigned homework and asked students to "use their time wisely" during the last 20 minutes of class. Of course, teachers can make lectures meaningful, but students should also be expected to consolidate their understanding collaboratively during the lesson.

Ms. Hayes knew that Mr. Switalski was not an uncaring teacher—just a resistant one. She also knew that he had expressed interest in continuing his learning. Ms. Hayes decided she would meet with her supervisor to talk further about Mr. Switalski's professional learning, as he was clearly at the *Not Yet Apparent* level of growth for this category. Among the notes she made was to connect with the local university math department to see if Mr. Switalski could observe college coursework. Following her discussion with her assistant superintendent, Ms. Hayes met with Mr. Switalski and reviewed his progress. She noted that the lack of collaborative learning was a significant concern, as were his planning and his assessments. Their conversation was respectful, and Ms. Hayes said, "Mike, there are several areas that are consistently not evident in your classroom. We've talked about this several times, and I'm not seeing any progress. I am recommending you for targeted improvement. I have requested a district peer coach to support you. I will continue to observe your progress, but you will have a peer to support you as well. I really think you can do this, if you want to."

3.3b: Task complexity

NYA	Developing	Teaching	Leading
The teacher does not monitor student collaborative work.	The teacher uses collaborative learning, but the tasks are insufficiently complex to challenge students' thinking. The teacher monitors students as they work collaboratively.	Collaborative work is sufficiently complex to allow students an opportunity to use a variety of resources to creatively apply their knowledge; the task challenges students' thinking. The teacher monitors groups' progress in the event that the task might need adjustment.	The teacher supports colleagues in their ability to design collaborative work that is sufficiently complex to allow students an opportunity to use a variety of resources to creatively apply their knowledge. The teacher supports colleagues in their ability to monitor groups' progress in the event that the task might need adjustment.

We have intentionally used the term *complexity* in this section to distinguish it from *difficulty*. Based on Webb's (2002) work on depth of knowledge, we define these two terms as follows:

- *Difficulty*—A measure of *time, effort, or work* required to complete a task.
- *Complexity*—A measure of the *thinking, action, or knowledge* that is needed to complete the task.

Simply making tasks more difficult will not ensure that students will think more creatively or critically. Assigning nine more math problems does not necessarily make the task more complex, but it will take more time. Marisa Ramirez, reflecting on her expectations, said, "I always required that essays be 1,500 words. And I knew that students would just add sentences to meet that requirement. I realized I was making the task more difficult but not always more complex. Some students can write amazingly complex pieces in 1,200 words. I redesigned my rubric to focus on the type of thinking and arguments I expected to see, which really helped students experience more complexity."

Having distinguished between complexity and difficulty, we don't think that everything needs to be complex. Sometimes tasks should provide students an opportunity to practice something and get better at it. Thinking of tasks in terms of these two dimensions, difficulty and complexity, generates a grid with four quadrants (see Figure 3.4). We don't think that any one of these quadrants is better than another. For example, we think that note taking is a low difficulty/low complexity task and that it's an important one for students to learn. However, when students are working collaboratively, the task should be sufficiently complex to require their collective effort. In other words, we look toward keeping collaborative tasks above the complexity axis, rather than below it, because doing so provides students with a reason to interact with one another. For instance, when studying their notes, students can pose questions to one another, seek clarification on specific points, and investigate information together. Another example is in analyzing multiple documents for similar or opposing arguments. A group of students engaged in this highly complex task are going to rely on one another to enumerate and debate these arguments. We use the four quadrants in Figure 3.4 to discuss with teachers how meaningful

Figure 3.4 | Complexity Versus Difficulty

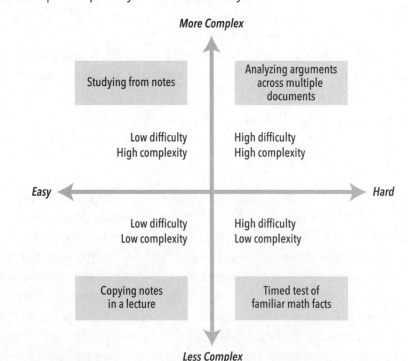

tasks can be developed so that students are challenged by something more than simply doing more work.

The importance of complexity in collaborative tasks is something we've been reminded of many times in our own classrooms when we constructed tasks that were inadvertently too easy for the group to accomplish. Instead of meaningful interaction, we witnessed a "divide and conquer" approach, with groups parsing out tasks to one another to be completed independently, only to meet again just before the assignment was due to assemble the final product. Tasks that work well for small groups can often be completed in more than one way, allowing students to use their creativity to resolve the problem. To aid in this, teachers will intentionally move to more ambiguous and less structured tasks as the groups show gains in their ability to work together. How ambiguous and how unstructured is dependent on a number of factors, including the developmental age of the students, their capacity to work together as groups, and the presence of a learning climate that encourages risk taking and experimentation.

Collaborative learning is a sophisticated instructional behavior because it draws on so many related components and factors. The complexity of the task has implications for the component of Planning with Purpose, especially in factor 1.3, *Meaningful Learning*. Although students are taking the lead on these tasks, the teacher remains continuously active in monitoring student progress, which touches on Assessing with a System, which we discuss in depth in the next chapter. Another aspect of this monitoring is in viewing each group's joint attention to the tasks. A student who is sitting apart from the group with arms crossed is signaling that he is not actively participating in the task. An effective teacher knows to head over to the group to find out what's going on. In some cases, this may have more to do with Cultivating a Learning Climate than with Instructing with Intention. Effective teachers make adjustments as needed during the collaborative learning phase, providing scaffolds when necessary to propel a group forward when their learning has stalled. As you can see, this adjustment signals the use of *Guided Instruction* (3.2), because the teacher is now using questions, prompts, and cues. Observers need to be sensitive to the fact that any number of components and factors come into play during collaborative learning. They must also remember that the teacher is making myriad decisions during this phase.

This range can be seen in classrooms at Abraham Lincoln Elementary School. For example, kindergarten teacher Fran Wilkie used Busy Bees regularly in her classroom of 5-year-olds. To practice addition math facts, Ms. Wilkie gave each child a handful of counting cubes and a sheet of paper to record their answers. As she called, "Busy bees, fly!" the children shuffled and buzzed until she announced, "Busy bees, land!" Each child partnered with the adjacent youngster and then focused on the task, which required that they collectively count their cubes and write the result as a math expression on their papers. Ms. Wilkie repeated this routine several times. "I like doing this because it allows them to gain some math fluency in partners. They also get to practice some of the social skills, like greeting each other and saying thank you." When asked to self-evaluate, she placed this task in the *Developing* range, because "it's not really super challenging for them, because it's material they're familiar with. I need to be able to challenge them more as they work together. I think they're probably ready for it, but I have to think through where I want them to go next." However, it is important to note that Ms. Wilkie was also fostering social skills, in keeping with her commitment to Cultivating a Learning Climate.

A few days later, Ms. Wilkie spent time in the classroom of Jen Collins, a 1st grade colleague who rated herself at the *Teaching* level on the criterion of *task complexity*. Ms. Wilkie decided to spend time in a 1st grade classroom to gain a better sense of what she should prepare her students for. The 1st grade teacher met with her kindergarten counterpart to discuss the types of collaborative learning routines she was using and the tasks that she designed for them. "I'm having success with using Fishbowl for some of the more complex tasks, because it lets me do a bit of guided instruction before students move to doing it collaboratively," she said. "I will invite a few students as a small group to the center of the room and then have everyone else sit in a larger circle outside," explained Ms. Collins. "As the students work on the task, I ask the others who are observing questions like 'Why do you think Vanessa just did that?' or 'What do you thing Simon was expecting when he asked that question?' I'm trying to use these events to cause them to think critically about how they are interacting and why, instead of only paying attention to the task," she said.

Ms. Wilkie also arranged to meet with her 2nd grade colleague, Juan Morales. He is a member of the school's instructional leadership team (ILT) and attends district professional development with his ILT as part of a district initiative. Mr. Morales has presented previously at school professional learning sessions on this topic, and Ms. Wilkie chose to meet with him because of his primary-grade focus. Using resources from several sites, including samples from their state's department of education, Mr. Morales had assembled several collaborative performance tasks for K–2 classrooms that featured a range of task complexity. Using the diagram in Figure 3.4, Mr. Morales and Ms. Wilkie used sticky notes of task descriptions and arranged them across the grid. "I recognized that many of the performance task examples called for more complex thinking, especially in the number of different stages of thinking my students had to do. It also got me thinking about designing more tasks that have more than one plausible answer, so the students can use their creativity and see it being used by others," Ms. Wilkie said. Mr. Morales, at the *Leading* level for this criterion, made notes about Ms. Wilkie's insights in order to share this activity at his school's next professional learning session.

When Ms. Wilke had a chance to talk with her team about the experiences she had had in rethinking task complexity, another kindergarten teacher reacted with skepticism: "Really? They're only 5 years old. School should be more about play and socialization for them. I don't think that there should be anything that is complex or hard for our students at this level." In this case, this teacher was at the *Not Yet Apparent* level of growth because he wasn't interested in considering appropriately complex tasks for his students.

3.3c: Language support

NYA	Developing	Teaching	Leading
The teacher does not provide language support to students.	The teacher provides generic written, verbal, teacher, or peer supports for all students, without attending to differentiated needs.	The teacher provides differentiated written, verbal, teacher, or peer supports to boost individual students' academic language usage.	The teacher supports colleagues in their ability to provide differentiated written, verbal, teacher, or peer supports to boost individual students' academic language usage.

The third ingredient of collaborative learning is *language support*. All students can benefit from these supports, not just English language learners and students with disabilities. These supports include the following:

- Language frames
- Word banks
- Specialized and technical vocabulary lists
- Peer supports
- Print and online glossaries
- Visual dictionaries
- Graphic organizers

Small-group communication is dependent on *what* is being said and *how* it is being said. Language supports such as those listed can bridge the content and the social aspects of communication. This support can range from using counting chips so that small children have a tangible means to self-monitor turn taking to using sophisticated technical vocabulary lists that include key terminology as well as general academic words that change their meaning in different contexts and content areas.

Teachers and school leaders from other states often visit the school where two of us work. We were especially impressed with a group that visited classrooms in our high school to view the range of language supports we offer. English language learners make up 32 percent of the student population, and students with disabilities account for 15 percent. And another significant number of students are "redesignated English learners," which means they have largely mastered the English language but still need some supports. As you can imagine, language supports mean a lot to us. The out-of-state visitors conducted a learning walk through classrooms. In each case, they sat at tables with students as the discussion occurred. After every third classroom, they paused to discuss patterns of what they had seen. Using their language, each person named a "glow" (something positive) and a "grow" (an opportunity to strengthen practice). Their goal was not to evaluate our teachers but to hone their own skills in developing post-observation questions. The teachers in some classrooms were at the *Developing* level of growth for this criterion, while others were at the *Teaching* level. The team identified the following "glow and grow" questions for each level:

- *Glow questions for teachers at the* Developing *level of growth:* What is an example of when a student benefited from a language support available to him or her? Why do you believe it was useful? Is there another student who might benefit from this?
- *Grow questions for teachers at the* Developing *level of growth:* How can you translate your success with this student into more widespread and consistent language support for all learners?
- *Glow questions for teachers at the* Teaching *level of growth:* Choose a student we saw today and tell me about how his or her language development has improved over the course of the year. To what do you attribute this growth? What will you do next for this student?
- *Grow questions for teachers at the* Teaching *level of growth:* In what ways have your colleagues benefited from your language support practices?

What are future opportunities that we could take advantage of to support your leadership development?

This visit was an excellent learning experience for us, too, because their "grow" questions focused on taking practice to the next level, not cataloging shortcomings. The growth mindset of these visitors reminded us that a *Leading* level of growth can be exhibited in and out of the classroom, and even in other schools.

Importantly, the visitors said that there were no classrooms in which language support was absent. They then related a story from their own district. They reported that some teachers assigned individual and collaborative tasks with no language support. As one of them said, "Some teachers assume that the students will figure things out, either by themselves or with their peers. In those cases, they don't really provide any language support. There are classrooms in our high school with no word walls, no language frames, and not much teacher or peer support."

When asked to describe the language support they observed that was at the *Developing* level, these visitors noted that every classroom had a word wall and that students were grouped in ways that ensure peer support. The difference they noted in the *Teaching* level of classrooms was not just the availability of these types of resources but also the fact that different language supports were provided to different students. As one of them said, "In one of the classrooms we observed, students were working collaboratively, and the teacher had provided different language frames, with choices for students to use. In that same classroom, we noticed that students had different vocabulary words listed in their notebooks, and the title of their vocabulary section was 'Self-Collected Vocabulary.' When asked about this, the students noted that their teacher discusses vocabulary with them and that she invites them to record the words they need to focus on, while also reminding them that they can add words that they need to learn from the texts they read and the conversations they have with their peers."

Summing Up

The third component of the FIT Teaching Tool focuses on the instructional processes that teachers use to facilitate student learning. Evidence for the criteria in this section frequently includes classroom observations. These observations can be completed formatively by peers, coaches, or leaders. Importantly, conversations about improvement should be based on several observations and not only one per year, as has become all too common. Of course, if a given criterion is missing from a specific observation, a growth conversation should occur immediately.

We have organized this component around specific elements of the gradual release of responsibility model. Thus, there are expectations for clear learning intentions, as well as teacher modeling and guided instruction. In addition, students are expected to interact with one another as they resolve problems and consolidate their understanding with peers. We did not include the final phase of the gradual release of responsibility in this category because independent learning is addressed in the Planning with Purpose area, specifically criterion 1.2a, which focuses on success criteria. In addition, independent learning is included in the next category, Assessing with a System, as the products from students' learning should guide the instruction that they continue to receive.

4
Assessing with a System

Assessment systems must, first and foremost, place the learner at the center of attention. By this we mean that any assessment system that values measuring and evaluating students over informing learning and teaching is doomed to fail. All the charts and graphs are for naught if the results are static. An old farming maxim says that you won't fatten cattle by simply weighing them. So it is with assessment systems that place a premium on summative assessments while paying lip service to formative assessment.

Formative assessment is the crux of what effective teachers do. They don't just present information and hope for the best. Nor do they adopt a cavalier attitude that "it's not my problem if some students don't get it, because after all, I taught it." (However, we suspect that many of us have been taught by a person with this attitude at some point in our lives.) The ability to leverage assessment for the purposes of learning, not just measurement, represents excellence in the profession. And it's not easy to do. Assessing with a system requires that teachers use tools and techniques to support learners, monitor progress, and inform subsequent practices. As Hattie (2012) notes, "Feedback thrives on error" (p. 115), and we agree, because missteps are a necessary part of the learning process. Without these missteps, and the accompanying feedback, students are robbed of the chance to fail forward, that is, to benefit from the learning that comes from partial understandings, misconceptions, mistakes, and errors. The following four questions are the ones we use in our own self-reflection, whether we are teaching 9th graders or doctoral students:

- Do I know what misconceptions or naïve assumptions my students possess?
- How do I know what they understand?
- What evidence will I accept for this understanding?
- How will I use their understandings to plan future instruction? (Fisher & Frey, 2014b, p. 14)

Interest in, and attention to, formative assessment continues to rise as educators and administrators have come to appreciate the power of checking for understanding for the purpose of adjusting instruction. Black and Wiliam (1998) report that the use of formative assessment accelerates student learning substantially. Importantly, formative assessment comprises several elements, including conveying learning expectations to students, systematically gathering data, monitoring progress, acting upon information to modify instruction, providing feedback, and giving students opportunities to self-assess.

Each of these formative assessment ingredients is represented in the Assessing with a System component, which requires that we begin with the learner, especially in relaying learning expectations that are comprehensible, and that we further use these expectations to help students establish goals for themselves (4.1: *Assessment to Support Learners*). A second factor is *Assessment to Monitor Learning* (4.2), as we check for understanding and monitor progress. The third factor is *Assessment to Inform Learning* (4.3) through judicious use of feedback and needs-based instruction. The design and implementation of systematic assessment necessarily affect planning and instruction. Throughout this chapter, you will find us referencing other parts of the tool, especially ingredients in the components Planning with Purpose and Instructing with Intention.

Factor 4.1: Assessment to Support Learners

Anytime we venture into unfamiliar territory, we look for guideposts to reassure us we're on track. Consider the trail markers used to signal to hikers that they're headed toward particular destinations. Although it is possible for experienced hikers to find their way without them, trail markers provide them with the reassurance they need to move forward with confidence. On the other hand, if hikers accidently veer off course, the trail markers reduce the time spent wandering around and prevent them from getting hopelessly lost. In a similar way, *clearly communicated learning outcomes* serve as a series of guideposts for learners as they move through new content territory. But these guideposts (in this case, purpose statements) are less useful if they are not well understood. Providing purpose statements isn't enough; we have to check in with students to make sure they're receiving the message we intended.

Let's extend the trail marker analogy a bit further to describe a second ingredient, *goal setting*. Most hikers, even the most inexperienced ones, have goals in mind. For some, it is the destination ("I want to make it to Clear Lake today") or a time ("I want to hike for the next three hours before I stop for lunch"). In some cases, a personal challenge is involved, such as achieving a new personal best for distance covered. Those are end points, or summative goals. But formative goals, such as reaching intermediate points along the route in a timely fashion, are just as important. In addition, there are likely to be at least a few conditional actions to accomplish, such as reapplying sunblock every two hours, checking the water level in the canteen, or monitoring weather conditions. Effective teachers encourage students to set formative and summative goals so they can similarly check students' progress toward the learning expectations and make corrections as needed.

4.1a: Comprehensible expectations

NYA	Developing	Teaching	Leading
The learning expectations are not understood by students.	The learning expectations are communicated to students, but the majority of students are only partially able to explain or demonstrate what they are learning, why they are learning the content, and how they will know they have learned it.	The learning expectations are clearly communicated and understood by students such that most randomly selected students can explain or demonstrate what they are learning, why they are learning the content, and how they will know they have learned it.	The teacher supports colleagues in their ability to convey comprehensible learning expectations such that most randomly selected students can explain or demonstrate what they are learning, why they are learning the content, and how they will know they have learned it.

Any sound assessment system is predicated on two things: (1) a clear-eyed vision of what the expected learning outcomes will be and (2) a method for communicating those outcomes to students in a way that is understandable to them. Therefore, determining whether the learning expectations in a given lesson are comprehensible requires talking with students. Although most of the ingredients cataloged in this tool are focused on adults, a few—including this one—are ascertained through discussion with students. Gauging how comprehensible the learning expectations are for the students is an important touch point for determining whether the content and language purposes designed in the planning phase (1.1d and 1.1e) are understood or need to be revised or elaborated upon.

All three of us spend lots of time in classrooms, so we know that students can provide great insight into what is happening. Doug talks about his evolution as an instructional coach. Years ago, it was his practice to ask students, "What are you doing?" He always got lots of answers from students eager to share their work, but their insights were limited because the question was too narrow. Invariably, students would describe the task or activity they were engaging in *right then*. Over time, he changed his question to "What are you *learning*?" This question invites an expanded response. It is fascinating to see students pause and consider the question carefully. Doug's interested not in how quickly they can answer but how thoughtfully. He also likes to ask students, "Why are you learning this?" to ascertain whether or not they understand the lesson's relevance. Over time, he added a third question: "How do you know when you've learned it?" To be clear, Doug often needs to give students additional prompts before they reveal these understandings, but the responses he gets tell him a lot about whether the expectations are comprehensible to learners and help him to determine whether the purpose has a level of specificity that fosters self-evaluation. Students who can explain what they are learning, why it matters, and how they measure their own success are contributing to their developing metacognitive awareness.

Doug recently used these questions with several classes of middle school students and recorded their responses to share in debriefing discussions with their teachers. When he asked students in a social studies class what they were learning, he heard a range of responses: seven students said they were learning about Egypt; eight said they were learning social studies; two stated that they were learning about the burial practices and rituals in ancient Egypt. When asked how they would know if they had learned it, nearly every student cited the test they would be taking soon. This surprised their teacher. "I write the purpose on the board every day," she said in dismay. Doug suggested it was possible that the students hadn't fully understood these posted learning expectations. "It seems like many were using your summative assessment as a gauge, rather than understanding how daily measures can move them forward," he noted. Doug and this teacher spent the next few minutes parsing the content and language purposes the teacher had used for the lesson. Given that the students didn't have a way to measure their daily progress, Doug and the teacher agreed that in this instance the teacher was at the *Developing* level of growth.

Doug used the same technique in a 7th grade math class, asking random students about their learning. This time, when asked what they were learning, many of the student responses were more specific: nine students referred to using proportions to determine populations; seven explained the formula their groups developed to calculate the answers to the extended word problem; only one did not have an answer. Doug also asked them, "How do you know you learned it?" Fifteen students talked about whether they would be able to accurately complete the group task, which was to compare international rates of soft drink consumption; one student said that he wanted to try it out using statistics he had recently read about participation in youth soccer across the country.

The math teacher was duly impressed with this last student's ability to extend mathematical principles beyond the classroom, and both adults recognized this ability was quite unusual. The teacher was pleased that students were using the task as a measure of their success but wanted to elevate their thinking even further. "I love that last student's answer about soccer; how can I get more students to think that way?" she asked Doug. Although clearly at the *Teaching* level of growth, this math teacher does what so many of us do: we challenge ourselves to continuously improve.

The following week, both the social studies teacher and the math teacher asked Doug if they could use video clips of his interviews at their next collaborative planning team meeting. "The two of us have been talking about what we've learned from our students, and we thought it would be great to reflect on these together. We're both next on the list for the sharing-student-work protocol our PLC uses, and we figured these would be great examples and nonexamples," said the social studies teacher. Although both had initially exhibited skills elsewhere on the scale, in this instance they were demonstrating a *Leading* level of growth by using their insights to benefit their colleagues.

4.1b: Goal-setting opportunities

NYA	Developing	Teaching	Leading
The teacher does not provide goal-setting opportunities to students.	The teacher provides goal-setting opportunities but only prompts students to use them summatively (end of project or assignment), thus limiting students' ability to measure progress formatively.	The teacher provides clear and focused opportunities for students to set and gauge their progress toward achievement of goals related to learning and mastery.	The teacher supports colleagues in their ability to provide clear and focused opportunities for students to set and gauge their progress toward achievement of goals related to learning and mastery.

A hefty body of research links student goal setting to achievement (see Huang, 2012, for a meta-analysis), but an important point is that not all goals work equally well. For example, students who use approach goals ("I will complete 9 of 10 quadratic equations correctly today") achieve at higher levels than those who use avoidance goals ("I will not fail today's math quiz"). And goal setting is not just a matter of achievement; it is also linked to motivation. Learners who work toward something positive rather than avoid something negative are found to have a higher sense of competency and show more persistence (Elliot, 1999). A learner of any age who establishes goals is able to direct cognitive resources toward achieving the goal while avoiding distractions that can undermine effort. However, goals that focus solely on more distant outcomes, such as earning an *A* on an end-of-unit test, are likely to backfire early on. "When assigning new or complex tasks in a classroom context, it might work best to also provide students with initial learning goals so that they can focus on discovering effective strategies. Once they know what to do, setting performance goals can be effective" (Morisano & Locke, 2013, p. 45). Effective teachers leverage student goal setting as a means for propelling students forward in their learning each day, as well as at the end of a unit of instruction. This approach parallels sound assessment practices for teachers, in that students are able to draw on their progress toward goals both formatively and summatively.

The 3rd grade team at Hartford Elementary formed a professional learning community to support their collective efforts in Assessing with a System. During one meeting, they turned their attention to goal-setting opportunities for students. The meeting began with a protocol often used at this school. After each teacher writes for 10 minutes in response to a question or prompt, they engage in successive rounds of structured discussion for each member, following these steps:

1. The focus teacher reads his or her writing.

2. Other members of the team ask clarifying questions to obtain additional information but do not offer comment at this time.

3. The group engages in discussion using four questions: What was your intention? How would students describe your intention? What was your evidence that your intention was successful? Looking back, what, if anything, would you have done differently?

4. Each member, in turn, is the focus teacher, and the process is repeated.

5. After all the rounds are complete, the group engages in a discussion about the topic and self-evaluates using an appropriate rubric.

6. The last five minutes of the meeting are dedicated to writing about action steps for deepening instructional practice.

Myra Santiago had been selected by the group to facilitate this meeting. Each member of the grade-level team took a turn at facilitation in order to build their collective capacity as teacher-leaders. "Our principal reminds us that there's a leader in every seat," said Ms. Santiago. Before this meeting, she had developed the following writing prompt to start the meeting: *Write about a time this year when your students set goals for themselves. How did you make this happen? In what ways did students use the goals? How did you use the goals?* After Ms. Santiago and the other teachers completed the writing portion of the meeting, John Desiderio volunteered to go first. After he read his response to the group and answered clarifying questions, the group used the four questions to structure the discussion. Mr. Desiderio had described the goal-setting activity he did with his students in September—"What I want to be able to do by May"—and remarked that his intention was for them to return to it a few times a month to see how they were progressing. However, he said that lately he had fallen behind and that his students had only checked in with their goals once in the past six weeks. "I'd have to say that, by now, my students are thinking that it was just an activity that has fizzled out," he offered. "I can't say that the goals they wrote for themselves have been a constant."

Ms. Santiago elected to go next. She, too, read her writing and answered the group's clarifying questions. She explained that her students have a goals notebook in their desk, and she guides them in each lesson to record a learning goal that she has crafted for them and write a personal goal for themselves. In response to the question about evidence of success, she explained that she uses these written lesson goals in impromptu conversations with individual students. "I'll give an example from earlier today. Trevor was showing signs of being confused, so I went to him and asked him some questions. I had him take his goals notebook out and asked him to read his 'I can' statement: 'I can describe what the main character does and why he or she does it.' I spent a few minutes with him breaking down this goal into examples from the book he was reading. That was enough to get him going again," she said.

Next, Lani O'Hearn read her writing, which explained that she hadn't done any goal setting with students and needed to know more about it. She admitted that although she had often read about the importance of goal setting in her decade-long teaching career, she just didn't do it. "I guess what's embarrassing is that I expect that goal setting is something that gets talked about in professional development, but I haven't actually done it. I'll cut to the chase on our questions," she said. "What I'll do differently is that I'll start setting goals with my kids. I'm just not sure I know how." Ms. O'Hearn is an example of the knowing-doing gap, possessing a high level of knowledge but an absence of application.

Each member of the grade-level team continued in similar fashion and then turned their attention to the FIT Teaching Tool. Based on the criteria, Mr. Desiderio placed himself at the *Developing* growth level, noting that he was using student goals infrequently, diminishing his students' ability to formatively assess their progress. "You've given me some good ideas, Myra," he said. Ms. Santiago, on the other hand, placed herself at the *Teaching* level, as she was regularly using student goals both formatively and summatively. Ms. O'Hearn put herself at the *Not Yet Apparent* level, as she had not yet written goals with students. When writing her action plan, she listed meeting with Myra Santiago to discuss student goal setting in more detail. She arranged to meet Ms. Santiago for lunch later in the week to get started. Now exhibiting a *Leading* level of growth, Ms. Santiago assembled some materials and resources after the PLC meeting that she would share with her colleague during their lunch.

Factor 4.2: Assessment to Monitor Learning

Imagine a trip with no midcourse corrections. Even if you have traveled the same route hundreds of times, you look for landmarks along the way, drawing reassurance that your journey is leading you closer to your destination. If a road is impassable, you take another route that will still get you to your intended destination, even if the midcourse correction meant you'd need to travel a bit longer than originally planned. The expected time for the journey is important, but it's not the sole consideration. A 20-minute journey isn't a guarantee that you'll end up where you wanted to. Yet, as Wiliam (2006) points out, too often we teach in exactly this way. You wouldn't be satisfied with a taxi driver who drove for 20 minutes and then told you to get out, even though the stopping point wasn't where you wanted to go. It wouldn't help matters if the taxi driver explained that he had another fare and needed to move on to the next job.

But isn't this exactly what happens to many students? Teachers often hold time as the constant and allow learning to vary among students. At the end of the lesson, some students master the content; others don't. Without attention to monitoring learning, teachers aren't capable of adapting to ensure that the learning is held constant and time is the variable (Fisher & Frey, 2010a). In the previous section, we discussed the importance of conveying expectations and providing opportunities for students to self-assess. In this section, we spotlight two ingredients: systematically gathering data through *checks for understanding* and *error analysis* to understand what adaptations need to happen next. Taken together, these practices make it possible to monitor learning progress so that reteaching can occur when needed. These midcourse corrections are essential for making necessary adaptations that ensure that the learning, not the time, is held constant.

4.2a: Checks for understanding

NYA	Developing	Teaching	Leading
The teacher does not check for understanding.	The teacher sporadically checks for understanding throughout the lesson, using a limited repertoire of techniques to do so. Opportunities to check for understanding are often overlooked, and the teacher relies primarily on anecdotal information about student progress.	The teacher systematically checks for student understanding throughout the lesson, using a variety of techniques, which may include the following: • Oral language (questioning, retelling, student conversation) • Student writing • Student projects/performances • Tests/quizzes/common assessments • Student self-assessment The teacher uses these checks for understanding to gauge progress of individuals and groups.	The teacher supports colleagues in their ability to systematically check for student understanding throughout the lesson using a variety of techniques, which may include the following: • Oral language (questioning, retelling, student conversation) • Student writing • Student projects/performances • Tests/quizzes/common assessments • Student self-assessment The teacher supports colleagues in their ability to use these checks for understanding to gauge progress of individuals and groups.

We describe checking for understanding as an ongoing series of events a teacher plans and implements to gauge progress in the moment. Techniques for checking for understanding run the gamut from listening to students' oral language as they converse, retell, and respond to questions to examining their written work, projects, and performances. Homework can also be used to check for understanding, so long as students have had opportunities to learn the content before they are asked to apply their knowledge independently. When homework does not count for a grade and students know that their teachers use the data formatively, they are more likely to show their actual understanding of the content. In contrast, when homework is counted for a grade, students often seek help from others, thus skewing the data and preventing teachers from taking action on the patterns of errors they see (or don't see).

However, we are questioned most often about the use of quizzes to check for understanding. This technique of using frequent, low-stakes assessments to accelerate learning is perhaps the most underused. We draw on the research about *washback*, the term used to describe the positive and negative effects of testing on learning. Roediger (2014) calls positive washback *retrieval-enhanced learning*, because these low-stakes quizzes can solidify new knowledge and promote transfer to new situations in ways that simply rereading cannot (transfer goals were discussed in Planning with Purpose 1.1a). A prime example of this is audience-response systems (clickers), an efficient means of assessing student understanding. Short quizzes, whether gathered digitally or through traditional paper-and-pencil tasks, accomplish two things at once, as they contribute to student learning while providing a means to check understanding. Figure 4.1 contains a comprehensive list of techniques for checking for understanding, including opportunities for using them.

"I have a test for them. I guess I don't see the problem," special education teacher Whitney Davidson said to her coteacher, Violet Bancroft. The two were discussing lessons for the following week. At the *Not Yet Apparent* level of growth, Ms. Davidson understood the importance of a summative assessment, but she had not identified ways that she would be checking for understanding throughout the unit. Although Ms. Bancroft was pleased that they had a summative assessment, she knew from experience that it wouldn't be sufficient to lead learning.

"How will you know they're learning, and more important, when they're not learning?" asked Ms. Bancroft. "I'll give you one simple example," she continued. "Remember today when I had the students write answers to the math problems we were doing on the small whiteboards? I did that not just to keep them engaged but also because it gave me information about when I could move to the next concept. They were doing fine when I asked them to write the reciprocal of the whole numbers. But when I saw that several of them were having trouble writing the absolute value of the number, do you remember what I did?" The special education teacher nodded, stating that her

Figure 4.1 | Techniques for Checking for Understanding

Using Oral Language to Check for Understanding		
Technique	**Description**	**How I Can Use It**
Accountable Talk	Provides a framework for and expectations of communication during academic discussions	To determine the next steps for instruction
Noticing Nonverbal Clues	Facial expressions and body language can provide clues to students' level of understanding	To check for understanding by noticing students' confused, dazed, or bored expressions
Value Lineups	Students evaluate a statement and line up according to the level of agreement or disagreement; provides opportunity to express own opinion and listen to differing opinions	To determine student knowledge, preconceived ideas, and gaps in information
Retellings	Students retell or summarize what they understand about text	To check for understanding after independent, small-group, or whole-group reading
Think-Pair-Share	Cooperative discussion activity in which students discuss responses with a partner before sharing with the class	To increase student participation and to improve quality of responses
Misconception Analysis	Provides opportunities for students to discuss and analyze any misunderstandings they may have	To help students explore ideas, correct or incorrect, and arrive at correct assumptions on their own through small-group discussions
Whip Around	Closure activity in which teacher poses a question, students write three items, students read one item, everybody checks item off if they have it on their list; continues until everyone has shared	To check the level of understanding after a lesson; to determine if reteaching is necessary

Using Questioning to Check for Understanding		
Strategy	**Description**	**How I Can Use It**
Constructing Effective Questions	Teacher asks questions to check for understanding and scaffolds when necessary with follow-up questions that evoke higher critical thinking	To determine next steps and depth of understanding
Providing Nonverbal Support	Nonverbal cues that can encourage participation and support communication	To model good listening skills, to show respect for the speaker, to give the teacher an opportunity to analyze responses

(continued)

Figure 4.1 | Techniques for Checking for Understanding (*continued*)

Using Questioning to Check for Understanding		
Strategy	**Description**	**How I Can Use It**
Developing Authentic Questions	Teacher develops questions that address all levels of Bloom's taxonomy to ensure that questions ultimately engage creative and critical thinking	To provide opportunities for students to think and the teacher to check for understanding
Response Cards	Students hold up a card, board, or other item that shows response to a question posed by the teacher as a whole-group activity	To check understanding and determine who "gets" it
Hand Signals	Students use pretaught hand signals to represent levels of understanding	To check understanding when teaching a new concept; to assess from beginning to end to determine when reteaching is necessary
Audience-Response Systems	Students respond to a multiple-choice question with a remote device that records and displays answers	To assess understanding after a concept has been taught; to help to determine what to review
ReQuest	Reciprocal questioning; teacher and students take turns questioning each other after reading a segment of text; students learn from teacher modeling	To help students comprehend difficult text, have them work in pairs and question each other as they read
Socratic Seminar	Questions and answers are posed within a group setting to examine opinions or ideas logically	To comprehend complex issues in a difficult text, teacher poses an opening question for discussion
Using Writing to Check for Understanding		
Strategy	**Description**	**How I Can Use It**
Interactive Writing	Students participate in the writing process in small- or whole-group settings where the writing is shared by teacher and student	To assess students' knowledge and understanding of grammar, language structure, writing conventions, spelling, etc.
Read, Write, Pair, Share	Students read text, write a response to their reading, and partner up and share before finally sharing their ideas with the group as a whole	To determine what students already know; listening to conversations becomes a window to student thinking
Summary Writing	Students write a summary of what they have read, viewed, or discussed	To help understand how students organize and condense knowledge

Using Writing to Check for Understanding		
Strategy	**Description**	**How I Can Use It**
RAFT	Writing prompts designed to help students gear their writing to different perspectives and audiences	To teach perspective in writing; to check for understanding

Using Projects and Performances to Check for Understanding		
Strategy	**Description**	**How I Can Use It**
Readers' Theater	A reading activity, much like a scripted play without the props, costumes, or sets, in which students read directly from a script to tell a story	To improve reading fluency, vocabulary knowledge, and comprehension
Multimedia Presentations	Students use technology to create presentations with graphics, video, animation, and text to show learning	To check for depth of understanding as a culminating project for a unit of study
Electronic and Paper Portfolios	A collection of work samples reflective of a student's best work throughout the year; samples should exemplify the cognitive processes of learning	To give next year's teacher a more in-depth view of students' performance levels
Graphic Organizers	A tool used to organize information or ideas from text to improve reading comprehension	To understand main idea and details in text; to assist students in prewriting activities
Inspiration®	Digital graphic organizer that uses graphics, text, and other visual tools	To provide an alternative to a traditional graphic organizer; for students who struggle with reading or who have disabilities
Foldables™	Three-dimensional graphic organizers; provide a kinesthetic element and alternative to worksheets	To compare and contrast two ideas, objects, or concepts
Dioramas	Miniature models of a scene that display a concept, idea, or story	To engage students while checking for understanding; can be used in most content areas
Public Performances	Opportunities to help gauge students' understanding and show what they have learned	To help students become comfortable with their public speaking while organizing the important ideas in a content unit of study

Source: Angela Fisher, Darnall Charter School, San Diego, CA. Used with permission.

coteacher called the struggling students into a "huddle" (her term for times during the lesson when she stops to do some short reteaching) while directing the rest of the class to go into "playbook mode" to review their notes and add an explanation about the differences between the two concepts. In a few minutes, the students in the huddle returned to their desks and provided an explanation to their table partners.

Ms. Bancroft then asked everyone to check their written explanations and make any corrections needed. When the lesson ended 15 minutes later, she asked all the students to stack their math notebooks at the end of the table, opened to the page where the explanation was written. The coteachers read and sorted them into correct, partial, and incorrect answers so that they could reteach as needed the following day (see the next section, on error analysis, for further information). Ms. Bancroft's example of using response boards, oral language of students, and written explanations was evidence of her *Teaching* level of growth.

After further discussion, Ms. Bancroft had an idea that would demonstrate her frequent checks for understanding. The following day, she filmed herself teaching a 15-minute segment of a lesson. During lunch, Ms. Bancroft and Ms. Davidson watched the video on Ms. Bancroft's phone. Each time Ms. Bancroft checked for understanding, whether through questioning, written responses, or a performance task, she paused the video and did an impromptu think-aloud about her decision-making processes. By the end of the exercise, Ms. Davidson had gained new insight not just into techniques for checking for understanding but also into the critical role they play in shedding light on progress toward the established purpose. Ms. Bancroft's coaching conversation with her coteacher exemplified a professional at the *Leading* level of growth.

Ms. Davidson adjusted her unit of instruction to include formative assessment. Like Ms. Bancroft, she used response boards and written explanations in her small-group lessons. However, when debriefing with her coteacher, she more often cited individual student examples—mostly oral responses to questions—to draw conclusions about the understanding of the class. Ms. Bancroft asked probing questions to help her colleague see the difference between drawing on systematically collected data and using anecdotal incidences to make determinations. "It's a common error of judgment that teachers make when they're new to the classroom," Ms. Bancroft explained later. Although her coteacher could be said to be at the *Developing* level because she did plan to check for understanding, she was still overgeneralizing knowledge of the group by extrapolating from isolated sources.

4.2b: Error analysis

NYA	Developing	Teaching	Leading
The teacher does not analyze student errors.	The teacher analyzes student errors, misconceptions, and miscues but does not link these findings to feedback or future instruction.	The teacher strategically analyzes student errors, misconceptions, and miscues to provide more accurate and specific feedback and future instruction to students.	The teacher supports colleagues in their ability to strategically analyze student errors, misconceptions, and miscues to provide more accurate and specific feedback and future instruction to students.

Learners make mistakes and errors all the time, but do you know the difference between the two? The answer lies in the response you get from the student. It is a *mistake* when an incorrect response is pointed out and the learner immediately knows what to do to fix it. For example, you point out a misspelling in an essay and the student recognizes it and immediately corrects it. On the other hand, it is an *error* when the student doesn't know what he should do next. In this case, the same student uses the word *seize* instead of *cease* and when this is pointed out, isn't able to discern the different meanings. When the response is an error such as this, more instruction is in order. When it is a mistake, the student just needs some time to fix it. The problem is that you won't know if the student has made a mistake or an error until you ask. More to the point, if you don't have a means for capturing and coding your findings, you will compromise your ability to bring a level of precision into your teaching practice.

Errors fall into four broad categories that further inform the subsequent instruction needed. The first is a *factual error*, which occurs more frequently when the student is at the beginning stages of learning new material. A second type is the *procedural error*, which happens when the student applies the factual information incorrectly. As an example, an elementary science student may confuse or misuse the terms *herbivore*, *carnivore*, and *omnivore* in a unit about food webs, which is a factual error. The student makes a procedural error when he incorrectly maps relationships between producers and decomposers in the food web. A third type, the *transformational error*, happens when students overgeneralize new knowledge in an attempt to apply it to situations where it is not valid or fail to apply the information when it is instructive. For instance, later in the unit the student understands that the food web shows how energy flows through an ecosystem but makes a transformational error when he does not apply this knowledge in the next physical science unit about energy. The fourth type, the *misconception*, is the most stubborn to unearth, because learners tend to selectively choose to attend to new knowledge in a way that supports existing misconceptions. Therefore, a student's study of food webs is compromised by an existing misconception that all carnivores are large and fierce and all herbivores are small and meek.

Effective teachers actively seek to gather information about mistakes and errors and analyze them to make decisions about future instruction. Many primary reading teachers routinely use running records to capture the oral reading behaviors of emergent readers (Clay, 2000). First grade teacher Melissa Hunter collected running records for each student every six weeks to make decisions about reading instruction. Ms. Hunter listened to a student as he read new text aloud, using a prescribed coding system to identify errors and self-corrections. "It's important that I capture those self-corrections, because it tells me when a child has made a mistake and was able to fix it. It lets me know he's monitoring his own reading," said Ms. Hunter. Early in her career, she collected running records and scored them, but she didn't use them to plan future instruction. "In retrospect, I was at the *Developing* [growth] level because I was using them mostly to measure progress. It took me a few years and some great guidance from the Reading Recovery teacher at our school to help me re-form groups and advance them to the next reading level," she said. "For a long time, I didn't realize that I wasn't moving them forward as quickly as I should have. My practice has changed over the last few years, and I feel I'm now at the *Teaching* level of growth."

Ninth grade English teacher Lance Kennedy, who teaches in the same district as Ms. Hunter, coded and analyzed his students' errors differently. "Our district has remained committed to formative assessment procedures for several years, and I think we're getting really good at this," he said. The high school English teachers in his district developed error analysis sheets to reflect major errors students make. "These error-coding sheets help us to make decisions about who needs some reteaching and in what form," Mr. Kennedy said. He took out a current coding sheet he was using as he read draft argumentative essays his students were developing (see Figure 4.2). "As I read them, I write

Figure 4.2 | Error-Coding Form for High School Writing

Note: For each period, students are indicated by their initials. In Column 1, (F) = factual error, (P) = procedural error, and (T) = transformational error.

Error	Period 1	Period 3	Period 4	Period 6
Makes errors in vocabulary words or phrases, figurative language, or idioms. (F)	PB, KF	ED, HP, MS, AJ	RR, DG, DD, EH	SP, KD, KL, CE, SD, JL
Uses inaccurate or incomplete information. (F)	PB, KF, DR, SP	OS, DT, HP	SA, HB, LC, CB	DB, CC
Sentences contain dangling modifiers. (P)	HY, KO, LM	RE, WW, BV, ES	GT	PE, AL, DT, PH, LW
Style or tone is not consistent throughout. (T)	PB	LE, KS, NR, JH	TR, WJ, DG, DD, SP	MO, DS, GL, MA, RA
Makes errors in using parallel structures. (T)	LU, DR	SI, SJ, BE, HP	MS, AP, CR, DD, JI, RR, LC	DB, CC
Evidence cited does not support claims. (T)	SS, AC, KF	ER, WQ, FG, ES, LE	AP, WJ, JI, PL	KD, JR, BA, CL, BB
Organizational errors interfere with the flow of reasoning. (T)	YC, PB, FR, GS, IN, VE	OS, WQ	MS, GT, HB, LC, AP, WJ, HH, WE, PL, CR, DD, SA, TR, JI, ST, AE, FR, RR, EH, CB, SZ, PL, DE, DG, EH	JP, MO, GL, PH

their initials down when I see that they're making certain kinds of errors. I can figure out what small groups to pull for some needs-based instruction." As he scanned down the error sheet, he pointed to the number of organizational errors being made in his fourth-period class. "That's going to be a whole-group lesson. But the good thing that comes out of my coding these is that I know I only need to do that in fourth period, not all day long." At the *Teaching* level, Mr. Kennedy is analyzing errors to make instructional decisions.

Zara Ali was delighted to hear the results of the conversations with Ms. Hunter and Mr. Kennedy. She is a 6th grade science teacher at one of the district's middle schools and a member of the district's formative assessment work group. For two years, she and the work group designed a series of professional learning sessions, webinars, and short online coaching videos about formative assessment. In addition, she facilitated meetings with district science teachers to develop similar error-coding forms in their content areas. "Putting the forms together really got all of us talking about the essential errors we needed to watch for. Not the minutia, but the big stuff," said Ms. Ali. "It's also helped us clarify success criteria for each unit. We don't want to drown in all the data. But we do need to keep our message clear to students about setting academic goals and gauging their success. This project has been a win-win for us." At the *Leading* level of growth, Ms. Ali was helping her colleagues across the district analyze errors, leading to better learning for many students.

Factor 4.3: Assessment to Inform Learning

The previous two factors—*Assessment to Support Learners* and *Assessment to Monitor Learning*—lead to the third, and culminating, factor: *Assessment to Inform Learning*. A formative assessment system must close the loop by providing students with the information they need to move forward. This is accomplished through various feedback mechanisms that are matched to reduce the distance between the learning goals and students' current level of understanding (Sadler, 1989). Learning intentions play a critical role in this process, as teachers use them to inform the feedback they offer to students. To maximize its impact on learning, the feedback must allow learners to take action by shining a light on a cognitive path they can take. Throughout the process, the teacher is making decisions about the next instructional steps that need to occur and, in doing so, analyzing errors to detect patterns. The error analysis profiled in the previous section results in further needs-based instruction that is targeted to the right learners at the right time.

4.3a: Types of feedback

NYA	Developing	Teaching	Leading
The teacher does not provide different types of feedback.	The teacher provides feedback about the task, about the processes of the task, and about self-regulation, but these feedback offerings may not be scaled to match the learning progress of the student. The teacher dilutes the feedback with praise.	The teacher selects the type of feedback most conducive to providing students with a clear understanding of how they are doing relative to the learning goal, providing progressive feedback • about the task, • about processing of the task, and • about self-regulation. The teacher keeps praise separate from feedback to increase its effectiveness.	The teacher supports colleagues in their ability to select the type of feedback most conducive to providing students with a clear understanding of how they are doing relative to the learning goal, providing progressive feedback • about the task, • about processing of the task, and • about self-regulation. The teacher supports colleagues in their ability to keep praise separate from feedback to increase its effectiveness.

Feedback is the engine of a formative assessment system because it propels learners forward. A student may have stalled and may not be sure how to get back on the road, or she may be pumping the brakes because she doubts whether her path is the correct one. These are the precise moments when feedback from the teacher can get students under way again. However, feedback is more effective when it aligns with where the learner is, cognitively and meta-cognitively. Hattie (2012) has devoted his career to understanding the relationship between teacher behaviors and their relative impact on student learning, and he has reported that feedback is among the most useful, at a .79 effect size. (Effect size can be thought of as "the amount of bang for your buck." Effect sizes above .40 are considered to be worthy of attention.) He further describes three types of feedback, each of which is more or less effective depending on where the student is in the learning process.

Feedback about the task is the most common type offered and is sometimes described as corrective feedback. The attention is on the task at hand and is focused on accuracy and completeness. Task-centered feedback is most useful when the learner is new to the content (Heubusch & Lloyd, 1998, as cited in Hattie, 2012). For example, a world history teacher says, "This portion of the essay is incomplete because you don't discuss his purpose or his domestic and international audiences. Reread the section on Stalin's Five-Year Plan speech and then read your answer again to add these details."

Feedback about the process focuses attention on the critical thinking that is needed in the task. This type of feedback is best suited for learners who are deepening their learning after they have acquired the initial knowledge needed. The same world history teacher might return to the same student later and say, "You've added the information about Stalin's purpose and audiences, which will help you in addressing the first part of the analysis. And the next part asks you to compare it to Mao's Great Leap Forward plan. How will you compare the two? You could list similarities and differences in a Venn diagram to organize your thinking."

Feedback on self-regulation is delivered to foster a student's ability to self-evaluate and make decisions for next steps, thus encouraging ownership. This type of feedback is often delivered as a thought-provoking question. The same world history teacher could later say, "I can see how you have strengthened your essay by expanding on Stalin's and Mao's ideas. What I don't see yet is evidence to support your argument. Why would that improve your essay, and how can you go about accomplishing that? I'll check in with you in a few minutes so we can discuss your plan."

Hattie describes a fourth type of feedback, one that undermines the effectiveness of the first three. Feedback about the self as a person, commonly known as general praise, actually mutes the feedback when it is combined with the others. In other words, "You're a great listener!" diverts attention away from the rest of the feedback ("You developed a plan for revising your essay that is clear"). Although praise is of great value in building relationships between teachers and students, it is better when used to offer comfort and encouragement, rather than embedded within feedback. This is difficult to do, as we tend to use praise to soften the blow we fear our corrective feedback will have on our students. But feedback about tasks, processes, and self-regulation doesn't have a negative effect on learning simply because we are pointing out an error. This is where student-developed learning goals are of particular use. Rather than saying, "These four problems are wrong, but I like how hard you're trying," a teacher can say, "You set a goal today of getting at least 18 of the 20 math problems correct. You've got 16 of them correctly finished so far. Choose two others to focus on, and we'll dig into them together." In the first example, the student's learning is no further advanced after the interaction with his teacher. In the second, he is back at work. It is essential to curb our reluctance to deliver "bad news" and instead focus on delivering feedback that propels learning forward.

Hartford Unified School District has a systemwide focus on Assessing with a System. While the 3rd grade collaborative planning team at Hartford Elementary was examining goal-setting opportunities (4.1b), the science department team at Westbank High School focused their professional learning on delivering feedback more effectively and in ways that corresponded to the students' learning progression. The team rotated the responsibility of leading the learning, and this time classroom teacher Delia Ventura was doing so. "I've taught science for six years, and I'm interested in refining my teaching practice," she said. Thirty minutes of their twice-a-month meetings were dedicated to professional learning. Ms. Ventura compiled several professional readings and found an archived webinar on feedback, and she built a module on her school's learning management system to house these resources. Near the end of the second meeting, the members decided to make audio recordings with their smartphones to capture examples of feedback in each of the three categories. Each member posted these to the LMS, and the team listened to and discussed each of them together at the next meeting.

Physics teacher Robin Gardiner played each of her three audio recordings and explained her thinking about why she believed her feedback examples were aligned to student learning. After extended discussion and several playbacks, the team concurred that each was a solid example of the three types (task, process, and self-regulation). They pressed Ms. Gardiner to elaborate on the evidence she used to match the feedback type to the learners' progressions. She explained:

> In the first one, when I was giving feedback about the task, I was giving it to the whole class. They were just beginning to learn about waves, and as you know, there's lots of technical vocabulary. They were still getting their heads around the difference between phase velocity and group velocity, so I set up a whole-class activity where they saw examples of both and then used response cards to show which type it was. I gave them corrective feedback about their answers and explained why it was either one or the other.

Ms. Ventura shared her audio recordings as well but identified herself as being at the *Developing* level after discussion with her team. She was using types of feedback to mirror her students' learning, but her team helped her realize that she was using praise in ways that detracted from the feedback itself. After playing back her recordings, she recognized that in two of the three samples she had couched her feedback "inside a praise sandwich," as she later said. "I told [Jamison] that he did 'great work' when he and I both knew that it wasn't. I talked about his goal for the lesson—'to graph the data from the lab accurately'—and there were three incorrectly plotted data points. No wonder he looked at me so suspiciously."

Ms. Gardiner was working at the *Leading* level of growth because she was applying her knowledge to build the capacity of her colleagues to use feedback more effectively. Ms. Gardiner supported her team's learning by using her own examples to engage in discussion about her decision-making processes regarding feedback. Although it was Ms. Ventura who facilitated the team's professional learning, her own practice was at the *Developing* level. All the members of the science team made plans to visit each other's classrooms and use a tally sheet to take a 15-minute data-collection sample for one another so they could discuss the results again during lunch. During the following week, each pairing used these conversations to attune their practices. "I'm pretty fortunate to work with these people," Ms. Ventura commented.

4.3b: Usefulness of feedback

NYA	Developing	Teaching	Leading
The teacher does not provide useful feedback.	The teacher provides students with feedback that is diminished in its effectiveness because it is delayed, vague, incomprehensible to the learner, or does not allow for the learner to take action.	The teacher successfully provides students with feedback that is timely, specific, understandable, and actionable.	The teacher supports colleagues in their ability to provide students with feedback that is timely, specific, understandable, and actionable.

At one time or another, we have all found ourselves on the losing end of feedback. Worse, much of that feedback occurred in school. You may have had graded work returned to you after the semester or course was over. Or perhaps the feedback you got was vague and incomprehensible. Nancy recalls getting essays returned in English with single words such as "awkward" written in the margins. Or worse, a professor in Stefani's graduate-degree program wrote "hmmm" in the margins of her essays. What did that even mean? But perhaps the worst is when there's no ability to act upon the feedback. Although it is popular to say, "Failure is not an option," in fact, it often is. When teachers save up their best (or only) feedback for summative assessments and do not allow for further revisions or retakes, the feedback is wasted (as in "wastebasket," because that's where you're likely to find many of those papers you labored over all weekend), and some students may fail. Feedback gets stale pretty quickly, and Wiggins (1998) reminds us that, to survive its short shelf life, feedback should be timely, specific, understandable to the learner, and actionable.

Middle school principal Dayea Guinto was surveying teachers about the usefulness of their feedback. Results of a staff survey about professional development needs indicated that many would like more training on feedback, so she decided to meet with her school's instructional leadership team to discuss their own practices in more detail. Ms. Guinto used the factors and ingredients of Assessing with a System to foster conversation. Among the five participants was Paul Jackson, a 7th grade mathematics teacher. Although he agreed with the four elements that make feedback useful, he admitted that many were a struggle to consistently achieve. "I get the results of their quizzes right back to them," he said. "I'm proud that I have a 48-hour turnaround policy, and my [students] know it and expect it. I schedule time into my calendar for each test so that I can do that," he said. "But I don't have them do it again, like to correct their mistakes. When the quiz is done, I'm done," Mr. Jackson continued. His description of his practice puts him at the *Developing* growth level for this criterion.

"But how do you know that those who didn't 'get it' will eventually get it?" asked ILT member Ofelia del Rosario. Mr. Jackson replied that he could tell by how each student did on the end-of-unit test. "But isn't that too late?" Ms. del Rosario pressed. The team debated the merits of providing students with the ability to retake quizzes and tests. Ms. del Rosario explained how 8th grade students in her pre-algebra class took short quizzes each day on her school's learning management system. "Three questions, tops," she said, "but I have them set as adaptive items, so that when they get an answer wrong there's a feedback statement I've written that pops up. The system tracks correct and incorrect responses, and the ones a student gets wrong come back again on another day. I can show all of you how to do it," she offered, demonstrating a *Leading* level of growth. The principal made a note to herself about this feature on the LMS, one she herself was not aware of, as a possible idea to be featured at the next professional learning session.

ILT member Ed Martinelli suggested that student perspectives might be needed to gauge the quality of feedback and volunteered to find out from his own students. Because students in his 6th grade English class were working on extemporaneous speaking skills, he decided to include "feedback on the feedback." Each day, four students spoke about the day's debatable topic (e.g., *Should parents limit screen time for their children? Are single-gender schools better for middle school students?*) after reading about the pros and cons and discussing it with their table mates. Mr. Martinelli's written feedback sheet for each speaker included information about the content, delivery, organization, and effectiveness of the persuasion. He added the following item:

> Dear Student,
>
> I am working on improving my skills as a teacher. Can you please rate the quality of the feedback I have given you on a scale of 1 (least effective) to 5 (most effective)? Please let me know the following: (1) Did you receive this written feedback in a timely way? (2) Did you understand the feedback you received? (3) Was the feedback specific and detailed? (4) Did the feedback include next steps for improvement? Please include any suggestions for me to give you better feedback.

Over the next two weeks, Mr. Martinelli provided written feedback to all of his students and, in turn, received feedback from them. Many of the students rated his feedback as effective, and some of the suggestions he received from his students were useful to him. "I had a number of students tell me that they'd like to do this more than once. They felt like they'd like to get better, but they didn't know if they'd get a chance to. I'm considering using shorter extemporaneous speech events like this every month so they can put the feedback into play." Mr. Martinelli, at the *Teaching* level of growth, would later use these pieces of student data when he met with vice principal Ken Pappert the following month to debrief a classroom observation.

4.3c: Needs-Based Instruction

NYA	Developing	Teaching	Leading
The teacher does not alter instruction based on student needs.	The teacher relies on initial instruction, with limited opportunities for reteaching at individual and small-group levels. Needs-based instruction occurs at times, but the teacher relies on impressions rather than data.	The teacher organizes individual, small-group, and whole-class instruction based on trend data and matches students with the specific instruction that they need to progress academically.	The teacher supports colleagues in their ability to organize individual, small-group, and whole-class instruction based on trend data and match students with the specific instruction that they need to progress academically.

Although needs-based instruction is widely recognized in the research as a key element of effective teaching (e.g., National Research Council, 2005), it does not occur routinely in classrooms. Pianta, Belsky, Houts, and Morrison (2007) studied more than 2,500 elementary classrooms and found that 91 percent of the instructional time was dedicated to whole-group instruction or individual seatwork; only 7 percent of the time did students work with their teacher in groups of five or fewer. This approach not only diminishes the learning but also robs teachers of a vital conduit for building relationships with students.

As we have noted before, feedback "thrives on error," and learning thrives on the instruction that follows to correct the error. Further, as the term makes clear, needs-based instruction targets precious instructional time exactly where it's needed, whether for intervention or for enrichment purposes. Forming needs-based instructional groups allows the teacher to bring a level of precision to the teaching, as it reduces the likelihood that students are either bored by needless remediation or left behind because the teacher moved on before they grasped the content.

The value of needs-based instruction was a difficult sell for Claire Hutchinson. A veteran teacher of high school Advanced Placement (AP) English for two decades, she saw no reason to meet with small groups of students to address their instructional needs. Although her administrator had met with her several times over the course of two years, Ms. Hutchinson remained unswayed. Citing her students' pass rates on the AP English exam, she explained that her adherence to the rigor of the course "weeds out" the students who can't make the cut. In other words, she saw herself as a gatekeeper. Her school used the FIT Teaching Tool formatively and summatively, and the quarterly reviews that she performed matched those performed by the instructional coach and the vice principal. All showed a deficit pattern on progress monitoring, error analysis, and needs-based instruction, placing Ms. Hutchinson at the *Not Yet Apparent* level.

Her principal pointed to enrollment data in her course, noting that although her pass rate was high, only 54 percent of the students who were in her course on the first day of school remained at the end of the year. After accounting for those who transferred to other schools, a full 48 percent of her former students had switched to other courses taught in the department. The principal showed Ms. Hutchinson the subsequent achievement data on those students, pointing out that the majority of them had scored at the proficient level on the state tests. In addition, 72 percent of those who had transferred into another section of AP English passed the exam with a score of 3 or above. This last statistic gave Ms. Hutchinson pause, and it opened the door to a growth-producing conversation with her administrator about the merits of needs-based instruction even with otherwise high-achieving students. Her principal later remarked that although there was still much to be done to improve the teacher's instructional practice, the use of the data proved to be an important turning point. "We're meeting tomorrow to do a learning walk together," he said.

The following morning, the two of them began with an observation in an AP psychology class. Samuel Jenkins, at the *Teaching* growth level, spoke briefly to the two adults to catch them up on the work his students were doing. "Today I've got them working in small groups," he explained. "Those two groups over there," he motioned, "are locating research articles in the database on perceptions. They'll be selecting a published experiment of their choice and writing a summary of the hypothesis, participants, findings, and implications." Turning, he gestured to another group. "I'm meeting with these students to review how research studies are read and interpreted. I've selected a study from the *Journal of Experimental Psychology* for them to work through. It's on a series of experiments about how people believe they ward off negative outcomes through superstitious 'avoidant actions.' Participants read scenarios and then were directed to knock on wood. Those who knocked in a pattern away from themselves—as if they were pushing bad luck away—were less likely to predict negative outcomes for the scenarios than participants who knocked in a pattern toward themselves. It's fascinating stuff." The principal asked him how he had selected the groups. "I had them complete a similar assignment last week after I taught them how to write an article summary. I coded the errors I saw—not just their grades—so I could figure out who needed what in the way of reteaching. The group I'm meeting with now needs assistance with summarizing the findings in their own words. The next group meeting will be shorter. They just need some refinement in using APA style in their citations."

Ms. Hutchinson and the principal then visited an AP world history classroom. Kendra Foster was not meeting in small groups while they were observing, but she talked with both of her visitors about her practice. "I'm still pretty new to this," she said. "Rita [the instructional coach] and I were just meeting about this. I'm comfortable with saying I'm at the *Developing* growth level right now. When the principal asked her to elaborate, Ms. Foster replied, "I'm definitely meeting more routinely with small groups to do follow-up intervention and instruction, but Rita helped me see that I'm doing it mostly based on what I think they need. I wouldn't say I'm wrong, necessarily, but when she questioned me, I had a hard time justifying why I had formed the small groups I met with, other than just intuition," she confessed. "I'm realizing it's not good enough to rely on my gut instincts alone. A goal I have for myself this quarter is to bring a higher degree of intentionality to my decisions about these needs-based groups."

After touring several more AP classrooms, the principal asked Ms. Hutchinson about her thinking and next steps. "I have to admit I was impressed with several of the teachers who talked about why they were meeting with those groups. I don't really do that, and I'm not sure where to start," she said. Her principal paused and then suggested that she and the AP world history teacher meet together with the instructional coach to discuss starting points. "Ms. Foster's got a goal for this quarter that you could benefit from, and it's closer to where you are right now in this aspect of your practice. Although I could see that there's lots to learn from the AP psychology teacher who's been doing this for so long, that might not be your first stop," said the principal. With the assistance of Rita Montgomery, the instructional coach who was at the *Leading* growth level, Ms. Hutchison and Ms. Foster would both be able to inform each other's practice as they, in turn, grew their own.

Summing Up

Formative assessment is an essential tool for driving instruction, but its value is diminished when it is done sporadically or less than systematically. Assessing with a System ensures that the data collected are used to inform instruction. This system begins with the learner in mind, as the expectations are conveyed to students in a manner that is comprehensible to them. Students who lack understanding of these expectations will have far more difficulty formulating and achieving goals. A formative assessment system continues with a means for checking for understanding and analyzing the collected information to make decisions about needs-based groups. Integrated throughout a formative assessment system is the quality of the feedback we provide to learners, both in terms of the type and conditions. Feedback, well done, does as much for the teacher as it does for the learner because both are informed. Maybe we should all start calling it *informative assessment*.

5
Impacting Student Learning

The purpose of teaching is to foster learning, and any measure of teaching must address its impact on student learning. Of course, numerous factors magnify a student's ability or inability to learn. Some, such as a child's birth and health history and socioeconomic status, are beyond the direct influence of teachers. But many other school-based factors do (thank goodness) contribute positively to learning.

We are all in this profession because we have seen for ourselves how a great teacher changes the trajectory of someone's life. We're not speaking of the stuff of movies, with freakishly charismatic teachers standing on desks while the background music swells; we're talking about how real-life, effective teachers operate. They plan with purpose and instruct with intention. They assess with a system that operates in a carefully cultivated learning climate. And throughout their careers, many rise to lead other teachers to continuously improve their practice. What we do matters, even if our profession's real story never makes it to the multiplex.

Educators need to stop being afraid of articulating what they do and how they know it makes a difference. Just because a politician or a police officer was once in 3rd grade doesn't mean that person is qualified to teach—or to evaluate teachers. However, they and many others are stakeholders who do have a right to know how we are performing. Our collective ability to demonstrate our impact on student learning to various stakeholders will strengthen the position that investments in education should be near the top of a society's list of priorities. Unfortunately, impact on student learning tends to be narrowly assessed through single administrations of standardized tests. Nothing is inherently wrong with these large-scale assessments per se; the problem lies in the misapplication of one data point as a single measure of everything a teacher, school, district, province, territory, state, or nation does (e.g., Ballou & Springer, 2015; Popham, 2013). Having said that, we believe that student performance data can be a reasonable and valid dimension in teacher growth and leadership.

Teachers are positioned to demonstrate how student learning evolves in the short term and across an entire school year. This is actually what we do best—watch our students closely and make decisions to accelerate their learning when it stalls. And what's more, we pass this information on to our immediate stakeholders: our students, their families, and our colleagues. The one audience we don't give enough attention to consists of the policymakers who make major fiscal, governance, and programmatic decisions that affect our profession. Can you blame them when they turn to standardized test scores? If educators don't provide any other information about student progress, people will use the data they have, which means they'll often draw inaccurate conclusions from incomplete information.

Let's paint a more complete picture for all of our stakeholders. In this chapter, we discuss the two major factors that demonstrate the component of Impacting Student Learning: (1) short-term evidence of progress toward periodic goals throughout the school year and (2) long-term evidence of attainment of transfer goals.

The FIT Teaching Tool has been designed to capture what it is that teachers do. We avoid the old trope that "teachers matter"—that's the premise of most of those movies we talked about. In fact, it is what teachers *do* that matters (Hattie, 2012). The first four components of this tool capture the intellectual and technical work of teachers. This final component focuses attention on the impact that this work has on student learning.

Factor 5.1: Short-Term Evidence of Learning

The evidence in "evidence-based teaching" consists of three major elements: evidence *for* practice, evidence *in* practice, and evidence *of* practice (Todd, 2015).

The first, evidence *for* practice, involves teacher knowledge of research about effective practices, such as those that come from credible external sources (e.g., research journals, professional organizations, conferences, and workshops). The second, evidence *in* practice, is the application of these methods. For instance, providing feedback that is useful to learners is evidence *in* practice. If you know the research base behind it, you're also employing evidence *for* practice. But the third facet, evidence *of* practice, requires that the teacher be able to furnish qualitative and quantitative data about student outcomes (see Figure 5.1).

Ask effective teachers how they know when learning occurs, and you'll likely hear discussion of a student's demonstration of procedural or conceptual knowledge. Pressed further about evidence, the same teachers are likely to cite progress on a measurement of some kind. It might be a checklist or something more formal, such as a test. In other words, effective teachers don't rely solely on impressions and anecdotal information. They know where the learner is and where the learner needs to go next, and they have a method for gauging this movement.

This skill is more difficult to develop than it might seem. Novice teachers often conflate evidence of student learning with evidence of their own teaching practices ("I know they learned it because I taught it"), thus making it hard to move forward in their practice (Hiebert, Morris, Berk, & Jansen, 2007). In other words, they use evidence *in* practice instead of evidence *of* practice.

Figure 5.1 | Elements of Evidence-Based Practice

Evidence *for* practice	FOUNDATION *Informational* Existing formal research provides the essential building blocks for professional practice.
Evidence *in* practice	PROCESS *Transformational* Locally produced evidence—data generated by practice—is meshed with research-based evidence to provide a dynamic decision-making environment.
Evidence *of* practice	OUTCOMES *Formational* User-reported evidence shows that the learner changes as a result of inputs, interventions, activities, and processes.

Source: From "Evidence-Based Practice and School Libraries: Interconnections of Evidence, Advocacy and Actions," by R. J. Todd, 2015, *Knowledge Quest,* 43(3), p. 9. Copyright 2015 by the American Library Association. Used with permission.

So what counts as evidence? Todd (2015) calls evidence of practice the "user-reported evidence that shows a learner changes as a result of inputs, interventions, activities, and processes" (p. 9). We discussed opportunities to check for understanding within a lesson previously. Now we turn our attention to the ways in which summative information is used to gauge learning intentions and success criteria (1.2a) throughout the year (*short-term evidence*), as well as progress toward transfer goals (1.1a) at the end of instruction or the unit of study (*long-term evidence*).

5.1: Short-term evidence of progress toward periodic goals

NYA	Developing	Teaching	Leading
Students consistently do not meet periodic goals throughout the school year.	The teacher is only occasionally able to demonstrate impact on student learning measured across units of study. Evidence is drawn from limited sources.	The teacher consistently demonstrates significant impact on student learning measured across units of study, with evidence drawn from a wide variety of sources, including valid and reliable summative assessments as well as observations and formative assessments.	The teacher supports colleagues in their work with students such that they are able to demonstrate impact on student learning measured across units of study, with evidence drawn from a wide variety of sources, including valid and reliable summative assessments as well as observations and formative assessments.

The expectation that assessments should be analyzed to provide evidence of students' short-term learning has increased over the last decade. Preservice candidates in teacher preparation programs are routinely required to include evidence of learning for units of instruction they have planned and implemented. One well-known example of this is the edTPA, a performance assessment of preservice teacher candidates (e.g., Darling-Hammond, 2013). One task involves the use of assessment information in a unit of instruction. In addition to detailing the learning intentions and success criteria and the plan to assess these goals, aspiring teachers must describe pre- and post-unit performance of the entire group and analyze three student work samples with teacher feedback that illustrate learning patterns for the class or group. This feedback can be in written form, or the teacher candidate can submit a video recording of the feedback event.

For practicing teachers, this factor focuses on periodic reviews of student learning. The teacher, or groups of teachers, can define the period in question.

It is more than the daily checking for understanding described in Chapter 4 and less than the long-term outcomes, which are covered in the next section of this chapter. Some teachers engage with this factor at the end of a unit of instruction; others do so weekly. To ensure that evidence of student learning is the focus of schooling, this factor should be addressed several times each semester and should involve collaborative conversations between and among educators.

These reviews should never be reduced to a few forms to fill out and turn in to an administrator. Rather, they should be a starting point for examining what is working and what changes can be made when needed. The artifacts are selected by the teacher to illustrate the learning that is occurring, and the discussions can occur with colleagues and instructional coaches as well as administrators. Conversations such as these form the heart of professional learning communities as educators plan collaboratively, using the PLC's guiding questions (DuFour et al., 2008):

- What do we want our students to learn?
- How will we know they have learned it?
- How will we respond when some students don't learn?
- How will we extend and enrich the learning for students who are already proficient?

The data collected and analyzed focus on progress toward learning intentions and their associated success criteria. Measures include criterion- and norm-referenced instruments such as informal reading inventories, as well as benchmark assessments that are periodically administered throughout the year. However, the most frequently used assessments for measuring short-term evidence of learning are those created by teachers. End-of-unit tests are one way to gauge students' progress in their learning and to take action as needed for individuals and groups. Projects and performances are another way. Essays are also useful in determining students' developing proficiency. Of course, a bit of a formative assessment process happens in each of these traditionally summative tools. In truth, anytime teachers are looking at summative test results to inform future practice, they are engaging in formative assessment. Figure 5.2 presents a (nonexhaustive) list of some of the other testing sources that can be used to demonstrate short-term learning.

The usefulness of a teacher-created assessment depends on its soundness as a measurement instrument. All assessments are in some way flawed; the goal

Figure 5.2 | Short-Term Learning Measures

Criterion- and norm-referenced tests
- Reading inventories
- Phonological Awareness Literacy Screening (PALS)
- Developmental Spelling Analysis (DSA)
- Developmental Reading Assessment (DRA)
- Dynamic Indicators of Basic Early Literacy Skills (DIBELS)
- Observation Survey of Early Literacy Achievement
- Oral and silent reading fluency measures
- Math Reasoning Inventory (MRI)

Benchmark tests
- District benchmark tests
- Career and Technical Education competencies

Teacher assessments
- Unit tests
- Graded writing of an assignment
- Running records
- Pre-/post-testing of a unit of study
- Rubrics for individual assignments
- Response to Intervention (RTI) monitoring tools

is to reduce those flaws to a reasonable level. We'll discuss the trustworthiness of assessments later in the chapter. For now, it is important to note that the design of assessments that measure students' learning during a unit of study should adhere to the following basic principles of measurement:

• The content of the test should align with learning intentions and success criteria.

• Multiple methods and measures should be used to assess student progress.

• Response opportunities should be equitable in terms of reducing unintended influences drawn from students' cultural and background knowledge.

Many teachers rely on collaboration with colleagues to design sound teacher-made assessments and to review their results. For example, the 7th grade English teachers at Grand Elms Middle School met monthly to design their unit assessments. The team members used a checklist to review their draft assessments in order to keep basic design principles in mind. "It's easy to drift away from these ideas," said team member Denise Carter. "It's been a long time since I took a measurement class in my teacher preparation program." These collaborative planning team meetings focused on assessment construction, interwoven with reviews of student results.

Don Hargrove, another team member, explained, "We come to these meetings with our student results on a chart so that we can talk about individual students who are not making progress." Alberta Marks, another 7th grade teacher, added her perspective. "It's been helpful to me when we see patterns that might be related to instruction. There are times when one of us gets really strong results compared to the rest of the team," she said. "We used to get nervous about this, but we've learned that sooner or later all of us wind up on one side of the equation or the other," Ms. Carter said. "In fact, on the last unit, which was on poetry, Don's classes scored really well. So we talked about what he did instructionally that differed from the rest of us. When we teach the poetry unit next year, we'll add his ideas to make the unit even stronger."

The team worked together to plot where students were scoring so they could find out which students were making progress and which might need further remediation. The majority of the 7th graders were progressing (defined by this group as scoring at least 70 percent on the end-of-unit assessments), but each teacher had a few students who continued to struggle. "Over the year, I get a better idea of my needs-based grouping, and I'm discovering that I'm better able to anticipate who is going to need more pre-teaching," said Ms. Marks. These teachers were at the *Teaching* level of growth for this factor because they were demonstrating how they used short-term evidence of learning to monitor the success of their students and were making adjustments as needed.

Art teacher Keith Porter didn't have a team to collaborate with but used short-term evidence of learning to gauge his own practice. "My students are creating wire sculptures, and, of course, grading them is pretty subjective," he said. He used a rubric for each project, although the criteria remained the same: craftsmanship, elements of design, concept application, and productivity. "I don't include things like behavior and effort in the rubrics, because these misdirect me and the students about their learning progress," he said, also noting that there is a schoolwide citizenship rubric to measure these important, but nonacademic, attributes. "With each major assignment, I score students on the rubric and then meet with them individually to talk about their trajectory. These are really valuable for both of us because we each gain some insight about motivation and interest in art." At the *Teaching* level of growth, Mr. Porter was using his short-term evidence of learning to monitor his processes while also leveraging this information to positively affect students.

Unfortunately, 5th grade teacher Gwen Metcalf was at the *Not Yet Apparent* level of growth, and she didn't even know it. Ms. Metcalf had been teaching 5th grade for many years, but when her state adopted a new set of mathematics standards, she didn't substantially alter her teaching practices. The instructional coach, Jim O'Hearn, met with her to discuss student progress, and Ms. Metcalf provided anecdotal evidence of learning but not much else. "She mostly talked about individual students, but she talked at least as much about their compliance as she did about their math competence," the coach remarked later. However, he did get her to agree to administer a math diagnostic test developed by the county office of education.

The results shocked her. The diagnostic test, aligned to the new standards, showed that even though it was November, 82 percent of Ms. Metcalf's students were performing well below expected levels. When she met again with the instructional coach to review the results, she asked how she could improve her students' learning. "This opened up some great dialogue between us about mathematical reasoning, public discourse about problems, and worked examples," he said. "I've been providing PD to the math department for over a year on these topics, but she wasn't applying it yet," he said. "It took looking at data that showed that her students weren't making progress to get her attention."

Many students do not perform at expected levels, and lower student performance alone is not a measure of teacher effectiveness. However, a teacher should be able to demonstrate accelerated gains as the year progresses. First grade teacher Petra Wolfe was a case in point. "Our state doesn't have a mandatory kindergarten requirement, and many of the families of my students are either unaware that our district has free kindergarten or just aren't able to make a half-day class work around their complicated schedules," she said. Unsurprisingly, the percentage of Ms. Wolfe's incoming 1st graders scoring below grade level on the DIBELS screening was higher than the district average. But because Ms. Wolfe's district reported information across three benchmark administrations, she was able to see how individual students were performing and how their learning trajectories were changing. "I am proud to say that over the year with me they ratchet up," she said.

This factor of the FIT Teaching Tool has afforded her a new platform for teaching others about using benchmark data as evidence of short-term learning. "I am now a part of the district's benchmark committee, and I do a workshop for new primary teachers every summer on how these data can give you a perspective on the gains your kids are making," she said. "Using data from previous years, I show them that I don't close the gap completely. The majority of my kids still aren't at the district average by the end of the year," Ms. Wolfe explained. "But I am able to show the teachers how the performance levels are shifting to more positive results with each administration of the benchmark. I remind them that what we do in terms of teaching makes a difference," she said. Her ability to teach others about demonstrating their short-term impact on student learning places her at the *Leading* growth level.

One of the members of the summer data institute Ms. Wolfe leads was Markus Leeds. He had spent most of his teaching career in the intermediate grades, and his recent transfer to primary education had been bumpy for him. "Last year was the first time I taught kindergarten ever," he explained, "and I had difficulty getting my kids moving toward the short-term goals that lead to long-term transfer skills." In his annual performance review the previous year, he and his administrator had agreed that he was at the *Developing* level of growth, because although a few of his students were making gains, most were not. "When I analyzed the district benchmark assessments, the results were flat," said Mr. Leeds. "I had the same percentage of kiddos remaining at the same levels between the second semester and the end of the year," he said. "It's like they just stalled."

Although Mr. Leeds had been using short-term evidence of student learning to measure progress (unlike Ms. Metcalf, the 5th grade math teacher who didn't know her students were falling behind), he had not been successful in accelerating their progress. In addition to the summer data institute, Mr. Leeds planned to attend a summer institute focused on emergent reading and writing. "I need to hone my craft so I can get some better results. I've been an effective teacher with older students. Now I've got a new challenge with the younger ones. I'm up for it," he said.

Factor 5.2: Long-Term Evidence of Learning

Learning isn't just short term, and it's not necessarily linear. Students also learn across longer periods of time, often in fits and starts; sometimes they experience dips in their understanding as new information is considered and assimilated. But time should reveal a generally positive trend, with evidence of learning accumulating. As weeks and months pass, teachers can collect evidence that students are learning to transfer skills, strategies, content, and ideas to new situations and problems. Of course, we need assessment tools to measure this as well as tools that measure students' retention of information.

5.2: Long-term evidence of attainment of transfer goals

NYA	Developing	Teaching	Leading
Students consistently do not meet long term transfer goals.	Students inconsistently meet long-term transfer goals, or the teacher does not set challenging but achievable goals.	Most students consistently meet challenging but achievable long-term transfer goals.	The teacher supports colleagues in their work with students such that most of the students meet challenging but achievable long-term transfer goals.

Education is awash with standardized tests that measure progress toward annual goals, and these tests have expanded greatly in the United States and other countries in this century. Norm-referenced standardized tests and their cousin, criterion-referenced standards-based tests, are used variously to evaluate programs, individual students, and, increasingly, teachers. The explosion of large-scale assessments has led to the misapplication of their results as a means to quantify teacher quality. As Popham (2013) points out, these instruments are instructionally insensitive, in that they cannot differentiate between students who have been well taught and those who have not. These standardized and standards-based tests primarily measure what students know, and although a lot of their knowledge comes directly from school experiences, they acquire a significant amount from outside sources and experiences. There just isn't a way to tell what portion of their knowledge can be attributed directly and solely to classroom learning.

To address this shortcoming, some states have adopted value-added measures (VAMs) in an attempt to control for these variances. However, this approach continues to be hotly debated, with supporters (e.g., Glazerman et al., 2010) and detractors (e.g., American Statistical Association, 2014) lining up on either side. Given the unsettled nature of this issue, we cannot support a VAM approach for measuring teacher quality, because its effectiveness has not yet been satisfactorily demonstrated. Having said that, we are aware that a number of states and territories have adopted this process. As Goldhaber (2015) notes, "What makes value-added [measures] distinct from classroom observations (the nearly universal way teachers are evaluated today) . . . is that it is an objective measure that does not rely on human interpretation of teacher practices" (p. 88). This is a compelling argument—and one that resonates with stakeholders and policymakers who justifiably want us to be accountable for the results of our work.

However, Goldhaber (2015) completes the sentence by saying, ". . . and by design, it is a system in which teachers are evaluated relative to one another rather than relative to an absolute standard (i.e., it creates a distribution in which teachers can be ranked)" (p. 88). It is this ranking effect that we find most troubling, because we believe it unintentionally undermines the values the FIT Teaching Tool rests upon. As Johnson (2015) states, there are significant concerns about these possible unintended consequences of VAM, including

- Making it more difficult to fill high-need teaching assignments
- Discouraging shared responsibility for students
- Undermining the promise of standards-based evaluation
- Generating dissatisfaction and turnover among teachers (p. 120)

But we are compelled to return to our original premise: students, families, colleagues, and policymakers are correct in asking us to demonstrate the ways that teachers are effective. When it comes to demonstrating progress toward long-term transfer goals (1.1a), we align with Popham (2013) and Darling-Hammond (2013), who state that educators should welcome the opportunity to demonstrate their long-term impact on student learning. Relevant sources of evidence include criterion- and norm-referenced state tests, as well as state and teacher-created end-of-course exams. And don't forget the importance of student performance portfolios, as well as other curriculum-based summative measures. We need to use all of these data to shine a light on student learning. By doing so, teachers are able to provide a more nuanced report than a single number or letter grade can accomplish. When multiple measures are used, rather than a single test score, teachers are able to demonstrate *attainment* (i.e., criterion-referenced measures of proficiency or grade-level expectations) as well as *improvement* (i.e., growth across the year), including acceleration for those initially working below expectations (Guskey, 2013).

We are especially interested in reporting on transfer goals to gauge impact on student learning. You will recall that transfer goals have the following qualities (McTighe, 2014):

- They are long-term in nature.
- They are performance-based and require application, not just recall.
- They call for using habits of mind.

Students' abilities to apply mathematical reasoning to solve problems and to construct a cogent written argument to support a claim are just two examples of transfer goals. Many discrete facts and skills are associated with both, but not all of them need to be measured. For young children, especially those below the age of standardized test administration, transfer goals include the growing ability to be able to decode and read for meaning, and to apply principles of number sense to solve problems. A 2nd grade teacher can provide long-term evidence of her effect on her students' learning by analyzing comparative data (e.g., from September and May) on students' reading levels, as gauged through the many informal reading inventories conducted throughout the year. A 10th grade biology teacher does something similar by using the preliminary assessment she and her department designed for the beginning of the course, paired with the state end-of-course exam results, and then discussing the implications of her findings with her colleagues. A special educator provides long-term evidence of attainment by furnishing the family of a student with an individualized education program that includes the September and May results of a group-administered reading survey test. All of these are ways to legitimately demonstrate long-term progress toward annual goals. More examples of sources of long-term evidence of student learning appear in Figure 5.3.

High school PE teacher Valeria Caprara administered the President's Youth Fitness Challenge to her students at the beginning and end of the school year. She and her department were committed to helping adolescents learn more about how they could maintain a healthy weight and an active lifestyle. The online calculator for the "fitnessgram" produced a report on each student's body mass index (BMI), walking and running skills, flexibility, and strength. "This has proven to be motivating for lots of students, who are dismayed when they find out how out of shape they are," said Ms. Caprara. Her district graduation guidelines required several years of physical education, providing even longer-term data for students to watch. "It's rewarding when you see

Figure 5.3 | Evidence of Long-Term Student Learning

Criterion- and norm-referenced tests
- Advanced Placement tests
- State standards tests
- Standardized tests
- President's Challenge physical fitness tests
- Certification tests for career and technical education courses
- Pre- and post-testing applications of screening and diagnostic tools across a school year

Teacher-created assessments
- Semester/end-of-course examinations
- Student portfolio assessments with rubrics
- Formal end-of-study exhibitions with rubrics
- Formal recital performances with rubrics
- Culminating projects of problem-based or project-based learning

how some students really learn to monitor their BMI and activity levels from 9th grade on," she said. These reports were not the only evidence she relied on, noting that many other outside factors affected students' health. "My department designed a district end-of-course test on the content we cover each year, including body systems and dynamics, nutrition, and fitness principles," she said. "We use this and student surveys from the beginning and end of the year to look for shifts in attitudes, habits, and knowledge." At the *Teaching* growth level for this factor, Ms. Caprara was able to demonstrate her positive impact on student learning.

High school fire science teacher Captain Lonnie Harrison led cadets through a demanding four-year course of study for this career pathway. Students began in 9th grade with physical fitness training and an introduction to careers, progressing over the next three years to learn about building construction, principles of forestry management, fire suppression, and rescue techniques. Each course included an end-of-course examination of the content. Captain Harrison led the district's Career and Technical Education (CTE) effort to design these end-of-course exams to parallel the state's certification exams for entry-level firefighters. Although not all students who began the fire sciences pathway in 9th grade remained in it through 12th grade, many did. Therefore, Captain Harrison used pass rates for the state certification exam as an additional measure of his long-term effect on student learning. Since assuming the position five years earlier, Captain Harrison had steadily increased the number of students who passed this rigorous exam. He used the data as part of a district program review, thus securing additional funding to expand the program to a neighboring high school. "I'm working with the CTE administrator and the Fire Academy staff to develop their program for next year," said Captain Harrison. "It's not just the content. I'm helping them identify those long-term transfer skills the cadets need to successfully complete the program. These will be the measures they use to gauge student success each year and help students pass that state test," he said. Captain Harrison is using his knowledge of long-term impact on student learning to develop new programs, providing evidence of his *Leading* level of growth for this factor.

Tenth grade band teacher John Rush identified at the *Developing* level. "I was hired by [the district] last year, and I have to say I wasn't accustomed to looking at my long-term impact on student learning in my old district. I mostly just graded on participation. If they showed up for performances, they got an *A*."

He worked with the administrator at his new school to identify short-term and long-term assessments, including unit tests on music theory and performance-based assessments of fundamentals. "I consulted with the local university's music department and found out how they use beginning- and end-of-year video assessments." Mr. Rush explained that each student provided a short video of his or her performance. "I score them on body and hand position and on embouchure [mouth position] if it's relevant. I also assess breathing technique and note accuracy." Last year's results were not encouraging. "When I reviewed the results from the beginning of the school year and compared them with the end, most of my students hadn't made much progress on their performances," he said. "I'm talking over half my students." He was encouraged, however, by their written assessments of music theory, which were somewhat better. "I spent the summer mapping out a new sequence so that I'm devoting more attention to the performance part of it, not just the lecture phase," said Mr. Rush. "Of course, they have to know theory, but if they're not also steadily improving on their technique, then it's more of a music appreciation class than a band class."

English teacher Nicole Landry was in the Peer Assistance and Review (PAR) program, which was jointly administered by the teachers union and the district. Because Ms. Landry had failed to make progress on her summative teacher evaluations for the previous two years, she had been identified by her site administrator as a candidate for the program. Although she had 10 years of experience, her performance on a significant number of the criteria in the FIT Teaching Tool was at the *Not Yet Apparent* or *Developing* level. Since working with the expert mentor teacher assigned to her through the PAR program the previous year, she had made positive progress, especially in the Planning with Purpose, Instructing with Intention, and Assessing with a System components.

"I can't say this has been an easy process," she said. "I've really had to confront my practices and habits." However, she noted that she and her mentor were seeing results. "I've been tracking my short-term impact on student learning this year, way more than I ever did before," she confessed. "We've both seen that my students are making gains. I'm feeling very hopeful that they are going to perform much better this year on the district's end-of-course exam," she said. "Last year only 32 percent of my students passed it. Based on how they've done this year so far, I am expecting that number to be a lot higher."

At this point, Karen Winters, her PAR mentor, added, "I hope that you're also seeing that it's because of your attention to planning and instruction. You've always had a positive climate, but now you're a stronger and more effective teacher. These practices are all linked, and you're so much stronger than you were 18 months ago."

Fourth grade teacher Leilani Hale was preparing for her summative teacher evaluation meeting with her principal and had been assembling artifacts as evidence of her practice. Now in her third year as a teacher, Ms. Hale was experiencing a degree of confidence she had not had in her first two years. "This year I'm feeling a lot more solid than I had before. I'm really getting much better at understanding how 4th graders think," she smiled. She worked in a Hawaiian-English dual immersion school, and one source of evidence she planned to use to demonstrate her long-term impact on student language was an assessment of proficiency in ʻŌlelo Hawaiʻi (Hawaiian language). "Only a small percentage of our families speak ʻŌlelo Hawaiʻi fluently, although they are themselves Native Hawaiian," she explained. "We encourage families to learn to speak the language alongside their children, but not a lot of them do." Many of her students were at a disadvantage in this regard, as out-of-school application of a second language can reinforce newly learned skills. Even among those who speak ʻŌlelo Hawaiʻi, there is a belief that their primary job is to reinforce the use of English (Yamauchi, Lau-Smith, & Luning, 2008). "Many of my students are still struggling to reach proficiency," said Ms. Hale. She used language-proficiency measures from the beginning and the end of the year to track their progress. "I want to have more students scoring at proficient levels by the end of the year," said the teacher. "But I'm also interested in growth across the year." This year, the majority of her students demonstrated expected and even accelerated levels of growth. Ms. Hale's measures of growth and proficiency on state content standards and language proficiency placed her at the *Teaching* level of growth for this factor.

Children in kindergarten teacher Denise Lyons's class didn't take state standardized tests, but she was still able to draw on several assessments to demonstrate her long-term impact on learning. Ms. Lyons reported on each child's gains using the battery of screening and readiness instruments her grade employed at the beginning and end of the year. This information was useful for families as she met with them to report on their child's progress. In addition, the 1st grade team applied this information as they built classes for the following year. Most of her students performed at or near grade level by the end of the year, which was about average across her district. A few children didn't make expected progress, but this was not used as a single indicator of her skill as a teacher.

Ms. Lyons said, "For the three students I have this year who are showing limited progress, I include information about interventions as well." She produced her RTI data for these three students and met with their families and the Student Study Team (SST) to discuss next steps. The SST looked to her to provide the kind of summative and formative RTI data that were necessary for making decisions, including referrals for additional testing. During this school year, she developed a list of formative and summative assessments for use with kindergartners and identified long-term transfer skills for them to refer to. "It can be tricky assessing children who are emergent readers, writers, and mathematicians," she said. Her involvement with the SST in identifying tools for determining short- and long-term progress of kindergartners was evidence of her *Leading* growth level for this factor.

Sixth grade science teacher Sid Petrosian was struggling with demonstrating his long-term impact on student learning. He was hired after the school year started when another teacher moved out of state, and the school's focus on project-based learning posed a challenge for him. "I understand the principles, of course. The professional learning has been great, and I've had lots of support this year," he said. However, his students' performance on the capstone project proposals (to prevent or reduce wildfires in a drought-stricken state park) fell flat. The students' oral reports in particular were below expectations, as described in the district rubric. "I sure learned a lot from this," said Mr. Petrosian. Of course, one data point should not be used in determining long-term impact, but his students' scores on the state standards-based science test were also depressed. He and his administrator agreed that he was at the *Developing* level for this factor, although he performed more strongly on several other components, especially Instructing with Intention. "I'm going to revisit the Planning with Purpose criteria this summer," he said, noting that he had primarily relied on the planning work completed by his team this year. "I need to be more involved in the planning process," he said. "I'm sure that's going to make me much better equipped for teaching them what they need to know and be able to do."

Trustworthy Assessment Tools

When demonstrating long-term impact on student learning, much of the data gathered come from assessments created by individual teachers, teams, or departments. These assessments tools need to be trustworthy—that is, reliable and valid. Assessments that are not reasonably trustworthy can limit the ability of teachers to articulate their impact on student learning, as the results themselves may be invalid.

Teachers, students, parents, and leaders all want to know: What did students learn? The tools used to determine the answer to this very important question matter. The format of the assessment can affect students' ability to demonstrate their understanding. This reality is evident when students say, "I wish this could have been an essay rather than a multiple-choice test." Teachers have to carefully consider appropriate formats for assessments and match them to the learning that was to have occurred.

In addition, the tool has to measure what was supposed to have been taught and not measure other factors, such as personal experiences or cultural knowledge. Students should not be seen as more proficient on a given assessment because their family vacations in France, for example. There's nothing wrong with spending summers in France. It's just not fair if success on the assessment is based on that experience rather than what was actually taught.

When it comes to summative, formal assessments such as those used by state departments of education to monitor student achievement trends, companies spend millions of dollars in the development and revision of assessment items to ensure that the tools are reliable and valid. We are not suggesting that teachers focus their efforts on creating tests that meet the standards of quality required of major test publishers. We do think that teachers should know about reliability and validity and then do their best to create assessments that are trustworthy. Here is how these qualities are defined by the Joint Committee on the Standards for Educational and Psychology Testing of the American Educational Research Association, the American Psychological Association, and the National Council on Measurement in Education (2014):

> **Reliability/Precision:** The degree to which test scores for a group of test takers are consistent over repeated applications of a measurement procedure and then are inferred to be dependable and consistent for an individual test taker; the degree to which the scores are free of random errors of measure for a given group. (p. 222)

> **Validity:** The degree to which accumulated evidence and theory support a specific interpretation of test scores for a given use of a test. If multiple interpretations of a test score for different uses are intended, validity evidence for each interpretation is needed. (p. 225)

These are fairly heady concepts. But think about it this way. If you step on a scale each day and the scale reports a consistent weight, and you do, in fact, weigh the same, the scale is reliable. If the number on the scale changed all of the time when your weight did not, the scale could not be reliable. But reliability by itself is not enough. If the scale gives you the same weight each day but it's not your actual weight, it is reliable but it is not valid. Validity requires a fair representation of the phenomenon being measured. Imagine if your scale reported your height rather than your weight!

For the work that most teachers do, the concept of validity is considered more important than reliability. Kelley (1927), widely recognized for developing the idea, claimed that a test is valid if it measures what it claims to measure. We did not include a factor about validity, or even trustworthiness, in the FIT Teaching Tool. Instead, we think that this is a conversation that teachers should have as part of their professional learning community and with their evaluators. When presenting evidence collected to document the effect on learning in the short term or the long term, teachers should be able to explain how they know that the assessment measured what they intended. The development of the assessment occurs as part of the Planning with Purpose component, and the use of the assessment, including any reteaching needed, occurs as part of Assessing with a System. Naturally, teachers make adjustments throughout the year to their planning, instructing, and assessing. As part of this process, teachers consider the tools that they use to determine student performance, which is where this information is valuable.

For example, Algebra II teacher Diana Simon developed a midterm assessment given at the end of the first semester. When she analyzed the results, she realized that 90 percent of the questions came from the last six weeks of the class. Thus, the content validity was not adequate to determine students' mastery of the first-semester content. She met with her administrator to talk about revising the assessment for the following year and collaborated with her colleagues on an improved end-of-course exam. She also realized that she needed to review the items from the first semester with her students before they took the final, as they had not been held accountable for that information at the semester's end.

First-year teacher Jamie Ramirez asked his colleagues on the 3rd grade team to review assessment items before he gave them to students. He made changes to the assessments based on the comments he received, and his colleagues sometimes used some of his assessment items as well. This test for validity helped ensure that the assessments actually measured what they were intended to measure.

This example illustrates one reason that common formative assessments are powerful. When teachers meet to discuss items, the overall validity of the assessment can improve (Ainsworth, 2015). Imagine the power of a group of 6th grade science teachers meeting to determine what students should know and how they will demonstrate that knowledge. This collaborative work will likely increase the trustworthiness of the assessments used, not to mention the overall unit of study.

Sometimes teachers want to take this process a step further and determine how closely their assessments align with other, similar tests. One way to do this is to compare a teacher-created assessment with the results on a benchmark or summative assessment. For example, Brandi Hayes wanted to know if her Algebra I summative assessment had any predictive validity in comparison with the state test. She worked with her instructional coach to calculate the number and was pleased to learn that there was a strong correlation between the two. It is important to note that this is not always a necessary condition. In some classes or grade levels, the course covers more than is included on a state test. In this case, if the teacher wanted to include this type of information in a performance review, it would be wise to use only items from the assessment that relate to the external measure.

Teacher Growth and Leadership

The FIT Teaching Tool includes many elements that we believe are critical to successful teacher growth and leadership. As we have shown, this tool can be used as a self-assessment, with an individual teacher reviewing the criteria and determining his or her strengths and areas of growth. Gary Schneider did just that. He read through the tool and examples of effective teaching and noted that his instruction was strong. He regularly provided relevant learning targets, accurately modeled for students, and engaged them in collaborative learning. He also realized that his assessment system was not very systematic. He relied heavily on summative assessments, so he set out to learn more about error analysis and reteaching. On his own, he became a more effective teacher.

Mr. Schneider performed his own gap analysis by comparing his current performance with his desired performance. On some level, we all do this, whether we realize it or not. But the critical thing is that Mr. Schneider took action to address the gap he found. He identified resources, read about error analysis, and talked with others who were using similar approaches. It was self-directed learning at its best, and he grew a lot from the experience. But it could have been made easier for him.

What Mr. Schneider did was hard work. It's easier to work collaboratively with colleagues to figure out where to focus growth opportunities. At our school, teachers review the FIT Teaching Tool each year and identify areas of strength and areas of interest for growth. They then form collaborative learning teams of between five and eight people focused on a single topic. They use their observation time, and their professional learning time, to hone their skills. For example, one group of teachers focused on transfer goals. They found some resources on the Internet and read a few books together. They observed one another in their classrooms and debriefed afterward. Over time, with practice and feedback, they dramatically improved their skills in meeting the diverse needs of students. At the same time, their colleagues were engaged in improving their purpose setting, revising their formative assessments, building a more welcoming culture, and developing electronic systems to store student work. In each case, the group of people engaged in an area of growth did so because of their reflection on the FIT Teaching Tool and their desire to be the best possible educators they could be.

Teacher leadership is tied not to job titles but to disposition. Teacher growth becomes teacher leadership when educators have opportunities to shape each other's knowledge and thinking. Every one of us has worked on teams where individuals regularly contributed their expertise to forward the group's work. In other words, the leadership emanated as needed from individuals who recognized that they could deepen the understanding of the group. It wasn't whether the team had a person identified as "leader," while everyone else was a "follower." High-performing teams in any profession are composed of people who contribute in order to strengthen the team, and the roles are fluid, not static. For example, the collaborative learning teams that are formed to examine an element of their instructional practice are filled with teachers who take on leadership behaviors, such as locating and sharing research, inviting colleagues into their classrooms, and spending time in the classrooms of others. For example, two English teachers collaborated to examine guided instruction (ingredient 3.2). The observing teacher, Gabriella Gutierrez, wrote to her colleague, Leslie Parker:

> Today I went into your room and saw students engaged in annotating articles through Google Docs. The content was advanced, but the

support you included within each document guided students in their learning and enabled them to be successful. You required students to highlight the text that supported their response to each question within the document, which gave them focus. I enjoyed watching Yajaira and Yasmine work together in understanding the complex text on the condition of hysteria.

The following day, these two teachers ate lunch together and talked further about the lesson. Importantly, they were both exhibiting leadership skills. Ms. Gutierrez, the observing teacher, asked great questions and listened carefully. But Ms. Parker, the teacher who taught the lesson, was a leader too. She had invited her junior colleague into class, recognizing it as a great avenue for mentoring as well as an opportunity to hone her own practice. At its heart, teacher leadership is best appreciated as a mutually beneficial process.

Improvement comes when teachers engage in meaningful discussion about quality educational experiences, reflect on their skill levels, and then focus on getting better. Teachers have to be learners as well, knowing what is expected and where they currently perform and then figuring out how to close the gap. Teacher leadership blossoms under these conditions, especially as educators position themselves as "lead learners." They actively seek opportunities to engage with the profession, and with fellow professionals, because they are driven to strengthen their practice. After all, we're teachers, and learning is our business.

Summing Up

Teachers should have an impact on students' learning. The final component of the FIT Teaching Tool requires that teachers, and those who support them, consider both short-term and long-term evidence of learning. Having said that, we feel it is important to emphasize, again, that relying on one measure, especially an externally mandated formal assessment, is not likely to produce significant changes in teacher growth or student learning. Instead, teachers and leaders should focus on multiple measures of student achievement. They should discuss the impact they've had on student learning with colleagues as part of a larger PLC effort and use these collaborative conversations to improve learning outcomes for students. Demonstrating—and publicizing—this kind of effectiveness can go a long way in combating the perceptions that some teachers (and schools) are unsuccessful.

When teams of teachers, and their coaches and formal leaders, reach agreements about quality (for example, through an extensive discussion about what each indicator means and might look like), compliance is replaced by commitment. As a result, expectations naturally rise due to deeper understanding, and implementation, of each ingredient. In essence, the words on the page take on life and guide teacher planning, instruction, assessment, and collaboration. When this occurs, teacher growth can be exponential, and students benefit greatly.

Conclusion
Taking Up the Challenge

The FIT Teaching Growth and Leadership Tool includes five elements that we believe are critical to successful teacher growth and leadership:

1. Planning with Purpose
2. Cultivating a Learning Climate
3. Instructing with Intention
4. Assessing with a System
5. Impacting Student Learning

Each of these components is important and provides opportunities for educators to continue to grow and develop. Improvement in teaching and learning will not come if administrators try to fire their way to school improvement—identifying poor teachers and getting rid of them. Nor will better teaching and learning come when well-meaning administrators score summative evaluations based on limited evidence and then file the reports away. It will come when teachers take charge of their own growth, engage in meaningful discussion about quality educational experiences, reflect on their skill levels, and then focus on getting better.

As teachers, we lead learners, but we must also be learners ourselves. This means knowing what is expected of us and where we currently perform and then figuring out how to close any gaps that exist. Becoming a FIT Teacher means embracing learning as our business, our calling, our challenge, and our responsibility. It means leading our students, leading our colleagues, and leading our profession.

Acknowledgments

We would like to thank the educators who supported the development of the FIT Teaching Tool by providing us with feedback and feed forward during our work.

Carl Atkinson, Assistant Superintendent, Springfield Township School District, PA

Rosemary Cataldi, Education Manager, Nobel Learning Communities

Page Dettmann, Executive Director of Middle School Curriculum, Sarasota County Schools, FL

Judy A. Fancher, Assistant Superintendent, Curriculum, Instruction & Assessment, PreK–12, Hacienda La Puente Unified School District, CA

Toby Grosswald, Education Manager, Nobel Learning Communities

Karen Janney, Superintendent, Sweetwater Union High School District, CA

Kelly McAmis, Assistant Superintendent, Garden Grove Unified School District, CA

Kathleen Poole, Assistant Superintendent, Northshore School District, WA

Mike Ritzius, Associate Director of Professional Development and Instructional Issues, New Jersey Education Association

Julie Scullen, Teaching and Learning Specialist for Secondary Reading, Anoka-Hennepin Independent School District, MN

Rich Wilson, Associate Director of Professional Development and Instructional Issues, New Jersey Education Association

Nancy Young, Director of Elementary Curriculum Instruction and Assessment, Northshore School District, WA

Appendix
The FIT Teaching Growth and Leadership Tool

1. Planning with Purpose	2. Cultivating a Learning Climate
1.1: Learning Intentions and Progressions 1.1a: Identifying transfer goals 1.1b: Linking to theme, problem, project, or question 1.1c: Identifying lesson-specific learning intentions 1.1d: Identifying content learning intentions 1.1e: Identifying language learning intentions **1.2: Evidence of Learning** 1.2a: Identifying success criteria 1.2b: Designing evidence-collection opportunities **1.3: Meaningful Learning** 1.3a: Designing aligned experiences 1.3b: Planning for differentiation	**2.1: Welcoming** 2.1a: Positive regard 2.1b: Physical environment 2.1c: Community building **2.2: Growth Producing** 2.2a: Builds agency and identity 2.2b: Encourages academic risk taking 2.2c: Repairs harm **2.3: Efficient** 2.3a: Rules, routines, and procedures 2.3b: Record keeping

3. Instructing with Intention	4. Assessing with a System	5. Impacting Student Learning
3.1: Focused Instruction 3.1a: Clear learning intentions 3.1b: Relevant learning intentions 3.1c: Accurate representation of critical content **3.2: Guided Instruction** 3.2a: Notices student needs 3.2b: Scaffolds support **3.3: Collaborative Learning** 3.3a: Interactive learning routines 3.3b: Task complexity 3.3c: Language support	**4.1: Assessment to Support Learners** 4.1a: Comprehensible expectations 4.1b: Goal-setting opportunities **4.2: Assessment to Monitor Learning** 4.2a: Checks for understanding 4.2b: Error analysis **4.3: Assessment to Inform Learning** 4.3a: Types of feedback 4.3b: Usefulness of feedback 4.3c: Needs-based instruction	**5.1: Short-Term Evidence of Learning** **5.2: Long-Term Evidence of Learning**

The five components of the FIT Teaching Tool are designed for both formative and summative use by teachers and supervisors to guide their work iteratively, so that conversations about planning and instruction are considered not in isolation but rather as part of an ongoing process.

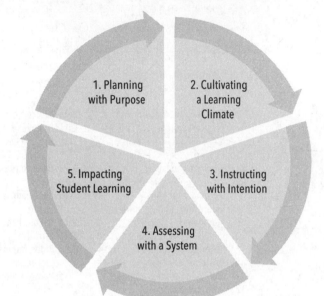

The FIT Teaching Tool embeds the highest forms of teacher practice into the *Leading* level of the rubrics. This level indicates teachers' willingness and ability to collaborate with colleagues and efforts to enhance the larger school community. In the FIT Teaching Tool, a teacher's professional growth is treated not as an isolated obligation but rather as fundamental to improving practice and collegial experiences. It would be unusual for a teacher to attain the highest level without a significant commitment to personal learning.

Rubrics

Teachers can use the rubrics formatively, as a self-assessment, as well as in conjunction with teacher peers and coaches. Supervisors can use the rubrics summatively. The four levels of growth are the following:

• *Not Yet Apparent (NYA):* Observed only occasionally. This level is indicated only when there is a *complete lack of evidence* that the teacher has considered a necessary aspect of instruction and incorporated it into practice. This should be differentiated from *NA* (*Not Applicable*), which indicates a rare situation when the ingredient is not expected as part of the teacher's practice.

• *Developing:* Most typical with teachers new to the profession or new to a grade level, subject area, or curriculum implementation. This level of growth is marked by inconsistency of practice and is selected when it is clear that teachers understand the criteria but the implementation is falling short of a desired level of success.

• *Teaching:* Most typical with experienced teachers implementing criteria with fidelity. This level is selected when it is clear that the teacher's practice is intentional, solidly implemented, and resulting in success for students.

• *Leading:* Most typical with seasoned teachers who have embraced a particular aspect of the criteria at its highest level and are providing support, guidance, and resources for colleagues. *Leading* teachers develop learning opportunities for adults that respect individual levels of personal practice and focus on extending collective growth. Teachers at this level have classrooms with open doors and consider themselves continuous learners, thereby affecting classrooms outside their own.

1.1: Learning Intentions and Progressions

Criteria	Not Yet Apparent	Developing	Teaching	Leading
1.1a: Identifying transfer goals	The teacher does not consider transfer goals during planning.	The teacher identifies transfer goals but does not use them to align plans for student application and assessment.	The teacher plans with grade- or course-appropriate transfer goals in mind and uses them to align activities and assessments.	The teacher supports colleagues in their ability to plan with grade- or course-appropriate transfer goals in mind and use them to align activities and assessments.
1.1b: Linking to theme, problem, project, or question	The teacher does not link learning intentions to themes, problems, projects, or questions.	The teacher identifies learning intentions that are minimally linked to themes, problems, projects, or questions.	The teacher identifies learning intentions that are linked to themes, problems, projects, or questions.	The teacher supports colleagues in their ability to identify learning intentions that are linked to themes, problems, projects, or questions.
1.1c: Identifying lesson-specific learning intentions	The teacher does not identify lesson-specific learning intentions.	The teacher identifies learning intentions that may be too broad to accomplish during a specific lesson.	The teacher identifies learning intentions that are achievable during a specific lesson.	The teacher supports colleagues in their ability to identify learning intentions that are achievable during a specific lesson.
1.1d: Identifying content learning intentions	The teacher does not identify content learning intentions.	The teacher identifies content learning intentions that may be vague or not grade- or content-appropriate or are primarily centered around isolated activities or tasks rather than on learning targets or enduring understandings.	The teacher identifies content learning intentions that are clearly stated and grade- or course-appropriate and are related to learning targets and enduring understandings rather than tasks or activities.	The teacher supports colleagues in their ability to identify content learning intentions that are clearly stated and grade- or course-appropriate and are related to learning targets and enduring understandings rather than tasks or activities.
1.1e: Identifying language learning intentions	The teacher does not identify language learning intentions.	The teacher identifies language learning intentions that may be vague or not grade- or content-appropriate.	The teacher identifies language learning intentions that are clearly stated; focused on vocabulary, structure, or function; and grade- or content-appropriate.	The teacher supports colleagues in their ability to identify language learning intentions that are clearly stated; focused on vocabulary, structure, or function; and grade- or content-appropriate.

1. PLANNING WITH PURPOSE

1. PLANNING WITH PURPOSE

1.2: Evidence of Learning

Criteria	Not Yet Apparent	Developing	Teaching	Leading
1.2a: Identifying success criteria	The teacher does not design summative assessments related to the lesson's learning intentions.	The teacher designs summative assessments that indirectly relate to the lesson's established learning intentions, permit limited application opportunities to foster transfer, or yield inconclusive data around student understanding.	The teacher collaborates with students to design summative assessments that relate directly to the lesson's established learning intentions and permit students the opportunity to demonstrate their understanding in order to foster long-term transfer.	The teacher supports colleagues in their ability to collaborate with students to design summative assessments that relate directly to the lesson's established learning intentions and permit students the opportunity to demonstrate their understanding in order to foster long-term transfer.
1.2b: Designing evidence-collection opportunities	The teacher does not plan to collect evidence of student understanding.	The teacher plans to infrequently collect evidence of student understanding or relies solely on summative assessment data.	The teacher has a clear plan for consistently collecting evidence of student understanding related to established learning intentions.	The teacher supports colleagues in their ability to develop a clear plan for consistently collecting evidence of student understanding related to established learning intentions.

1.3: Meaningful Learning

Criteria	Not Yet Apparent	Developing	Teaching	Leading
1.3a: Designing aligned experiences	The teacher does not design aligned learning experiences.	The teacher designs experiences that are minimally linked to the learning intentions. Activities rarely require students to construct meaning through interaction with the teacher, the content materials, and each other. Instead, they rely on replication rather than innovation.	The teacher designs experiences that are clearly aligned to the established learning intentions and require students to experiment with concepts and actively construct meaning through interaction with the teacher, the content materials, and each other.	The teacher supports colleagues in their ability to design experiences that are clearly aligned to the established learning intentions and require students to experiment with concepts and actively construct meaning through interaction with the teacher, the content materials, and each other.
1.3b: Planning for differentiation	The teacher does not differentiate instruction.	The teacher has a limited differentiation repertoire or provides differentiation that is only loosely based on formative assessment data.	The teacher designs for differentiated instruction based on formative assessment data, using flexible grouping and providing a variety of experiences that meet student needs or interests.	The teacher supports colleagues in their ability to design for differentiated instruction based on formative assessment data, using flexible grouping and providing a variety of experiences that meet student needs or interests.

2.1: Welcoming

Criteria	Not Yet Apparent	Developing	Teaching	Leading
2.1a: Positive regard	The teacher has strained relationships with students or does not hold students in high esteem.	The teacher exhibits positive regard but has limited interactions with more challenging students.	The teacher actively seeks to establish and maintain positive relationships with all students by showing interest in their academic lives, interests, and aspirations.	The teacher supports colleagues in their ability to establish and maintain positive relationships with all students by showing interest in their academic lives, interests, and aspirations.
2.1b: Physical environment	The classroom is disorganized, cluttered, or dirty and negatively affects student learning.	The teacher has designed but has difficulty maintaining an inviting classroom environment that will support student learning and movement.	The teacher designs and maintains an inviting classroom environment that supports student learning and movement.	The teacher supports colleagues in their ability to design and maintain an inviting classroom environment that supports student learning and movement.
2.1c: Community building	The teacher rarely creates opportunities for students to build relationships with one another and communicates with families only when there is a problem.	The teacher occasionally engages in relationship building between and among students or has limited contact with families.	The teacher strengthens the social fabric of the classroom by building relationships between and among students and their families in order to foster a positive community of learners.	The teacher supports colleagues in their ability to strengthen the social fabric of the classroom by building relationships among students and their families in order to foster a positive community of learners.

2.2: Growth Producing

Criteria	Not Yet Apparent	Developing	Teaching	Leading
2.2a: Builds agency and identity	The teacher belittles, shames, or humiliates students or uses sarcasm, diminishing student agency and identity.	The teacher often uses language that contributes to students' learned helplessness and, more rarely, builds resilience and persistence.	The teacher frames language so that students develop a sense of resilience and persistence in their learning lives.	The teacher supports colleagues in their ability to frame language so that students develop a sense of resilience and persistence in their learning lives.

2. CULTIVATING A LEARNING CLIMATE

	Not Yet Apparent	Developing	Teaching	Leading
2.2b: Encourages academic risk taking	The teacher does not encourage risk taking and potential failure, instead valuing student comfort and contentment over challenge.	The teacher values accuracy over potential growth and only occasionally challenges students to extend their thinking, even if it means initial failure.	The teacher fosters a growth mindset for students by creating a safe and respectful environment where failure is not ridiculed but considered an important component of the learning process.	The teacher supports colleagues in their ability to foster a growth mindset for students by creating a safe and respectful environment where failure is not ridiculed but considered an important component of the learning process.
2.2c: Repairs harm	The teacher does not address disruptions and misbehavior or routinely has others outside the classroom address behavior issues.	The teacher's responses to disruptions and misbehavior are primarily respectful but reactive, and the return to productive learning is often delayed.	The teacher expects, plans for, and responds to disruptions or misbehavior in a manner that respects students and focuses on a return to productive learning.	The teacher supports colleagues in their ability to expect, plan for, and respond to disruptions or misbehavior in a manner that respects students and focuses on a return to productive learning.

2.3: Efficient

Criteria	Not Yet Apparent	Developing	Teaching	Leading
2.3a: Rules, routines, and procedures	The teacher does not establish rules, routines, and procedures, resulting in a confusing learning environment.	The teacher establishes some rules, routines, and procedures, but they are used inconsistently or do not anticipate common situations, resulting in needless learning interruptions.	The teacher proactively establishes and maintains rules, routines, and procedures that enable students to self-regulate, resulting in smooth classroom operations that maximize learning.	The teacher supports colleagues in their ability to proactively establish and maintain rules, routines, and procedures that enable students to self-regulate, resulting in smooth classroom operations that maximize learning.
2.3b: Record keeping	The teacher's instructional and noninstructional records are consistently incomplete, delayed, not secured, or missing.	The teacher maintains instructional and noninstructional records, but these are sometimes delayed or incomplete, making them less useful to students, families, and colleagues.	The teacher maintains both instructional and noninstructional records so that data are immediately available for planning and to inform students, families, and colleagues.	The teacher supports colleagues in their ability to maintain both instructional and noninstructional records so that data are immediately available for planning and to inform students, families, and colleagues.

2. CULTIVATING A LEARNING CLIMATE

3.1: Focused Instruction

Criteria	Not Yet Apparent	Developing	Teaching	Leading
3.1a: Clear learning intentions	The teacher does not establish learning intentions with the students.	The teacher establishes the learning intentions with students at the beginning of the lesson segment but does not return to the learning intentions at any other time during the lesson.	The teacher uses the learning intentions to focus students throughout the lesson (such as during transitions and closure activities).	The teacher supports colleagues in their ability to use the learning intentions to focus students throughout the lesson (such as during transitions and closure activities).
3.1b: Relevant learning intentions	The teacher does not establish the relevance of the content.	The teacher loosely or vaguely establishes the relevance of the content to students. The relevance of the content is not revisited.	Relevance is established and maintained throughout the lesson as students are reminded about why they are learning the specific content.	The teacher supports colleagues in their ability to establish and maintain relevance throughout the lesson as students are reminded about why they are learning the specific content.
3.1c: Accurate representation of critical content	The teacher does not provide accurate content.	The teacher provides accurate content that is loosely linked with learning intentions. The instruction prevents students from engaging in related tasks or fails to provide them with the appropriate foundation.	The teacher provides accurate content that is clearly linked with the learning intentions. The instruction ensures students have the foundation necessary for the tasks they will accomplish.	The teacher supports colleagues in their ability to provide accurate representations of critical content that are linked with the learning intentions and provide a foundation for related tasks.

3. INSTRUCTING WITH INTENTION

3.2: Guided Instruction

Criteria	Not Yet Apparent	Developing	Teaching	Leading
3.2a: Notices student needs	The teacher does not notice students' misconceptions, errors, or confusions.	The teacher only occasionally notices students' misconceptions, errors, or confusions, as evidenced by minimal follow-up probes.	The teacher notices students' misconceptions, errors, or confusions by asking questions to probe their thinking, paying attention to nonverbal cues, or analyzing student work.	The teacher supports colleagues in their ability to notice students' misconceptions, errors, or confusions by asking questions to probe their thinking, paying attention to nonverbal cues, or analyzing student work.
3.2b: Scaffolds support	The teacher does not scaffold support for students.	The teacher at times offers questions, prompts, and cues to scaffold support of student learning, but at other times moves to direct explanations instead of scaffolding first.	The teacher scaffolds support for students using prompts and cues when student responses demonstrate incorrect or partial understanding, reserving direct explanations only for situations when prompts and cues are insufficient.	The teacher supports colleagues in their ability to scaffold support for students using prompts and cues when student responses demonstrate incorrect or partial understanding, reserving direct explanations only for situations when prompts and cues are insufficient.

3. INSTRUCTING WITH INTENTION

3.3: Collaborative Learning

Criteria	Not Yet Apparent	Developing	Teaching	Leading
3.3a: Interactive learning routines	The teacher does not use collaborative learning routines.	The teacher uses collaborative learning routines but does not teach the processes and procedures necessary for students to maximize instructional time.	The teacher systematically teaches the process and procedural skills needed for collaborative learning routines that will be used throughout the unit or school year. This is apparent as students demonstrate clear understanding of collaborative learning routines in order to maximize instructional time.	The teacher supports colleagues in their ability to support students in acquiring the process and procedural skills needed to engage in collaborative learning routines in order to maximize instructional time.
3.3b: Task complexity	The teacher does not monitor student collaborative work.	The teacher uses collaborative learning, but the tasks are insufficiently complex to challenge students' thinking. The teacher monitors students as they work collaboratively.	Collaborative work is sufficiently complex to allow students an opportunity to use a variety of resources to creatively apply their knowledge; the task challenges students' thinking. The teacher monitors groups' progress in the event that the task might need adjustment.	The teacher supports colleagues in their ability to design collaborative work that is sufficiently complex to allow students an opportunity to use a variety of resources to creatively apply their knowledge. The teacher supports colleagues in their ability to monitor groups' progress in the event that the task might need adjustment.
3.3c: Language support	The teacher does not provide language support to students.	The teacher provides generic written, verbal, teacher, or peer supports for all students, without attending to differentiated needs.	The teacher provides differentiated written, verbal, teacher, or peer supports to boost individual students' academic language usage.	The teacher supports colleagues in their ability to provide differentiated written, verbal, teacher, or peer supports to boost individual students' academic language usage.

3. INSTRUCTING WITH INTENTION

4.1: Assessment to Support Learners

Criteria	Not Yet Apparent	Developing	Teaching	Leading
4.1a: Comprehensible expectations	The learning expectations are not understood by students.	The learning expectations are communicated to students, but the majority of students are only partially able to explain or demonstrate what they are learning, why they are learning the content, and how they will know they have learned it.	The learning expectations are clearly communicated and understood by students such that most randomly selected students can explain or demonstrate what they are learning, why they are learning the content, and how they will know they have learned it.	The teacher supports colleagues in their ability to convey comprehensible learning expectations such that most randomly selected students can explain or demonstrate what they are learning, why they are learning the content, and how they will know they have learned it.
4.1b: Goal-setting opportunities	The teacher does not provide goal-setting opportunities to students.	The teacher provides goal-setting opportunities but only prompts students to use them summatively (end of project or assignment), thus limiting students' ability to measure progress formatively.	The teacher provides clear and focused opportunities for students to set and gauge their progress toward achievement of goals related to learning and mastery.	The teacher supports colleagues in their ability to provide clear and focused opportunities for students to set and gauge their progress toward achievement of goals related to learning and mastery.

4. ASSESSING WITH A SYSTEM

4.2: Assessment to Monitor Learning

Criteria	Not Yet Apparent	Developing	Teaching	Leading
4.2a: Checks for understanding	The teacher does not check for understanding.	The teacher sporadically checks for understanding throughout the lesson, using a limited repertoire of techniques to do so. Opportunities to check for understanding are often overlooked, and the teacher relies primarily on anecdotal information about student progress.	The teacher systematically checks for student understanding throughout the lesson, using a variety of techniques, which may include the following: • Oral language (questioning, retelling, student conversation) • Student writing • Student projects/performances • Tests/quizzes/common assessments • Student self-assessment The teacher uses these checks for understanding to gauge progress of individuals and groups.	The teacher supports colleagues in their ability to systematically check for student understanding throughout the lesson, using a variety of techniques, which may include the following: • Oral language (questioning, retelling, student conversation) • Student writing • Student projects/performances • Tests/quizzes/common assessments • Student self-assessment The teacher supports colleagues in their ability to use these checks for understanding to gauge progress of individuals and groups.
4.2b: Error analysis	The teacher does not analyze student errors.	The teacher analyzes student errors, misconceptions, and miscues but does not link these findings to feedback or future instruction.	The teacher strategically analyzes student errors, misconceptions, and miscues to provide more accurate and specific feedback and future instruction to students.	The teacher supports colleagues in their ability to strategically analyze student errors, misconceptions, and miscues in order to provide more accurate and specific feedback and future instruction to students.

4. ASSESSING WITH A SYSTEM

4.3: Assessment to Inform Learning

Criteria	Not Yet Apparent	Developing	Teaching	Leading
4.3a: Types of feedback	The teacher does not provide different types of feedback.	The teacher provides feedback about the task, about the processes of the task, and about self-regulation, but these feedback offerings may not be scaled to match the learning progress of the student. The teacher dilutes the feedback with praise.	The teacher selects the type of feedback most conducive to providing students with a clear understanding of how they are doing relative to the learning goal, providing progressive feedback • about the task, • about processing of the task, and • about self-regulation. The teacher keeps praise separate from feedback to increase its effectiveness.	The teacher supports colleagues in their ability to select the type of feedback most conducive to providing students with a clear understanding of how they are doing relative to the learning goal, providing progressive feedback • about the task, • about processing of the task, and • about self-regulation. The teacher supports colleagues in their ability to keep praise separate from feedback to increase its effectiveness.
4.3b: Usefulness of feedback	The teacher does not provide useful feedback.	The teacher provides students with feedback that is diminished in its effectiveness because it is delayed, vague, incomprehensible to the learner, or does not allow for the learner to take action.	The teacher successfully provides students with feedback that is timely, specific, understandable, and actionable.	The teacher supports colleagues in their ability to provide students with feedback that is timely, specific, understandable, and actionable.
4.3c: Needs-based instruction	The teacher does not alter instruction based on student needs.	The teacher relies on initial instruction, with limited opportunities for reteaching at individual and small-group levels. Needs-based instruction occurs at times, but the teacher relies on impressions rather than data.	The teacher organizes individual, small-group, and whole-class instruction based on trend data and matches students with the specific instruction that they need to progress academically.	The teacher supports colleagues in their ability to organize individual, small-group, and whole-class instruction based on trend data and match students with the specific instruction that they need to progress academically.

4. ASSESSING WITH A SYSTEM

5.1: Short-Term Evidence of Learning

Criterion	Not Yet Apparent	Developing	Teaching	Leading
5.1: Short-term evidence of progress toward periodic goals	Students consistently do not meet periodic goals throughout the school year.	The teacher is only occasionally able to demonstrate impact on student learning measured across units of study. Evidence is drawn from limited sources.	The teacher consistently demonstrates significant impact on student learning measured across units of study, with evidence drawn from a wide variety of sources, including valid and reliable summative assessments as well as observations and formative assessments.	The teacher supports colleagues in their work with students such that they are able to demonstrate impact on student learning measured across units of study, with evidence drawn from a wide variety of sources, including valid and reliable summative assessments as well as observations and formative assessments.

5.2: Long-Term Evidence of Learning

Criterion	Not Yet Apparent	Developing	Teaching	Leading
5.2: Long-term evidence of attainment of transfer goals	Students consistently do not meet long-term transfer goals.	Students inconsistently meet long-term transfer goals, or the teacher does not set challenging but achievable goals.	Most students consistently meet challenging but achievable long-term transfer goals.	The teacher supports colleagues in their work with students such that most of the students meet challenging but achievable long-term transfer goals.

5. IMPACTING STUDENT LEARNING

References

Ainsworth, L. (2015). *Common formative assessments 2.0: How teacher teams intentionally align standards, instruction, and assessment.* Thousand Oaks, CA: Corwin.

American Statistical Association. (2014). ASA statement on using value-added models for educational assessment. Retrieved from https://www.amstat.org/policy/pdfs/ASA_VAM_Statement.pdf

Ashman, A. F., & Gillies, R. M. (1997). Children's cooperative behavior and interactions in trained and untrained work groups in regular classrooms. *Journal of School Psychology, 35*(3), 261–279.

Asiyai, R. (2014). Students' perception of the condition of their classroom physical learning environment and its impact on their learning and motivation. *College Student Journal, 48*(4), 716–726.

Ballou, D., & Springer, M. G. (2015). Using student test scores to measure teacher performance: Some problems in the design and implementation of evaluation systems. *Educational Researcher, 44*(2), 77–86.

Bandura, A. (2001). Social cognitive theory: An agentic perspective. *Annual Review of Psychology, 52*, 1–26.

Black, P., & Wiliam, D. (1998). Assessment and classroom learning. *Assessment in Education: Principles, Policy and Practice, 5*(1), 7–73.

Block, P. (2008). *Community: The structure of belonging.* San Francisco, CA: Berrett-Koehler.

Brattesani, K. A.,Weinstein, R. S., & Marshall, H. H. (1984). Student perceptions of differential teacher treatment as moderators of teacher expectation effects. *Journal of Educational Psychology, 76*(2), 236–247.

Brown, A. L. (1987). Metacognition, executive control, self-regulation, and other more mysterious mechanisms. In F. E. Weinert & R. H. Kluwe (Eds.), *Metacognition, motivation, and understanding* (pp. 65–116). Hillsdale, NJ: Erlbaum.

Bryk, A. S., Sebring, P. B., Allensworth, E., Luppescu, S., & Easton, J. Q. (2010). *Organizing schools for improvement: Lessons from Chicago.* Chicago: University of Chicago Press.

Chappuis, J., Stiggins, R. J., Chappuis, S., & Arter, J. A. (2012). *Classroom assessment for student learning: Doing it right—using it well.* Boston: Pearson.

Clay, M. M. (2000). *Running records for classroom teachers.* Portsmouth, NH: Heinemann.

Costello, B., Wachtel, J., & Wachtel, T. (2009). *Restorative practices handbook for teachers, disciplinarians, and administrators.* Bethlehem, PA: International Institute for Restorative Practices.

Danielson, C. (2007). *Enhancing professional practice: A framework for teaching* (2nd ed.). Alexandria, VA: ASCD.

Darling-Hammond, L. (2000). Teacher quality and student achievement: A review of state policy evidence. *Education Policy Analysis Archives, 8*(1). Available: http://dx.doi.org/10.14507/epaa.v8n1.2000

Darling-Hammond, L. (2013). *Getting teacher evaluation right: What really matters for effectiveness and improvement.* New York: Teachers College Press.

Davis, T. (2013). McREL's Research-Based Teacher Evaluation System. Denver, CO: McREL International.

Denton, P. (2007). *The power of our words: Teacher language that helps children learn.* Turners Falls, MA: Northeast Foundation for Children Inc.

DuFour, R., DuFour, R., & Eaker, R. (2008). *Revisiting professional learning communities at work: New insights for improving schools.* Bloomington, IN: Solution Tree.

DuFour, R., & Marzano, R. (2011). *Leaders of learning: How district, school, and classroom leaders improve student achievement.* Bloomington, IN: Solution Tree.

Dweck, C. S. (2006). *Mindset: The new psychology of success.* New York: Random House.

Echevarria, J., Short, D., & Powers, K. (2006). School reform and standards-based education: A model for English-language learners. *Journal of Educational Research, 99*(4), 195–210.

Elliot, A. J. (1999). Approach and avoidance motivation and achievement goals. *Educational Psychologist, 34*, 169–189.

Epstein, J. L., et al. (2009). *School, family, and community partnerships: Your handbook for action* (3rd ed.). Thousand Oaks, CA: Corwin.

Fisher, D., & Frey, N. (2010a). *Enhancing RTI: How to ensure success with effective classroom instruction and intervention.* Alexandria, VA: ASCD.

Fisher, D., & Frey, N. (2010b). Unpacking the language purpose: Vocabulary, structure, and function. *TESOL Journal, 1*(3), 315–337.

Fisher, D., & Frey, N. (2011). *The purposeful classroom: How to structure lessons with learning goals in mind.* Alexandria, VA: ASCD.

Fisher, D., & Frey, N. (2014a). *Better learning through structured teaching: A framework for the gradual release of responsibility* (2nd ed.). Alexandria, VA: ASCD.

Fisher, D., & Frey, N. (2014b). *Checking for understanding: Formative assessment techniques for your classroom* (2nd ed.). Alexandria, VA: ASCD.

Fisher, D., & Frey, N. (2014c). Using teacher learning walks to improve instruction. *Principal Leadership, 14*(5), 58–61.

Fisher, D., Frey, N., & Pumpian, I. (2011, November). No penalties for practice. *Educational Leadership, 69*(3), 46–51.

Fisher, D., Frey, N., & Rothenberg, C. (2008). *Content area conversations: How to plan discussion-based lessons for diverse language learners.* Alexandria, VA: ASCD.

Frey, N., & Fisher, D. (2010, October). Identifying instructional moves during guided instruction. *The Reading Teacher, 64*(2), 84–95.

Gess-Newsome, J. (2013). Pedagogical content knowledge. In J. Hattie & E. M. Anderman (Eds.), *International guide to student achievement* (pp. 257–259). New York: Routledge.

Glazerman, S., Goldhaber, D., Loeb, S., Raudenbush, S., Staiger, D., & Whitehurst, G. (2010). *Evaluating teachers: The important role of value-added.* Washington, DC: Brookings Institute.

Goddard, Y. L., Goddard, R. D., & Tschannen-Moran, M. (2007). A theoretical and empirical investigation of teacher collaboration for school improvement and student achievement in public elementary schools. *Teachers College Record, 109*(4), 877–896.

Goldhaber, D. (2015). Exploring the potential of value-added performance measures to affect the quality of the teacher workforce. *Educational Researcher, 87*(2), 87–95.

Good, T. L., & Brophy, J. E. (2007). *Looking in classrooms* (10th ed.). Boston: Pearson/Allyn & Bacon.

Goodenow, C. (1993). The psychological sense of school membership among adolescents: Scale development and educational correlates. *Psychology in the Schools, 30*, 79–90.

Guskey, T. R. (2013). Defining student achievement. In J. Hattie & E. M. Anderman (Eds.), *International guide to student achievement* (pp. 3–6). New York: Routledge.

Hattie, J. (2012). *Visible learning for teachers: Maximizing impact on learning.* New York: Routledge.

Heubusch, J. D., & Lloyd, J. W. (1998). Corrective feedback in oral reading. *Journal of Behavioral Education, 8*(1), 63–79.

Hiebert, J., Morris, A. K., Berk, D., & Jansen, A. (2007). Preparing teachers to learn from teaching. *Journal of Teacher Education, 58*(1), 47–61.

Hintz, A., & Kazemi, E. (2014, November). Talking about math. *Educational Leadership, 72*(3), 36–40.

Huang, C. (2012). Discriminant and criterion-related validity of achievement goals in predicting academic achievement: A meta-analysis. *Journal of Educational Psychology, 104*(1), 48–73.

Johnson, D. W., Johnson, R. T., & Smith, K. A. (1991). *Active learning: Cooperation in the college classroom.* Edina, MN: Interaction Book Company.

Johnson, S. M. (2015). Will VAMs reinforce the walls of the egg-crate school? *Educational Researcher, 44*(2), 117–126.

Johnston, P. H. (2004). *Choice words: How our language affects children's learning.* Portland, ME: Stenhouse.

Joint Committee on the Standards for Educational and Psychology Testing of the American Educational Research Association, the American Psychological Association, and the National Council on Measurement in Education. (2014). *Standards for educational and psychological testing.* Washington, DC: American Educational Research Association.

Kelley, T. L. (1927). *Interpretation of educational measurements.* New York: Macmillan.

Lippman, P. C. (2013). Collaborative spaces. *T.H.E. Journal, 40*(1), 32–37.

Marshall, K. (2011). Teacher evaluation rubrics. Available: http://www.marshallmemo.com/articles/Marshall%20 Teacher%20Eval%20Rubrics%20Aug.%2031,%2011.pdf

Martin, A. J., & Marsh, H. W. (2006). Academic resilience and its psychological and educational correlates: A construct validity approach. *Psychology in the Schools, 43*(3), 267–281.

Marzano, R. J. (2013). *The Marzano teacher evaluation model.* Englewood, CO: Marzano Research Laboratory.

Marzano, R. J., Pickering, D. J., & Pollock, J. E. (2001). *Classroom instruction that works: Research-based strategies for increasing student achievement.* Alexandria, VA: ASCD.

McMahon, S. D., Wernsman, J., & Rose, D. S. (2009). The relation of classroom environment and school belonging to academic self-efficacy among urban fourth- and fifth-grade students. *Elementary School Journal, 109*(3), 267–281.

McTighe, J. (2014). Long-term transfer goals. Retrieved from http://jaymctighe.com/wordpress/wp-content/ uploads/2013/04/Long-term-Transfer-Goals.pdf

Morisano, D., & Locke, E. A. (2013). Goal setting and academic achievement. In J. Hattie & E. M. Anderman (Eds.), *International guide to student achievement* (pp. 45–50). New York: Routledge.

Nathan, M. J., & Petrosino, A. (2003). Expert blind spot among preservice teachers. *American Educational Research Journal, 40*(4), 905–928.

National Research Council, Committee on *How People Learn: A Targeted Report for Teachers.* (2005). *How students learn: History, mathematics, and science in the classroom.* Washington, DC: National Academies Press.

New Zealand Ministry of Education. (n.d.). Success criteria. Retrieved from http://assessment.tki.org.nz/Glossary/ Success-criteria

Oliveira, A., Wilcox, K., Angelis, J., Applebee, A. N., Amodeo, V., & Snyder, M. A. (2013). Best practice in middle-school science. *Journal of Science Teacher Education, 24*(2), 297–322.

Olweus, D. (2003). A profile of bullying at school. *Educational Leadership, 60*(6), 12–17.

Pai, H., Sears, D., & Maeda, Y. (2015). Effects of small-group learning on transfer: A meta-analysis. *Educational Psychology Review, 27*(1), 79–102.

Paley, V. G. (1992). *You can't say you can't play.* Cambridge, MA: Harvard University Press.

Palincsar, A. S., & Brown, A. L. (1984). Reciprocal teaching of comprehension-fostering and comprehension-monitoring activities. *Cognition and Instruction, 2*, 117–175.

Pearson, P. D., & Gallagher, G. (1983). The gradual release of responsibility model of instruction. *Contemporary Educational Psychology, 8*, 112–123.

Pianta, R. C., Belsky, J., Houts, R., & Morrison, F. (2007). Opportunities to learn in America's elementary classrooms. *Science, 315*, 1795–1796.

Pianta, R. C., La Paro, K. M., & Hamre, B. K. (2008). *Classroom assessment scoring system (K–3).* Baltimore, MD: Paul H. Brookes.

Popham, W. J. (2013). *Evaluating America's teachers: Mission possible?* Thousand Oaks, CA: Corwin.

Posner, G. J. (1994). *Analyzing the curriculum* (2nd ed.). New York: McGraw-Hill.

Potter, S., & Davis, B. H. (2003). A first-year teacher implements class meetings. *Kappa Delta Pi Record, 39*(2), 88–90.

Roediger, H., III. (2014). The science of successful learning. *Educational Leadership, 72*(2), 42–46.

Sadler, D. R. (1989). Formative assessment and the design of instructional systems. *Instructional Science, 18*(2), 119–144.

Sapon-Shevin, M. (1998). *Because we can change the world: A practical guide to building cooperative, inclusive classroom communities.* Boston: Allyn & Bacon.

Shulman, L. S. (1987). Knowledge and teaching: Foundations of the new reform. *Harvard Educational Review, 57*(1), 1–22.

Slavin, R. E. (1996). Research on cooperative learning and achievement: What we know, what we need to know. *Contemporary Educational Psychology, 21*(1), 43–69.

Smith, D., Fisher, D., & Frey, N. (2015). *Better than carrots or sticks: Restorative practices for positive classroom management.* Alexandria, VA: ASCD.

Stronge, J., & Tucker, P. D. (2003). *Handbook on teacher evaluation: Assessing and improving instruction.* London: Eye on Education.

TED (Producer). (2012). Use data to build better schools [Video file]. Retrieved from https://www.ted.com/talks/andreas_schleicher_use_data_to_build_better_schools

Tekkumru Kisa, M., & Stein, M. K. (2015). Learning to see teaching in new ways: A foundation for maintaining cognitive demand. *American Educational Research Journal, 52*(1), 105–136.

Todd, R. J. (2015). Evidence-based practice and school libraries. *Knowledge Quest, 43*(3), 8–15.

Tomlinson, C. A. (2000, August). Differentiation of instruction in the elementary grades. *ERIC Digest.* Champaign, IL: ERIC Clearinghouse on Elementary and Early Childhood Education. (ERIC Identifier: ED443572)

Tomlinson, C. A. (2015, January 28). Differentiation does, in fact, work. *Education Week, 34*(19), 26, 32.

Tomlinson, C. A., & Imbeau, M. B. (2010). *Leading and managing a differentiated classroom.* Alexandria, VA: ASCD.

Tschannen-Moran, M. (2014). *Trust matters: Leadership for successful schools* (2nd ed.). San Francisco: Jossey-Bass.

Van Es, E. A., & Sherin, M. G. (2002). Learning to notice: Scaffolding new teachers' interpretations of classroom interactions. *Journal of Technology & Teacher Education, 10*(4), 571–596.

Veenstra, R., Lindenberg, S., Huitsing, G., Sainio, M., & Salmivalli, C. (2014). The role of teachers in bullying: The relation between antibullying attitudes, efficacy, and efforts to reduce bullying. *Journal of Educational Psychology, 106*(4), 1135–1143.

Viadero, D. (2010, January 27). Chicago study teases out keys to improvement. *Education Week, 29*(19), 1, 9.

Webb, N. L. (2002). *Alignment study in language arts, mathematics, science, and social studies of state standards and assessments for four states.* Washington, DC: Council of Chief State School Officers.

Whitehurst, G. J., Chingos, M. W., & Lindquist, K. M. (2015). Getting classroom observations right. *Education Next, 15*(1). Retrieved from http://educationnext.org/getting-classroom-observations-right/

Wiggins, G. (1998). *Educative assessment: Designing assessments to inform and improve student performance.* San Francisco, CA: Jossey-Bass.

Wiggins, G., & McTighe, J. (2005). *Understanding by design* (2nd ed.). Alexandria, VA: ASCD.

Wiliam, D. (2006). *Does assessment hinder learning?* Princeton, NJ: ETS Global Institute. Retrieved from http://www.dylanwiliam.org

Yamauchi, L. A., Lau-Smith, J., & Luning, R. I. (2008). Family involvement in a Hawaiian language immersion program. *School Community Journal, 18*(1), 39–60.

Index

Notes: The letter *f* following a page number denotes a figure. Numerical references to FIT Teaching Tool components, factors, and ingredients are included in parentheses.

academic risk taking, encouraging (2.2b)
    examples, 66–69
    grades and, 67
    growth mindset, 66–67
    rubric, 66, 173
accountability in positive interactions, 103
achievement, goal setting and, 120
achievement gap, 48
agency
    building (2.2a), 61–66, 172
    meaning of, 62–63
assessment. *See also* Evidence of Learning (1.2); understanding, checking for (4.2a)
    benchmark tests, 147*f*
    criterion- and norm-referenced tests, 147*f*, 151
    differentiation-based, 42–43
    end-of-course exams, 152
    FIT Teaching rating scale, 8–11
    large-scale, misapplication of, 143, 151
    performance portfolios, 152
    standardized tests, 151
    teacher-created, usefulness of, 146–147
    of teacher quality, 8–14, 151–152
    trustworthy tools for, 153–154

Assessment to Inform Learning (4.3)
    feedback, types of (4.3a), 133–136, 179
    feedback, usefulness of (4.3b), 136–138, 179
    ingredients, 167
    needs-based instruction (4.3c), 138–141, 179
Assessment to Monitor Learning (4.2)
    error analysis (4.2b), 129–132, 131*f*, 178
    ingredients, 167
    time vs. learning constant, 122–123
    understanding, checking for (4.2a), 123–129
Assessment to Support Learners (4.1)
    conditional actions, 117
    elements underlying, 117–118
    expectations, comprehensible (4.1a), 117–119
    goal setting, 117
    goal-setting opportunities (4.1b), 119–122
    ingredients, 167
    purpose statements, 117
    trail marker analogy, 117

Assessment with a System (component 4). *See also specific factors*
    Assessment to Inform Learning factor (4.3), 133–141
    Assessment to Monitor Learning factor (4.2), 123–132
    Assessment to Support Learners factor (4.1), 117–122
    factors, 167
    focus, 6
    ingredients, 7*f*, 167
    introduction, 115–116
    learner's position in, 115
    requirements, 115
    summary overview, 141
assessment tools, trustworthy, 153–154
audience-response systems (clickers), 124

background knowledge, 100
behaviors, problematic, 63–64
belongingness, 47
bulletin boards, 52
bullying, 70

circles, 56
circulation patterns, classroom, 52

classrooms. *See also* Cultivating a Learning Climate (component 2)
  class meetings, 55, 56*f*
  community building outside the (2.1c), 56
  lesson-specific learning (1.1c), 23–26, 170
classrooms, efficient; *see* Efficient learning climate (2.3)
classrooms, environmental factors
  color, 52
  common and individual spaces, 52
  décor, 52
  examples, 51–54
  furniture arrangements, 52
  movement and circulation patterns, 52
  rubric, 51, 172
  signage / bulletin boards, 52
  social aspect and physical layout, 51–54
clickers (audience-response systems), 124
collaboration. *See also* Collaborative Learning (3.3)
  community building (2.1c), 58–60
  FIT Teaching recognition of, 10
  reflection and, 13
  success criteria, identifying (1.2), 35–36
Collaborative Learning (3.3)
  benefits, 102–103
  in gradual release of responsibility model, 82*f*
  ingredients, 167
  interactions, developing positive, 103–104
  language support (3.3c), 111–113, 176
  learning routines, interactive (3.3a), 103–107, 176
  phases, focus of, 82
  success prerequisites, 104
  task complexity (3.3b), 107–111, 108*f*
communication
  in collaborative learning, 104
  for community building (2.1c), 58–59
  purposeful talk, 104
  small-group, 112

community building (2.1c)
  circles, 56
  class meetings, 55, 56*f*
  collaboration for, 58–60
  communication for, 58–59
  dimensions, 55
  examples, 54–60
  family partnership practices, 56–57
  outside the classroom, 56
  peer relationships, 58–60
  repairing harm and, 69
  rubric, 54, 172
  between and with students, 58–59
  welcoming learning climate in (2.1), 54–60, 56*f*, 69, 172
conflict resolution, 70–71
Consortium on Chicago School Research, 45
content, accurate representation of critical (3.1c)
  demonstration, 92*f*
  examples, 91–95
  lecture, 92*f*
  modeling approach, 92*f*
  read aloud, 92*f*
  rubric, 91, 174
  think-aloud skills, 92, 93*f*, 94
  video viewing, 92*f*
content differentiation, 42
content learning intentions, identifying (1.1d)
  examples, 26–28
  rubric, 26, 170
cues, environmental, gestural, verbal, and visual, 101
Cultivating a Learning Climate (component 2). *See also* learning climate, *specific factors*
  cultivating, term meaning, 45
  Efficient factor (2.3), 74–79
  factors, 167
  focus, 5–6
  Growth Producing factor (2.2), 61–73
  ingredients, 7*f*, 167
  introduction, 45–46
  social aspect, 70
  summary overview, 79–80
  Welcoming factor (2.1), 47–60

data management, 1–2, 77–78
décor, classroom, 52

Developing growth level, 9, 11
differentiation
  dimensions, 42
  of expectations, 48
  in expectations, 48
  planning for (1.3b), 41–43, 171
  planning for in meaningful learning (1.3b), 41–43, 171
  student needs, noticing (3.2a), 42
differentiation-based assessment, 42–43

Efficient learning climate (2.3)
  classroom management practices, 73
  ingredients, 167
  record keeping (2.3b), 77–79, 173
  rules, routines, and procedures (2.3a), 74–77, 173
engagement for meaningful learning, 38
environmental factors, classroom (2.1b)
  color, 52
  common and individual spaces, 52
  décor, 52
  examples, 51–54
  furniture arrangements, 52
  movement and circulation patterns, 52
  rubric, 51, 172
  signage / bulletin boards, 52
  social aspect and physical layout, 51–54
equality in education, 48
error analysis (4.2b)
  errors, types of, 129–130
  examples, 129–132
  misconceptions, 130
  mistakes vs. errors, 129
  rubric, 129, 178
error-coding form (example), 131*f*
errors
  factual, 129
  feedback and, 115
  mistakes vs., 129
  procedural, 129
  transformational, 129–130
evidence-based practice, 143–145

evidence-collection, designing (1.2b), 36–38, 171
Evidence of Learning (1.2)
    evidence-collection, designing (1.2b), 36–38, 171
    focus, 33
    ingredients, 167
    success criteria, identifying (1.2a), 33–36, 82, 82f, 171
expectations
    comprehensible (4.1a), 118–119, 177
    differentiated, 48
expert blind spot, 96

face-to-face interactions, 103
fail forward, 115
family partnership practices, 56–57
feedback
    about the process, 134
    about the self as a person, 134
    about the task, 133–134
    error's role in, 115
    examples, 133–136
    maximizing, 132–133
    rubric, 133, 179
    on self-regulation, 134
    types of (4.3a), 133–136, 179
    usefulness of (4.3b), 136–138, 179
FIT Teaching (Framework for Intentional and Targeted Teaching), 3–4
FIT Teaching Tool (FIT Teaching and Growth and Leadership Tool)
    assumptions underlying, 8–11
    components, 5–7, 7f, 167. See also specific components
    ingredients, 167
    leading, 10
    overview, 167
    growth levels, 8–11, 168–169
    purpose, 7–8
    rubrics, 168–169. See also specific ingredients
    structure, 6–7, 167
Focused Instruction (3.1)
    content, accurate representation of critical (3.1c), 91–95, 92f, 93f
    examples, 84–95

Focused Instruction (3.1) (continued)
    gradual release of responsibility model, 82f
    ingredients, 167
    learning intentions, clear (3.1a), 84–90, 174
    learning intentions, relevant (3.1b), 10, 87–91, 174
    phase focus, 81
framework, term meaning, 3
furniture arrangements, classroom, 52

goals
    approach goals, 120
    performance goals, 120
    short-term evidence of progress toward (5.1), 145–150, 147f, 180
    student-developed, 134
goal setting
    achievement and, 120
    formative/summative, 117
    motivation and, 120
    opportunities for (4.1b), 119–122, 177
grade books, electronic, 77–78
grades, 67
gradual release of responsibility model, 81–82, 82f
growth mindset, 66–67
Growth Producing learning climate (2.2)
    academic risk taking, encouraging(2.2b), 66–69, 173
    agency and identity, building (2.2a), 61–66, 172
    harm, repairing (2.2c), 69–73, 73f, 173
    ingredients, 167
    teacher attitudes and actions in, 60–61
Guided Instruction (3.2)
    examples, 94–102
    expert blind spot, 96
    gradual release of responsibility model, 82f
    ingredients, 167
    phase focus, 81–82
    requirements for, 95–96
    scaffolds (3.2b), 99–102, 109, 175
    student needs, noticing (3.2a), 96–99, 175

harm, repairing (2.2c)
    bullying, 70
    community building for, 69
    conflict resolution, 70–71
    examples, 69–73
    prompts for, 73f
    restorative practices principles, 70
    rubric, 69, 173
homework, 123–124

identity, building (2.2a)
    examples, 61–66
    rubric, 61, 172
identity, meaning of, 61–62
Impacting Student Learning (component 5). See also specific factors
    factors, 167
    focus, 6
    ingredients, 7f, 167
    introduction, 142–143
    Long-Term factor (5.2), 150–157, 180
    Short-Term factor (5.1), 143–150, 180
    summary overview, 162–163
information management, 77–78
instruction
    focused; see Focused Instruction (3.1)
    guided; see Guided Instruction (3.2)
instruction, needs-based (4.3c)
    examples, 138–141
    rubric, 138, 179
Instruction with Intention (component 3). See also specific factors
    Collaborative Learning factor (3.3), 103–112
    factors, 167
    focus, 6
    Focused Instruction factor (3.1), 84–95
    gradual release of responsibility model, 81–82, 82f
    Guided Instruction factor (3.2), 94–102
    ingredients, 7f, 167
    introduction, 81–83
    summary overview, 113–114
intention. See Instruction with Intention (component 3); Learning Intentions and Progressions (1.1)

intentional, term meaning, 3–4
intention statements, 31*f*
interactions, developing positive social and academic, 103–104
interdependence, positive, 103
interpersonal skills, 104

knowledge, pedagogical content (PCK), 81–83

language learning intentions, identifying (1.1e)
  examples, 28–32
  intention statements, 31*f*
  rubric, 28, 170
language support (3.3c)
  examples, 111–113
  rubric, 111, 176
Leading growth level, 9–10
learning. *See also* Assessment to Inform Learning (4.3)
  collaborative *see* Collaborative Learning (3.3)
  evidence of; see Evidence of Learning (1.2)
  independent, 82, 82*f*
  long-term evidence of; see Long-Term Evidence of Learning (5.2)
  meaningful; see Meaningful Learning (1.3)
  primary goal of, 102
  retrieval-enhanced, 124
  short-term evidence of; see Short-Term Evidence of Learning (5.1)
learning climate
  classroom management practices, 73
  efficient; see Efficient learning climate (2.3)
  growth producing; see Growth Producing learning climate (2.2)
  ingredients, 167
  record keeping (2.3b), 77–79, 173
  rules, routines, and procedures (2.3a), 74–77, 173
  welcoming; see Welcoming learning climate (2.1)
learning intentions, clarity in (3.1a)
  content and language learning, 84
  establishing, 83–84
  examples, 84–87

learning intentions, clarity in (3.1a) *(continued)*
  misuse of, 84–85
  posting and discussing, 84–85
  relevance and motivation accompanying, 88–90
  rubric, 84, 174
learning intentions, relevant (3.1b), 10, 87–91, 174
Learning Intentions and Progressions (1.1)
  content learning (1.1d), 26–28, 170
  ingredients, 167
  language learning (1.1e), 28–32, 31*f*, 170
  lesson-specific learning (1.1c), 23–26, 170
  theme, problem, project, or question, linking to (1.1b), 20–23, 170
  transfer goals, identifying (1.1a), 17–20, 170
learning routines, interactive (3.3a), 103–107, 176
lesson-specific learning (1.1c), 23–26, 170
Long-Term Evidence of Learning (5.2)
  assessment tools, trustworthy, 157–160
  end-of-course exams, 152
  performance portfolios, 152
  teacher assessments, 151, 153*f*
  tests, criterion- and norm-referenced, 151–152, 153*f*
  transfer goals, long-term evidence of attainment of (5.2), 150–157

Meaningful Learning (1.3)
  aligned experiences, designing (1.3a), 39–41, 171
  complexity of task in, 109
  differentiation, planning for (1.3b), 41–43, 171
  ingredients, 167
  relevance, 38
mistakes vs. errors, 129
modeling, 92*f*
motivation
  clarity in learning intentions and (3.1a), 88–90
  goal setting and, 120
  teacher, 142
movement patterns, classroom, 52

Not Yet Apparent (NYA) growth level, 8–10

peace table, 70–71
pedagogical content knowledge (PCK), 81–83
performance, checking for understanding (4.2a), 127*f*
Planning with Purpose (component 1). *See also specific factors*
  Evidence of Learning factor (1.2), 33–36
  factors, 7*f*, 167
  focus, 5, 16
  Intentionality in Learning factor (1.1), 17–28
  introduction, 15–16
  Meaningful Learning factor (1.3), 39–41
  summary overview, 43–44
The Power of Our Words (Denton), 65
praise, motivation and, 67
problems, linking to learning intentions (1.1b)
  examples, 20–23
  rubric, 20, 170
procedures, term meaning, 74
procedures in efficient classrooms (2.3a)
  examples, 74–77
  rubric, 74, 173
process differentiation, 42
product differentiation, 42
professional development, 11
professional learning communities (PLCs), 8, 13–14
projects
  in checking for understanding (4.2a), 127*f*
  linking to learning intentions (1.1b), 20–23, 170
prompts, heuristic, procedure, and process, 100

questions
  glow and grow, 112
  linking to learning intentions (1.1b), 20–23, 170

read aloud, 92*f*
record keeping (2.3b), 77–79, 173
reflection, 11, 13, 115–116
reflection prompts, 100
regard for students, positive (2.1a), 47–51, 172

relationships
    positive, developing, 103–104
    prompts for reestablishing, 73f
    teacher-student, developing,
      49–50, 58–59, 134
relevance, 10, 87–91, 174
restorative practices principles, 70
risk taking, encouraging (2.2b)
    examples, 66–69
    grades, 67
    growth mindset, 66–67
    rubric, 66, 173
routines in efficient classrooms
    (2.3a)
    examples, 74–77
    routines, term meaning, 74
    rubric, 74, 173
rules
    meaning of, 74
    posting, 76
rules in efficient classrooms (2.3a)
    examples, 74–77
    posting, 76
    rubric, 74, 173

sarcasm, 64, 66
scaffolds (3.2b), 99–102, 109, 175
schools
    culture vs. climate in, 60–61
    PLCs for improving, 13
    social health, elements affect-
      ing, 45
    successful, conditions present
      in, 46
    trust factor in improving, 9
self as person, feedback on, 134
self-regulation, feedback for, 134
Short-Term Evidence of Learning
    (5.1)
    benchmark tests, 147f
    criterion- and norm-referenced
      tests, 147f, 151

Short-Term Evidence of Learning
    (5.1) *(continued)*
    evidence-based practice,
      143–145, 144f
    goals, progress toward (5.1),
      145–150, 147f, 180
    teacher assessment, 147f
signage, in classrooms, 52
space in classrooms, common and
    individual, 52
student needs, noticing (3.2a), 42,
    96–99, 175
student profiles, developing, 48
students, welcoming, 47–51, 172
student-teacher relationships,
    49–50, 58–59, 134
success criteria for Evidence of
    Learning (1.2a)
    examples, 33–36
    independent learning, 82, 82f
    rubric, 33, 171

targeted, term meaning, 4
task complexity in collaborative
    learning (3.3b)
    difficulty vs. complexity, 107–
      108, 108f
    examples, 107–111
    rubric, 107, 176
teachers
    assessments created by, 153f
    attitudes and actions in a
      growth environment, 60–61
    effective, behaviors of, 83
    FIT Teaching assumptions
      about, 10–11
    FIT Teaching growth levels,
      8–11, 168–169
    motivation, 142
    new, welcoming, 49
teacher-student relationships,
    49–50, 58–59, 134

teaching, purpose of, 142
Teaching growth level, 9, 11
technology
    grade books, electronic, 77–78
    use of personal, 76
themes, linking to learning inten-
    tions (1.1b), 20–23, 170
think-aloud planning sheet, 93f
think-aloud skills, 92, 94
transfer goals, identifying (1.1a),
    17–20, 170
tribes, 60, 70
trust, 9, 59

understanding, checking for (4.2a)
    audience-response systems
      (clickers), 124
    examples, 123–129
    grades, 124
    homework, 123–124
    oral language, 125f
    projects and performances, 127f
    questioning, 125–126f
    rubric, 123, 178
    writing, 126–127f

value-added measures (VAMs),
    151–152
video for representing content, 92f
vocabulary, 29

washback, 124
Welcoming learning climate (2.1)
    belongingness and, 47
    community building (2.1c),
      54–60, 56f, 69, 172
    ingredients, 167
    physical environment in (2.1b),
      51–54
    positive regard (2.1a), 47–51,
      172
    school social health and, 45

About the Authors

Douglas Fisher is a professor of educational leadership at San Diego State University and a teacher leader at Health Sciences High & Middle College. He is a member of the California Reading Hall of Fame and was honored as an exemplary leader by the Conference on English Leadership. He has published numerous articles on improving student achievement, and his books include *The Purposeful Classroom: How to Structure Lessons with Learning Goals in Mind; Enhancing RTI: How to Ensure Success with Effective Classroom Instruction and Intervention; Checking for Understanding: Formative Assessment Techniques for Your Classroom; How to Create a Culture of Achievement in Your School and Classroom;* and *Using Data to Focus Instructional Improvement.* He can be reached at dfisher@mail.sdsu.edu.

Nancy Frey is a professor of educational leadership at San Diego State University and a teacher leader at Health Sciences High & Middle College. Nancy is a recipient of the Christa McAuliffe Award for Excellence in Teacher Education from the American Association of State Colleges and Universities and the Early Career Award from the Literacy Research Association. She has published many articles and books on literacy and instruction, including *Productive Group Work: How to Engage Students, Build Teamwork, and Promote Understanding; The Formative Assessment Action Plan: Practical Steps to More Successful Teaching and Learning;* and *Guided Instruction: How to Develop Confident and Successful Learners.* She can be reached at nfrey@mail.sdsu.edu.

 **Stefani Arzonetti Hite** is a professional education consultant who specializes in supporting systemic educational change initiatives in schools, districts, learning associations, and state departments. Her work is primarily focused on building teacher and administrator instructional capacity, standards-based grading practices, curriculum development, and strategic assessment strategies. She is a member of ASCD's FIT Teaching Cadre, wrote the ASCD white paper "Using the FIT Teaching™ Framework for Successful Teacher Evaluations," and aligned the framework with major teacher evaluation models in use across the United States. She served as deputy head (principal) of a preK–13 international school in the United Kingdom, curriculum director for a countywide support institution, curriculum supervisor for several school districts in Pennsylvania, and a classroom teacher in elementary, middle, and high school. She can be reached at stef@tigrisllc.org.

Related ASCD Resources: FIT Teaching®

At the time of publication, the following ASCD resources were available (ASCD stock numbers appear in parentheses). For up-to-date information about ASCD resources, go to www.ascd.org. You can search the complete archives of *Educational Leadership* at http://www.ascd.org/el.

ASCD EDge Group
Exchange ideas and connect with other educators interested in effective classroom instruction, classroom management, school culture, and assessment on the social networking site ASCD EDge® at http://ascdedge.ascd.org/

Print Products
Better Learning Through Structured Teaching: A Framework for the Gradual Release of Responsibility (2nd ed.) by Douglas Fisher and Nancy Frey (#113006)

Checking for Understanding: Formative Assessment Techniques for Your Classroom by Douglas Fisher and Nancy Frey (#107023)

The Formative Assessment Action Plan: Practical Steps to More Effective Teaching and Learning by Nancy Frey and Douglas Fisher (#111013)

Guided Instruction: How to Develop Confident and Successful Learners by Nancy Frey and Douglas Fisher (#111017)

How to Create a Culture of Achievement in Your School by Douglas Fisher, Nancy Frey, and Ian Pumpian (#111014)

The Purposeful Classroom: How to Structure Lessons with Learning Goals in Mind by Douglas Fisher and Nancy Frey (#112007)

Video
FIT Teaching in Action: A Framework for Intentional and Targeted Teaching (#615055)

WHOLE CHILD
TENETS

THE WHOLE CHILD

ASCD's Whole Child approach is an effort to transition from a focus on narrowly defined academic achievement to one that promotes the long-term development and success of all children. Through this approach, ASCD supports educators, families, community members, and policymakers as they move from a vision about educating the whole child to sustainable, collaborative actions.

Intentional and Targeted Teaching: A Framework for Teacher Growth and Leadership relates to the **safe, engaged, supported,** and **challenged** tenets.

1 **HEALTHY**
Each student enters school healthy and learns about and practices a healthy lifestyle.

2 **SAFE**
Each student learns in an environment that is physically and emotionally safe for students and adults.

3 **ENGAGED**
Each student is actively engaged in learning and is connected to the school and broader community.

4 **SUPPORTED**
Each student has access to personalized learning and is supported by qualified, caring adults.

5 **CHALLENGED**
Each student is challenged academically and prepared for success in college or further study and for employment and participation in a global environment.

For more about the Whole Child approach, visit
www.wholechildeducation.org.